M000279420

Beyond
Soul Growth

Beyond
Soul Growth

Awakening to the Call of Cosmic Evolution

Lynn Sparrow Christy

A.R.E. Press • Virginia Beach • Virginia

Copyright © 2013
by Lynn Sparrow Christy

1st Printing, December 2013

Printed in the U.S.A.

All rights reserved. No part of this book may be reproduced or
transmitted in any form or by any means, electronic or mechanical,
including photocopying, recording, or by any information storage and
retrieval system, without permission in writing from the publisher.

A.R.E. Press
215 67th Street
Virginia Beach, VA 23451-2061

ISBN 13: 978-0-87604-732-3

Edgar Cayce Readings © 1971, 1993-2007
by the Edgar Cayce Foundation.
All rights reserved.

THE HOLY BIBLE, NEW INTERNATIONAL VERSION®, NIV® Copyright © 1973,
1978, 1984, 2011 by Biblica, Inc.®
Used by permission. All rights reserved worldwide.

Cover design by Christine Fulcher

To my dear friend Elaine Lukasik.

Without her wise, intuitive counsel and steady encouragement I may never have made it through the extended birthing process that brought forth this book.

Contents

Acknowledgments

No work such as this can take wing in a vacuum. While the core concepts of what has come to be known as evolutionary spirituality arose for me through a process of inner inquiry and from my interpretation of the Edgar Cayce readings, they found a wider context in which to flourish when I was exposed to the work of many others who have plowed this ground before me. Most notably, I am indebted to Ken Wilber for his sweeping integral vision. Undoubtedly, his writings have been my greatest source of spiritual sustenance since I first discovered Edgar Cayce at the age of sixteen. And while the integral-evolutionary community has spawned what I consider to be some of the most thought-provoking and inspiring thinkers of the modern age (many of whom are quoted in this book), I wish to give special thanks to Craig Hamilton, Michael Dowd, and Terry Patten, whose work has inspired me and whose respective Internet interview series with the spiritual giants of our time have enriched my own experience of evolutionary spirituality beyond measure.

In acknowledging those who have been most helpful to me in expanding my understanding of the profound connection between biological and spiritual evolution, I would be remiss not to mention Pierre Teilhard de Chardin. I first heard his work mentioned by a friend back in my college days. It is my loss that it took more than three decades for me to get around to reading him—and that was only after encountering a fictionalized account of his life and work in Morris West's novel *The Shoes of the Fisherman*. I would urge anyone with a serious interest in the subject matter of this book not to wait as long as I did to read Father Teilhard de Chardin's landmark book *The Phenomenon of Man*.

I would also like to thank Kevin Todeschi, Cassie McQuagge, and the publishing committee at A.R.E. Press for the blessing of knowing that I had a publisher even as I was writing this book. The motivational value of that cannot be underestimated when taking on a project like this! Similarly, it is largely because Rachel Alvidrez of Edgar Cayce eGroups commissioned me to develop an Internet-based seminar on this topic that I first put on paper some of the material that forms the foundation of this book.

The contribution of my longtime friend, Elaine Lukasik—to whom this book is dedicated—is difficult to adequately describe. It has been my good fortune to have a friend with the clarity of intuition that Elaine has demonstrated over the years. As a writer with a gap of more than twenty years between books, many were the times I despaired of ever completing another one. It was Elaine's unwavering insistence that all was well and that I was only gathering more experience and knowledge over those years of writing drought as well as her assurance that I *would* write "the book" that often kept me from abandoning the idea altogether.

In that regard, I thank my husband Larry Christy for his continual support in all of the endeavors of my life. Easygoing and ready to flow with things as they unfold, Larry always knows how to encourage without nagging. He put application to his belief that it was important for me to write by cheerfully accepting disruptions to our routine, our meals, and our time together. In addition, Larry's reading of early chapter drafts served more than once to keep me going when I felt bogged down or discouraged.

Few people besides Larry saw any portion of this book before publication, but to those few who did, I am grateful for feedback. I received some particularly helpful advice early on from my dear friend Mary Holden. I am also thankful for encouragement from my "Facebook friends" Anthony Brancale and John Greenhalgh, whose reading of some chapters constituted a small trial balloon concerning potential reader response from both inside and outside the Edgar Cayce community.

Finally, I want especially to thank my editor Stephanie Pope. Her editing was not only skillful and meticulous, but was also done with a level of sensitivity to my original text that every writer hopes for, but few are fortunate enough to get. Thanks to Stephanie's professionalism, the last stages of birthing this work were almost painless.

Prologue

*B*eginning in early adulthood, I began to have recurring dreams about visiting theme parks. I distinctly remember the first one. Shortly after I had moved to Virginia following college, I had a dream about going to Kings Dominion, a theme park just north of Richmond. I had never been to Kings Dominion, nor did I have any plans to do so, but I couldn't help but notice the clear metaphor in the name. To one whose spiritual sensibilities were very much attuned to the ideal of God's kingdom manifesting "on earth as it is in heaven," the symbology of "king's dominion" seemed obvious. It represented earth under divine rule, and I took the dream as a call to an awakened, Spirit-directed life.

The theme park dreams continued over a span of more than three decades—in fact I still have this dream periodically today. Over the years, most people with whom I shared these dreams have jumped to the conclusion that the theme park image was a cautionary one—a warning about the unreality of this world. They saw it as a reminder that this world is just the arena of souls' play, a wispy fantasy place that diverts our attention from our true domain until we get tired of make-believe and then return to the "real" world beyond this earthly plane. To them, the dreams meant "This life has no ultimate reality."

But that construction never fit with the "king's dominion" frame set by the very first dream in the series, nor did it account for the spiritual intensity that these dreams always awakened in me. No matter how the details of my theme park dreams may have varied over the years, two conditions are always present: First, I feel intensely alive and engaged with everything around me. I am struck with the beauty and wonder of it all, there is so much to see and do, and I feel exhilarated by the sheer number of possibilities. Second, time is always short. It is near closing time, and I often regret not having gotten there sooner. There is an urgency to do and experience as much as possible before time runs out. Right alongside my ecstatic joy in being there, I feel a deep ache over the shortness of time.

For me, these dreams have embodied in both symbol and felt experience the intangible something that bubbles up within me when I hear the evolutionary call of Spirit in this world. The universe becomes a place of endless possibilities, a place that invites us all to delight in the wonders of the creative impetus that brings worlds into manifestation. From this perspective there is something new to discover around every bend. It can be a wild ride at times, when the best we can do is fasten our seatbelts and hold on for dear life. And it *can* be a place where we indulge appetites that are less than spiritually nutritious. But then it is also the place where the best of human ingenuity and problem solving can find a fertile field for expression and where visions of perfection can be molded into visible reality for others to experience and enjoy. And while it's true that if we look closely behind the scenes, we may find ourselves disillusioned by a mercenary taint on some of this world's most delightful offerings, there is also much innocent joy to be found, if that is what we look for. Perhaps most important of all, this world is a place that holds magic for each generation of children born into it, if only we will take care of it and pass it on to them in better shape than we find it in now.

Just as I wrote these words, the day's mail arrived. As if to remind me to mention that this universe is alive and speaking to us, the delivery included a special offer for a "Fun Pass" to the Busch Gardens theme park.

Introduction

(Q) As created by God in the first, are souls perfect, and if so, why any need of development?
(A) In this we find only the answer in this: The evolution of life as may be understood by the finite mind. In the first cause, or principle, all is perfect. In the creation of soul, we find the portion may become a living soul and equal with the Creator. To reach that position, when separated, must pass through all stages of development, that it may be one with the Creator.   900-10

Has creation a final goal? And if so, why was it not reached at once? Why was the consummation not realized from the beginning? To these questions there is but one answer: Because God is Life, and not merely Being.   Friedrich Schelling*

I could never really accept the idea that this world is fundamentally fallen or broken and that the human beings who call it home are deluded dreamers at best or depraved sinners at worst. Yet everywhere I turned, that seemed to be the prevailing idea. In the churches of my childhood, I heard that God had created a paradise but that the disobedience of Adam and Eve had turned it into the vale of toil and woe which we now experience it to be. In the ostensibly more enlightened circles of my adulthood, I heard essentially the same story, but couched in New Age terminology: We are perfect, immortal beings who have fallen into the trap of earthly life and now must make our way back to our pristine state beyond materiality. As the story is most often told in both the orthodox and New Age worlds, in the beginning everything was just the way God intended it to be. But, unfortunately, we used our God-given free will to turn our backs on our maker. Where in the orthodox version our first parents disobeyed a key com-

---

*Friedrich Schelling, (1809), *Philosophical Inquiries into the Nature of Human Freedom*, retrieved from en.wikipedia.org.

mandment and ate forbidden fruit, in the New Age version we started out in a state of perfection but found the allures of this world to be far more interesting than sitting around somewhere that was nowhere, just being one with God.

The tragic upshot of this cosmic mistake was that we got ourselves stuck here in the earth. We'd only meant to visit this deceptively sparkling prison, but now we find ourselves inmates. With our own misguided choices we have consigned ourselves to the long, arduous path of undoing the bonds of incarceration here on earth. The good news in all of this (as the narrative often goes) comes in the reassurance that sooner or later we'll succeed. Then we'll be back "home," and everything will be right again, just as it was before we messed things up. This story is not quite as condemnatory, perhaps, as the one that involves the doctrine of original sin and a fallen world. But it still holds the unavoidable implication that our presence in this world is a mistake—something to be undone with as little delay as possible. To continue with the metaphor of my prologue, this philosophy tells us it's time to leave the amusement park and go home.

Is It Really All About Going Back to Where We Started?

If I couldn't accept the idea that this world is flawed and that we are its corrupted denizens, then neither could I accept the seemingly more benign idea that all of life is about getting back to where we started. Could it be that untold millennia of human history—all of our aspirations and attainments, all of our struggles and failures, all of our hopes and fears, the love, the pain, and all of the joys that characterize the human experience—all of these are nothing more than the way back to where we began? If you've ever missed your exit on a limited access highway and had to double back for many miles in order to correct your oversight, you know how frustrating and pointless that feels. Is it possible that the purpose of this life has no point beyond retracing our steps back to where we went wrong at the dawn of time? In retrospect, I can see that my passion for evolutionary spirituality had its roots in this very question.

It's not that I find the idea that we are here to undo past choices that separated our consciousness from God totally without merit. To an extent, it answers some of the big questions about why life can be so hard at times and full of pain. A world peopled by beings walled off from their divine source is bound to be a world fraught with difficulties. I can even find great meaning in the idea that successive lives in this world afford us an opportunity to make the corrections that will re-awaken our true nature as sons and daughters of God. It is certainly more logical and more consistent with belief in a loving God than the idea, pervasive in the Western Christian culture I grew up in, that we have only this one life and that our eternal fate is determined by either (depending on which sect of that Christian culture one happens to belong to) the virtues we manage to develop or the faith we happen to affirm while we are here on this earth. A God who gives us every opportunity to come back to our divine inheritance is surely a more loving God than one who gives us one shot at it and then leaves us to figure out the rules for making the grade. Better to think of this world as a school for wayward souls than as a cruel tryout for heaven, where only a fraction will make the cut.

But still the question *why* overshadows these explanations of life's travails. Why, if we were created in the image of God and have an ultimate destiny to return to God, are we even in this loop, cycling in and out of this world, making such slow progress, and suffering so much along the way? After all, it is supposedly God's image in which we were created. Couldn't God have made us such that we didn't have the all-too-obvious propensity to mess things up? It seems odd that the first thing a being made in the image of God would do is turn its back on God—a kind of design flaw, we might speculate. More disturbing still, what if, once we suck it up and do what has to be done to re-attain the state of oneness, we fall into separation all over again? Will we have to redo the whole process of return? Will it just go on and on like that forever? If the answer to that question is yes, I cannot think of a more bleak and futile existence. Yet if the answer is no, that there will be something in the re-attained state of oneness that includes a safeguard against falling away from God again, then we're back to the same basic problem: Why didn't the all-powerful Creator just make us that way in the first place and spare all of us a lot of trouble and pain?

I remember the first time I articulated this question. I was an idealistic seventeen-year-old attending my first conference at the Association for Research and Enlightenment in Virginia Beach. I had been reading for a couple of years about the American psychic Edgar Cayce and many of the topics covered in his remarkable trance discourses. The ideas I'd encountered there had revolutionized my life and kindled the fire in my soul. I was at that glorious stage when I was discovering the answers to all of life's big questions and my encounter with the knottier questions that would arise later on was still safely tucked away in the future. Everything fit together beautifully but for that one sticking point: If it's possible to be a free-willed being, safely resting in oneness with God, which is the promised outcome of all this that we call life, then why didn't God make us that way in the first place?

I was sitting over a meal with an older conferee (he must have been at least twenty-five or maybe even thirty!) when I voiced this question. He looked at me and said, simply, "That's exactly the kind of being God is creating right now." In a flash, my cosmology had changed. This "aha!" moment was, for me, the first glimmer of realization that the process of becoming has inherent meaning in the scheme of things.

From "Soul Growth" to Participation in Creation

It would be more than three decades before the full evolutionary significance of this idea had taken shape in my thinking. By then, the original realization that creation is a here-and-now process rather than an event in the distant past had continued to extend as an influence over every major development in my spiritual understanding. For example, the next shift in my cosmology had been the realization that this process is not about what God is making of us, but what we are making of ourselves. Later still I would see that the goal of all this making is not a static state but a dynamic one; that is, it's not just about resting in oneness but rather our being fitted out for conscious participation in something God is doing in and through time and space. The locus of attention began to shift from soul growth as an end in itself to soul growth as a means to an end. Eventually, the connection between our co-creative role and the great cosmological and biological evolution going on all around us slowly dawned on me, coming into sharpest focus in the pages of an inspirational writing practice I had adopted along the way.

In my ongoing study of diverse points of view concerning the spiritual path, I had been listening to a CD course in which the teacher reiterated the view that had always troubled me. He described an endless cycle of involution–evolution–involution in which God pours aspects of Godself (that would be us) out into materiality and then slowly grows back to timeless, spaceless oneness—only to eventually become "bored" and venture out again into this illusory world, thus starting the cycle all over again. Upon hearing this, all of my original objections to this world view arose. I still found it hard to believe that this life was about nothing more than going back to the beginning. But other things this teacher had said had been helpful enough that I was reluctant to simply dismiss his position in favor of my own biases. I figured it deserved a second look. Was he right about this endless cycle? If he was, I was back to the question that had haunted my earliest seeking.

As I took the question to the interior inquiry that inspirational writing facilitates for me, the first clarification came in a reminder that this was not a true/false question, but rather a matter of choice between two broadly different paths—each acceptable, each honorable. Release from bondage to the flesh and the earth is the reward of any spiritual path that honors the pre-eminence of Spirit, adheres to life practices and disciplines that awaken Spirit and moves the aspirant into the consciousness of oneness, my inner source told me. At the same time (the explanation continued), there is a distinctive path which breaks outside the endless cycle of descent into the world and ascent back to oneness. This path leads to full participation in the next developmental stage of creation. One on this path is not bound by the earth, yet is fully engaged with the earth. It is a path that embraces the ongoing evolutionary process, moving forward, so to speak, rather than endlessly cycling through the same territory. It is the path of conscious, chosen co-creatorship.

When this articulation of a distinctive path that seeks to participate in ongoing, forward-moving creation first took shape via my inspirational writing dialog more than a decade ago, I had not encountered it in any formalized teaching and I was eager to start talking and writing about it. In one sense, it was so obvious. How often do we hear the term co-create in the contemporary spiritual world? And yet, despite the ubiquitous appearance of the term, in the spiritual conversation of our day a true commitment to living from an evolutionary perspective is still largely overlooked by both traditional and contemporary forms of spiritual practice. I couldn't wait to share my epiphany. But my impulse to share notwithstanding, the same inner realization that opened my awareness to the evolutionary possibilities before us advised me to hold off on writing and teaching about it. I'm glad it did, for it turns out that I had merely stepped into a stream of thought that, unbeknownst to me, had been developing for at least a few hundred years. Time and time again, I was amazed to come upon ideas and perspectives that had felt original when they first dawned on me via the process of personal attunement. Is there anything more affirming of universal truth than to find that it has sprung up independently in numerous contexts and among otherwise diverse sources? I have also come to realize that this phenomenon is just a small foretaste of the unity consciousness that will characterize the next stage of our collective development.

Over the ensuing decade, I discovered a vast and invigorating world of those who embrace the evolutionary approach to life. Many of these thinkers, both contemporary and historical, will enter into the pages that follow. One special delight was to come upon this reflection from the German philosopher Friedrich Schelling (1775–1854), concerning the very question that had been the original, proverbial stone in my shoe. Schelling wrote, "Has creation a final goal? And if so, why was it not reached at once? Why was the consummation not realized from the beginning? To these questions there is but one answer: Because God is Life, and not merely Being."[1] We will return to this concept that "God is Life"—that is, a life force that seeks manifestation in this visible world of three dimensions—many times in the pages to come, as it is foundational to the evolutionary world view. Concerned with far more than the evolution of the individual soul, evolutionary spirituality fo-

---

[1] Friedrich Schelling, (1809), *Philosophical Inquiries into the Nature of Human Freedom*, retrieved from en.wikipedia.org.

cuses instead on the evolution of the entire cosmos and our role in that unfolding story. It is a world view that looks at this vast cosmos, where new stars are continually being born and old ones are dying; at this earth, where life continues to evolve toward ever-greater diversity and complexity; and at human consciousness, which continues to grow to ever more expansive reaches, and sees an underlying unity of purpose. Evolutionary spirituality concludes that the universe is going somewhere and that we are a key part of that journey.

This evolutionary perspective can have a deeply catalyzing effect on one's spiritual life, and perhaps nowhere do we find a more compelling version of this perspective than in the readings of Edgar Cayce. Despite the fact that I was steeped in the readings' story of the soul in the earth and their repeated reference to the soul's purpose as a "companion and co-creator with God," I was nonetheless amazed, when I turned to the Cayce source with my evolutionary sensibilities awakened, to see a complex and profound body of evolutionary thought that had been there all along, "hiding in plain sight." Yet the contemporary conversation about evolution, inclusive of diverse spiritual and scientific perspectives (one of its great strengths, as we shall be seeing), has not so far included the contribution from the Cayce legacy. It is largely for that reason that I have framed this book around Edgar Cayce's distinctive perspective on evolution. I believe it is an important addition to the evolutionary inquiry that may well shape the direction of this century's spirituality.

In presenting the Cayce readings' perspective on our evolutionary purpose, I have tried to give a comprehensive treatment of their take on the origin and destiny of the human soul. However, there is one aspect of that story that I found to be too large and complex to assimilate into the general evolutionary perspective given here. It has to do with the role of the Christ, his own evolution, and the impact his evolution has had on the rest of the cosmos. Try as I would to weave that important narrative into this work, there was no way I could do it justice without literally doubling the length of this book. Therefore I have opted not to open that discussion here, instead making it the primary focus of a follow-up work that I am tentatively titling *The Rest of the Evolutionary Story*. For those not familiar with the Cayce readings concerning the Christ, the material dealt with here stands on its own.

For those who are already familiar with the importance the Cayce readings ascribe to the Christ, the evolutionary path described here is offered as a significant context within which to place his story.

Regardless of your prior exposure to the Cayce material, my hope is that the concepts and practices described in the chapters ahead will assist you toward finding your place in this great evolutionary framework; for as we each find our own co-creative path, we serve the great ongoing evolutionary agenda of the cosmos, while simultaneously finding our own greatest peace, happiness, and fulfillment in life.

PART ONE:
EMBRACING EVOLUTIONARY SPIRITUALITY

" . . . for time and space are as the evolution upon which the forces of the divine make for that change that brings same into the experiences of those souls who seek to become one with the Creative Energies."

254-95

"For those who believe in God, or a cosmic intelligence, it would be blasphemous to suppose that the universe has been created without purpose or plan, or that the race has been brought into existence only to eat, drink and make merry with the extravagant expenditure of resources, both mineral and organic, of the earth. There must be a reason why intelligence has been granted to mankind and why a whole planet with all its wealth has been placed at her disposal."

Gopi Krishna, *Kundalini: Empowering Human Evolution*[*]

---

[*]Gopi Krishna, *Kundalini: Empowering Human Evolution* (St. Paul: Paragon House, 1996), 148.

Chapter 1:
Why Evolution Matters

" . . . The earth's sphere, with the first creation in the mind of the Creator, has kept its same Creative Energy, for God is the same yesterday, today and forever . . . "   900-340

"The creation of the world did not take place once and for all time, but takes place every day."   Samuel Beckett, Proust*

Mine is the generation that came of age as strains of "this is the dawning of the Age of Aquarius" wafted through the airwaves to our car radios. A lot of us eagerly looked for the signs of that dawning any day. Now, more than forty years later, we can look back on a number of dates and years that various prophetic voices declared to be the Big One. We've harmonically converged and fired the grid. We've awaited 1998, and once that year came and went, set our sights on 2012. It seems to me that for my whole lifespan thus far we have been waiting for the Big Event that would transform our world.

As I write this, anticipation continues to build all over the world around the great hope that many of the spiritually minded hold for December, 2012, as a pivotal point of prophetic destiny. As you read this, December 21, 2012, (selected largely because the Mayan long count calendar ended on that date) will have come and gone. Now what? (The joke will be on me if December, 2012, turns out to meet its advance press. But in that event, this book probably won't have been published, so it's all right!) Depending on how far this date has receded into the past, by the time you are reading this there may well be yet another future date that has become the object of much hope and—dare I say it?—hype.

It's understandable, really, this human tendency to latch on to particular times and dates as the fulfillment of our spiritual yearnings and the answer to the problems we face as a human race. Who can deny

---

*Samuel Beckett, *Proust*, retrieved from goodreads.com.

1

the allure of the expectation that in a single day or year all of our
spiritual yearning will be fulfilled and that all of our unfinished business, our failures of will, discipline, and purpose, and our too-often
lackadaisical service to a higher good will be swept aside in an influx
of transformative grace such as this world has never known? And lest
we think this date watching is a distinctly New Age phenomenon, we
need only look to the *Left Behind* books, enormously popular among
evangelical and fundamentalist Christians, as just one recent link in a
chain of apocalyptic expectations that stretch all the way back to Jesus'
disciples asking, "What will be the sign of your coming and the end of
the age?"[2]

Nor can we deny that, historically, there have been many threshold
times of great transformative significance. The harnessing of fire, the
development of agriculture, the first writing of language, the Renaissance, the Industrial Revolution—these are just a smattering of examples of transformative epochs that forever changed the face of
humankind on the earth. Each furthered the reach of our combined
knowledge, culture, and know-how, and thus in each of these we can
see what was, in its time, a truly new age that brought the peoples of
the world a little closer together.

Living on the Threshold of Change

Looking around us at the world today, it does not take much of a
stretch to think that we, too, are on a major threshold. Global challenges on the economic, political, and environmental fronts rivet our
attention. An unprecedented worldwide cross-pollination of spiritual
perspectives as well as scientific breakthroughs and technological advances hint at solutions that will be a quantum leap beyond old ways
of dealing with our problems. Perhaps most significant of all, the effective shrinking of the world through the Internet and other modern
communications systems suggests that, for the first time in human
history, a unified humanity is within the realm of possibility. Add to
that the astronomical fact that, because of the precession of the equi-
noxes, Earth's vernal equinox is transitioning from the constellation of

---

[2]Matthew 24:3

Pisces to that of Aquarius, and maybe the dawning of the Aquarian Age does not seem so far-fetched after all.

The interesting thing about dawns and crossing over thresholds, however, is that these movements are *processes* that occur over some period of time. There are multitudinous factors leading to the approach of a threshold, and complex internal forces propel individuals to become pioneers in its crossing. Who can delineate, for example, all of the influences of philosophy, science, mathematics, art, and politics that came together to produce the Renaissance? And what forces were at work within the makeup of an Isaac Newton or a Leonardo da Vinci to propel them over the threshold, thereby making them such influential figures in the widespread and lasting transformation that the Renaissance became?

Unlike a fix that swoops down from above, transformative epochs have always tended to rise up from within the participants. Even the birth of Jesus, held by those of Christian faith to have been the major transformative event so far in human history, was described by Edgar Cayce as coming in response to "continued preparation and dedication" on the part of those who knew the potentials of their day and organized their lives around it accordingly.[3] We should expect no less a requirement of us if our day is truly to be one of transformation to a new age. In that context, we might look at the Aquarian Age as an invitation for us to participate in the next stage of a process that is synonymous with evolution.

At least that seems to be the Cayce readings' take on it. The only time that the readings spoke about the Aquarian Age by name occurred in 1939, when Edgar Cayce was asked if he could name the date when the crossover from the Piscean to Aquarian Age would happen. His response was that "In 1998 we may find a great deal of the activities as have been wrought by the gradual changes that are coming about. . . . " He went on to further clarify that " . . . This is a gradual, not

---

[3]5749-7 (Edgar Cayce readings are referenced throughout this work according to the numeric designation assigned to each reading. The first number represents either a person [whose name has been removed to protect privacy] or a topical grouping of readings. The number following the hyphen indicates where the reading falls in the sequence of readings for that individual or topic. In this case, it is the seventh reading in the 5749 series, a topical collection of readings about Jesus.)

a cataclysmic activity in the experience of the earth in this period."[4]
This emphasis on process and gradual transformation rather than sudden, cataclysmic change matches the very essence of evolution (which
is defined as a *process* in all of its dictionary definitions).

Elsewhere in this same reading he said that where the Piscean Age
brought the consciousness of Emmanuel or "God with us," the
Aquarian Age would mean the full consciousness of the ability to communicate with or be aware of our relationship to "Creative Forces" *and
the use of these creative forces in a material world.* The opportunity of our day,
then, would seem to be conscious engagement with the Creative Force
behind all things and our own use of such creative capacity right here
in this world. This is, in essence, a call to an evolutionary lifestyle, a
spirituality based not on seeing how quickly we can "graduate" from
the earth, but instead on how well we can participate in the process of
creation. What else might we expect from a body of spiritual teaching
that consistently links co-creatorship to our core purpose?

For us in this early twenty-first century world, so fraught with both
peril and potential, the stakes have never been higher. The potentials
of our time call us to engage with *processes* that will take us over the
threshold into the attributes of the Aquarian epoch, rather than wait
for particular dates that will bring it all together for us. In the language of the Cayce reading cited above, our astounding opportunity is
to learn how to use creative forces—the same forces that have brought
worlds into being—right here in this material world where we find
ourselves. The perils of our day make the maxim that we cannot solve
a problem from the level of consciousness that created it all too obvious. Rather than fix our gaze on some hoped-for event on the horizon, where a previously unattainable state of spiritual consciousness
will fall like refreshing dew, *today* is when we must actively engage in
pushing past the boundaries in our own consciousness to *be* that consciousness which will approach the world's problems in an entirely
new way. It is time for us to find the ways we are called to be the
embodiment of evolution—a process that is leading us toward a new
threshold for life on this planet. As we learn to nurture those forces
within us that will help nudge us over the inevitable hurdles that any

threshold will entail, we will rise to the evolutionary potential of our age.

What's Distinctive about the Evolutionary Approach to Life?

Just what is it that makes the evolutionary approach different from other spiritual paths? Isn't all spirituality, by its very definition, evolutionary? Well, yes—and no. We might say that the main difference is one of context. From any spiritual standpoint that includes the long view of the soul's history, we're used to thinking of evolution in terms of our personal path of development. Traditional spirituality often presents the path to enlightenment as an evolutionary one, whereby we transcend the bonds and limitations of the flesh and this three-dimensional world and return to fully realized consciousness of our oneness with God.

The evolutionary world view would agree that this opening up of consciousness is crucial. But it sees that as not an end in itself but rather as the *means* to an ongoing evolutionary advance that can be traced back to the Big Bang. And the primary arena of that evolutionary advance is *here*, in this world of flesh and blood and rocks and plants. In other words, a spiritual path that emphasizes getting out of this world is not evolutionary in the sense that I will be using the term here. "Evolutionary spirituality," as presented in these pages, is a world view—an interpretation of the facts at hand—that holds central the idea that the manifest universe is evolving. Not just the cosmos, not just plants and animals, *but consciousness itself* is evolving on a cosmic scale, influencing every atom of manifest creation. Therefore, evolutionary spirituality is a commitment to take responsibility for bringing consciousness into our thoughts, our bodies, the world, and creation itself.

For that reason, this world of three dimensions has intrinsic meaning and purpose. It is far more than just an illusion to be rolled away or a dream to be awakened from. Furthermore, our purpose here in this earthly realm goes beyond personal spirituality and "soul growth." We are called beyond soul growth to participation in an ongoing creation. In one sense all living things are participants in ongoing creation. But in the case of humanity, that participation is a bit more pointed if, in fact, we are at the leading edge of evolution as most contemporary evolutionary world views claim. In us and through us comes the evolutionary advance of all that is. Therefore, evolutionary spirituality entails a commitment to embrace the unique opportunity of incarnation. This book is both a call to that commitment and an exploration of what it might look like in our daily habits, priorities, and actions, if we were to truly seize the evolutionary opportunity before us.

The story of that opportunity begins with an infinitesimal point outside of time and space, where nothing burst forth into something and when time and space and matter were born. From that moment on, a forward-moving process began, and this process is still taking place today. While traditional approaches to spirituality (even New Age ones) will often assume that this earth plane is a fixed environment through which the soul moves for its own growth, evolutionary spirituality sees us as developing entities in a developing environment. The universe is up to something that has significance beyond us, yet it also carries us along on its astounding journey toward the future. As this occurs, we become significant shapers of what that future will be. We—all sentient beings and the cosmos we inhabit—are all going somewhere together.

The evolutionary perspective differs from other spiritual paths in another significant way as well. Because it is characterized by a deep appreciation for the science of evolution, it may well offer the world's first science-based spirituality. It's not that cooperation between people of faith and people of science is unprecedented. There have always been theistic scientists as well as those among the religiously devout who respect the contribution of science to our knowledge of the world. There have also always been those who sought and found bands of connection between scientific and theological inquiry, and so it would not be at all accurate to allow either the anti-scientific stance of some fundamentalist groups or the strident atheism of some scientists to represent the entire spectrum of positions when it comes to views of science and religion. But regardless of whether their relationship was friendly or adversarial, the domains of science and religion have been treated as separate since the beginning of the modern scientific era.

Never before have the interests of science and spirituality been so completely intertwined. The theist and atheist alike can (and do) come to the story of evolution and find in it a perspective that unites them in a common work toward the collective good.

Our Evolutionary Story

The story that unites theist and atheist in a commitment to cooperate with the evolutionary trajectory is truly an amazing one. Approximately 13.7 billion years ago the evolutionary advance began with the utter chaos that followed the Big Bang, giving rise to the galaxies 200–500 million years later as hydrogen gasses coalesced into stars. As the earliest life cycles of stars gave rise to carbon and oxygen through the death of stars, about 4.6 billion years ago, a planet like Earth could form from the debris in the burgeoning cosmos. And then, over the next several billion years, life began to emerge from matter, molecules combining into cells. And then came that miracle of miracles when the first multi-cellular cooperatives emerged. What forces were at work when single-celled life forms joined together? Some specialized in transporting nutrients while others specialized in sensing environmental conditions or making up a protective skin, for example, so that together they became one more complex and more adaptive life form. But come together they did, and from there life proliferated, complexified, and diversified until, a mere 1.8 million years ago, our ancestors first left the trees to walk upright on the ground.

Then, most anthropologists believe, human culture first emerged a mere 50,000 years ago—although fossil evidence of *homo sapiens* dates the arrival of human beings at about 195,000 years ago.

Along the way, every evolutionary advance has involved a growth in cooperation, natural selection notwithstanding. This is perhaps one of the great realizations of modern evolutionary thinking, and it is crucial to the spiritual application of evolution. The long, slow climb upward from the primordial beginnings of life has not been ruled entirely by the well-known principle of survival of the fittest. A look at the long story of evolutionary advance will show us that as life proliferates and complexifies, with the most adaptive outcomes of this experimentation ("the fittest") surviving, those surviving life forms are in turn made more viable by their cooperative groupings. From the cells that first came together and specialized their functions for greater survival to the emergence of complex life forms with interdependent organs, and from family groups that banded together to increase their viability and on to tribes and nations, cooperative collectives have evolved in lockstep with evolutionary advance. The spiritual implications of this will be apparent: greater cooperation and unity are not simply abstract spiritual ideals; they are not only the signposts of personal growth; they are a major mechanism by which evolution itself takes place.

Nor is cooperation the only spiritually relevant growth that has accompanied the evolutionary advance. As the complexity of life forms evolves, so does the capacity for consciousness. Rather than an all-or-nothing view that attributes consciousness to some life forms (such as humans) and absence of consciousness to others (such as the grass growing in your front yard), the evolutionary perspective sees the potential for consciousness commensurate with the complexity of the particular life form. In the human being, we have evolution's current apex and therefore the greatest capacity for consciousness. This will be a theme that we return to many times in these pages, for it is one of the core aspects of the evolutionary spiritual path: How, specifically, do we actualize the potential for consciousness that is our evolutionary inheritance? And where is that growth in consciousness leading us? Up until now, evolution has been a largely unconscious process, with the forces of nature shaping the evolution of all things. ("Forces of nature" including, for the theist, the God who manifests as nature.) But now we are awake, aware. We know that we are conscious and we know about evolution. And that changes everything.

Chapter 2:
The Evolution of
Evolutionary Awareness

. . . In this manifestation of the material world, and of the creative energy as is manifested, is the stumbling block to many peoples, for evolution is as of a fact in the mind of the creative energy, and the will of the energy creating is of the higher forces, same as the will of the individual in the higher species . . .   900-249

As life arose in a world without life; as Simple Consciousness came into existence where before was mere vitality without perception; as Self Consciousness leaping widewinged from Simple Consciousness soared forth over land and sea, so shall the race of man which has been thus established, continuing its beginningless and endless ascent, make other steps (the next of which it is now in the act of climbing) and attain to a yet higher life than any heretofore experienced or even conceived.

Richard Bucke, *Cosmic Consciousness**

*E*veryone now living has grown up in a world where "the theory of evolution" is known. While in some quarters there is still a tenacious insistence that evolution is a mere theory, the evidence for it has become so overwhelming as to make it an accepted underlying premise in the study of genetics, neurology, psychology, anthropology, and sociology. Yet one place where the evolutionary perspective has been less well assimilated to date is in the realm of spiritual inquiry. That statement may seem surprising, given the amount of religious controversy that continues to surround evolution, particularly in American culture. Yet if we examine the hot-button issues in this controversy, they tend to be about the origin of life and how we got to where we are now rather than about *how life works right now*. There are

*Richard Maurice Bucke, *Cosmic Consciousness* (New York: Penguin Compass, 1991), 22.

religious people who believe in evolution and those who hotly con-
test it, but even among those who believe in it, evolution has not yet
taken on a widespread influence over how they live their lives, how
they deal with their challenges and weaknesses, or how they navigate
any number of other essential aspects of the spiritual path. In short,
for the vast majority of those who pursue the life of the spirit, evolution has not yet become a practical spiritual world view.

Nonetheless, the evolutionary spirituality movement has taken a
firm foothold in contemporary spirituality, and its values and priorities are gaining a momentum that promises to become a growing force
in twenty-first century ideas about the spiritual path. One need only
do a web search using key terms such as "evolutionary," "evolution,"
and "spirituality" to see numerous sites, teleseminar series, articles,
and books that address the topic. As we will be seeing, the spiritual
view of evolution has been around for at least a few centuries, but it
remains for us in this day and time to assimilate the meaning that
knowledge of evolution sheds on life and allow it to actively shape a
new spirituality that nurtures our capacity to fulfill our potential as
co-creators. This is a truly momentous opportunity—one that is integral to the dawning of a new age. The evolutionary drive that has
been operating beneath the surface of things for nearly fourteen billion years is now waking up to become aware of itself. *We* are evolution becoming conscious! Let's step back a moment and look at what a
profound awakening that is.

The Coming of Evolutionary Thought

Having been born into a world where, from the scientific point of
view, evolution is a given, we may not fully appreciate what a radical
development it was for human beings to realize for the first time that
things are evolving and that although history may repeat itself in the
short term, on a cosmic scale it has an ever forward-moving direction.
In earliest human societies, change was so slow that life could remain
pretty much the same over spans of time measured in thousands of
years. The first technological advances—things like sharp edges, fire,
and the wheel—took tens of thousands of years to develop. And people
had pretty much the same way of life, the same tools to do the work of

life, and the same cultural traditions for generation upon generation. Life certainly gave every appearance of being cyclical, as seen most obviously in the seasons. A cycle of planting and harvesting might bring bounty or it might bring scarcity, but one thing was sure: planting season would come again and with it would come either good fortune or ill. No wonder a people caught in this endless, capricious loop would seek to appease the gods who held power over their fate. And so on it went for the first many thousands of years of human civilization.

But however slowly the increments of change occurred over the course of the early millennia of civilization, the rate of change in human knowledge and technological advance is an exponential one rather than one of simple accretion. When knowledge and technology are limited, their doubling does not change things very much; but as the doubled knowledge doubles again, and that in turn doubles, the rate at which change becomes apparent speeds up considerably over time. So whereas major changes took thousands of years in the very ancient world, by the middle of the second millennium AD, a major societal shift required only a century or two—such as happened when the printing press revolutionized western culture in the relative eyeblink of a few hundred years. Yet still, when major shifts took a few hundred years to happen, you would live pretty much as your grandparents had, and your grandchildren would live pretty much the same kind of life you did. Life tended to be short and hard with very little to suggest it would ever be otherwise here on this earth, and so the religions of humankind focused on a better life after death and on death as release from the pain and suffering that characterized so much of human existence. This earth didn't seem to have much to offer in the way of a future.

When we consider that the religions of the world formulated their doctrines in a cultural context which did not know that all was evolving, we can more easily understand why relatively little ultimate importance was placed on this life. Disconnected from the ongoing evolutionary advance, life becomes little more than a way station for those whose main hope rests in otherworldly dimensions. Under non-evolutionary assumptions, this fleshly life on earth finds its main significance (particularly for those in traditional Western religions) as a testing ground for heaven, a time and place for us to make decisions of eternal import. And having once formulated their dogmas and practices around belief in a nonevolving world, adherents of such faiths were predisposed to see the new idea of evolution as the denial of everything they held sacred. As evidence for evolution has continued to mount over the past century, people of faith have had only two choices: revise their dogmas or deny evolution. Today, we can readily see the warring of these two responses to evolution in American religion and politics. In some groups Darwin is nothing short of the Antichrist!

Yet in the scientific discourse the idea of evolution was not new with Darwin. Decades before Darwin brought the theory of physical evolution into the public eye, there was debate between "evolutionists," who observed species' tendency to develop over time, and the "immutabalists," who believed that the species and their characteristics were fixed. In fact, as far back as the mid-1700s, the French naturalist and mathematician Comte de Buffon suggested that species change over time and that the earth was considerably older than Bishop Ussher's then largely accepted 6,000 years. Darwin's own grandfather, Erasmus Darwin, along with other such evolutionary pioneers as Comte de Buffon's student Jean–Baptiste Lamarck[5] and geologists Charles Lyall and James Hutton were among those whose evolutionary thinking paved the way for more detailed treatment in *The Origin of Species.*

If evolution was not an entirely new concept in the world of scientific thought when Darwin published his book *The Origin of Species*, neither was it altogether new in philosophical and theological thought. In the philosophical world, the ancient idea of a fixed or cyclic view of nature had already given way at least a hundred years earlier to a

---

[5]Although Lamarck's idea that acquired traits can be passed on to offspring was largely discredited for many years, by the 1920s some vindication for his theories began to show up in laboratory experiments in which successive generations of rats learned to navigate mazes with fewer and fewer learning trials (the acquired learning of the parents presumably passing on to their offspring) and reports from Pavlov that his famous conditioned response similarly affected subsequent generations of dogs. Today, a growing neo–Lamarckian perspective is supported by the field of epigenetics, which studies environmental influence on the activation of genetic codes.

view of history as forward moving, setting the stage for Darwinian ideas of evolution. For example, the philosopher Leibniz speculated in the 1600s that over the long course of history the species of animals had transformed many times and "a cumulative increase of the beauty and universal perfection of the works of God, a perpetual and unrestricted *progress* of the universe as a whole must be recognized, such that it advances to a higher state of development."[6] In that same century the German mystic Jakob Boehme departed from his Lutheran roots to espouse an evolutionary cosmology. By the eighteenth century, German thinkers like Kant, Goethe, and Fichte were developing evolutionary philosophical systems, and that trend continued into the nineteenth century with Schelling, Hegel, and Schopenhauer who were all suggesting an evolving manifestation of spirit in the world of materiality. Schelling wrote: "History as a whole is a progressive, gradually self-disclosing revelation of the Absolute."[7]

In the world of Christian spiritual thought, the evolutionary perspective was not universally dismissed, even among the most orthodox. Although he may have been ahead of his time, nineteenth century Scottish theological writer and revivalist Henry Drummond was quick to see the spiritual significance of evolution when he wrote in *Natural Law in the Spiritual World*:

> We have Truth in Nature as it came from God. And it has to be read with the same unbiased mind, the same open eye, the same faith, and the same reverence as all other Revelation. All that is found there, whatever its place in Theology, whatever its orthodoxy or heterodoxy, whatever its narrowness or its breadth, we are bound to accept as Doctrine from which on the lines of Science there is no escape.[8]

In the late nineteenth and early twentieth centuries, the theosophi-

---

[6] As quoted by Arthur Lovejoy in *The Great Chain of Being: A Study of the History of an Idea* (Cambridge, MA: Harvard University Press, 1936), 257.

[7] Friedrich Schelling, (1800), *System of Transcendental Idealism*, retrieved from en.wikipedia.org.

[8] Henry Drummond, (1883, p. 68), *Natural Law in the Spiritual World*, e-book.

cal writers were among the first to present comprehensive evolutionary perspectives on the spiritual path that encompassed what were, at
the time, the latest scientific understandings of the physical dimensions of evolution. One can't read Alice Bailey's theosophical treatise,
The Consciousness of the Atom, without being struck by its prescient grasp
of the essential unity of the evolutionary process from the sub-atomic
to the cosmological levels. Within the framework found in the evolutionary writings of the early twentieth century theosophists, we find
some of the earliest articulations of how inward spirit co-evolves with
outward form. For example, C.W. Leadbeater wrote:

> The whole process is one of steady evolution from lower forms to
> higher, from the simpler to the more complex. But what is evolving
> is not primarily the form, but the life within it. The forms also evolve
> and grow better as time passes; but this is in order that they may
> be appropriate vehicles for more and more advanced waves of life.[9]

Rudolf Steiner, whose Anthroposophy was an outgrowth of the theosophical movement, expressed a similar concern for the interior dimensions of evolution when he pointed out that Darwinian thought was
valid but incomplete if we left out the spiritual essence of the evolutionary process in humankind. "From epoch to epoch," he wrote, "progressive evolution leads humanity, in respect to the path of higher cognition,
to ever changing modes, just as outer life likewise changes its form."[10]

The Indian sage Sri Aurobindo was also a major influence in the
blending of evolutionary science with spiritual philosophy. Although
Hindu philosophy from ancient times had expounded a distinctly evolutionary view, such evolution came within a cyclic context, with the
emphasis of evolution being a return to spirit, followed by another
period of involution when spirit would once again flow out into manifestation. Aurobindo saw evolution as leading the enlightened one
beyond nirvana to continued engagement with the evolutionary force
that has been at work in the cosmos. He called man a "transitional
being," saying that the step from man to superman is the next ap-

---

[9]C.W. Leadbeater, (1912, p. 20), *A Textbook of Theosophy*, e-book.
[10]Rudolph Steiner, (1922), *An Outline of Occult Science*, e-book.

proaching achievement in the earth's evolution and that it flows from an inherent logic of the evolutionary principle whereby intellectual mind transitions to spiritual mind.

Among the American transcendentalists, both Thoreau and Emerson were also synthesizers of evolutionary thinking with spiritual philosophy. The biological aspects of evolution paralleled and brought enrichment to their own observations of the natural world, while its spiritual aspects dovetailed with transcendental ideas of evolution toward unity and perfection.

Richard Bucke, whose classic *Cosmic Consciousness* was recommended in the Cayce readings, saw a growing phenomenon of cosmic consciousness experiences as a reflection of evolution continuing its advance through the human race and predicted that such experiences would become more and more common as we evolved. Gopi Krishna, whose writings perhaps more than anyone else's illuminate the mysteries of kundalini, saw the kundalini forces as an evolutionary force and our ability to experience them in a balanced, healthful way as the key to the next evolutionary advance.

Perhaps the best-known spiritual evolutionary thinker of modern times was the French priest Pierre Teilhard de Chardin. Published in 1955, Teilhard de Chardin's *The Phenomenon of Man* puts forth a comprehensive view of the evolution of the cosmos with humankind's arrival and growing consciousness at the leading edge of an evolutionary advance toward what he called the "Omega Point," the ultimate development of consciousness into a unified God consciousness. As a Jesuit who studied both paleontology and geology, Teilhard de Chardin grasped the spiritual implications of evolutionary theory for the entire human race and the future of the earth. "The outcome of the world, the gates of the future, the entry into the super-human—these are not thrown open to a few of the privileged nor to one chosen people to the exclusion of all others," he wrote. "They will open only to an advance of all together, in a direction in which all together can join and find completion in a spiritual renovation of the earth."[11]

[11]Pierre Teilhard de Chardin, *The Phenomenon of Man* (New York: Harper and Row, 1961), 244. Fun fact: The priest, Father Telemond, in Morris West's 1963 novel, *The Shoes of the Fisherman*, was based closely on Teilhard de Chardin. Within that work, the reader will find an excellent and very reader friendly distillation of Teilhard de Chardin's thinking as well as an unfortunately typical reaction from the orthodox theological world.

A "spiritual renovation of the earth:" how timely that message is! Yet until recently this evolutionary perspective has been largely ignored by most of the spiritually minded. In our culture, the religionists with a "ticket to heaven" theology and the New Agers with a "this world is only an illusion to be outgrown" spirituality have largely ignored the huge importance of our place in this evolving world of manifest form. Nonetheless, that importance cannot be overstated in a world that seems to be tripping over its own limited resources in solving the problems that beset humanity. It's been said that religion is for those who are afraid to go to hell and spirituality is for people who've been there. Well, *evolutionary spirituality* is for people who've been to both hell and heaven and now know that we have a choice as to which decides the destiny of our world. Or to put it in the language of that *other* herald of evolutionary spirituality, Edgar Cayce, " . . . The soul of each individual is a portion then of the Whole, *with* the birthright of Creative Forces to become a co-creator with the Father, a co-laborer with Him. As that birthright is then manifested, growth ensues. If it is made selfish, retardments must be the result."[12]

Evolutionary Thought in the Cayce Readings

Certainly the Cayce readings were on board with our crucial role in the renovation of the earth. It is no small thing from the evolutionary perspective that one of the most common terms for God in the readings is "Creative Force." And it would seem that the Creative Force always intended the continuation of creation. One reading suggested that God rested on the seventh day in the creation story " . . . to let His purpose flow through that which had been made, *that it might be perfected in itself.*"[13] This same divine intention that creation evolve toward completion rather than be a finished product at the start is reflected in the somewhat cryptic comment:

When the heavens and the earth came into being, this meant the universe as the inhabitants of the earth know same; yet there are

---

[12] 1549-1
[13] 3491-1, emphasis added

> many suns in the universe,—those even about which our sun, our earth, revolve; and all are moving toward some place,—*yet space and time appear to be incomplete.*[14]

An incomplete realm of time and space, a manifest world that is still unfolding, an aspect of the Ultimate that has an innate drive to express in form—that is the essence of the evolutionary story. As we already saw in the statement by Friedrich Schelling, God did not bring about the consummation of creation "in the beginning" because "God is Life, and not merely Being." Made in the image of God, we too are characterized by the quickening impulse of life and not simply being. We do not exist simply to transcend the manifest universe and exist in changeless, eternal bliss, but rather to express the onward movement of life as it expresses through us in this world of form. " . . . For the purpose is that each soul should be a co-creator with God," the Cayce readings tell us.[15]

Co-creativity is no mere incidental aspect of our being in the Cayce world view. It is at the very core of our purpose for being, for we are described as " . . . [children] of Creative Force . . . " and are told that we came into being in order to " . . . be a companion with the Creative Force, God, in its activity . . . "[16] So intrinsic is our co-creative role that we are described as corpuscles in the body of God, where acts that reflect love are God's bloodstream and consciousness is like God's nervous system.[17] Astonishingly, he even says that we are instrumental in the redemption of the world: "Know that self in the physical activative state is a part of the plan of salvation, of righteousness, of truth, of the Creative Forces or God in the earth."[18]

Notice the repeated emphasis on *activity* in this world. We are not called to armchair philosophize about evolution, but to live out our evolutionary potential in the character of the lives we lead. This character is closely linked in the readings, as it is in most contemporary

---

[14]5757-1, emphasis added
[15]4047-2
[16]262-88
[17]2174-2
[18]2174-2

spirituality, with the quality of our consciousness:

> For, the *soul* being a part or a shadow of the real spiritual self, it controls or rules the universe rather than being ruled by same. But, they that have entirely put on a consciousness are ruled by same. Hence, as each individual entity accepts and lives by this or that awareness, or consciousness, it gives power and spirit to same. Thus is each *soul,* each entity, a co-creator with that *universal consciousness* ye call God.[19]

In us, consciousness is waking up; and as it does evolution takes an enormous leap forward. In the words of Teilhard de Chardin:

> Man is not the centre of the universe as once we thought in our simplicity, but something much more wonderful—the arrow pointing the way to the final unification of the world in terms of life. Man alone constitutes the last-born, the freshest, the most complicated, the most subtle of all the successive layers of life.[20]

We are evolution waking up to itself.

---

[19]2246-1
[20]Teilhard de Chardin, *The Phenomenon of Man,* 223.

Chapter 3:
Evolution Awakens to Itself

> . . . The Spirit of God is aware through activity and we see it in those things celestial, terrestrial, of the air, of all forms . . .   262-99

> That the Unconscious Will of the Universe is growing aware of Itself I believe I may claim as my own idea solely——at which I arrived by reflecting that what has already taken place in a fraction of the whole (i.e. so much of the world has become conscious) is likely to take place in the mass;——and there being no Will outside the mass——that is, the Universe——the whole Will becomes conscious thereby: and ultimately, it is to be hoped, sympathetic.
>
> Thomas Hardy, from his personal correspondence*

A diverse sampling of evolutionary thought will show that there is one thing upon which most evolutionary thinkers seem to agree: a growing capacity for awareness—or consciousness, as we may also call it—is the product of evolution. Pointing out that every evolutionary advance has resulted in increased consciousness, Christian evolutionist Teilhard de Chardin characterized consciousness as "nothing less than the substance and heart of life in the process of evolution."[21] The Indian sage Sri Aurobindo described the essence of evolution as "the strife of a Consciousness somnambulised in Matter to wake and be free."[22] Similarly, contemporary evolutionary thought leader Barbara Marx Hubbard says that "By understanding evolution as the expression of universal intelligence, now becoming conscious of itself within us, and as us, we overcome the dichotomy between current evolutionists who see no design in evolution, and creationists who

---

*Thomas Hardy, *The Life and Work of Thomas Hardy*, ed. Michael Millgate (Athens: The University of Georgia Press, 1985), 360.

[21]Teilhard de Chardin, *The Phenomenon of Man*, 178.

[22]Sri Aurobindo, *Sri Aurobindo's Major Works, Volume 10: "Essays Divine and Human"* (Pondicherry: Sri Aurobindo Ashram, 1993), 166.

often propose an anthropomorphic God as creator."[23] Mystical evolutionist Jakob Boehme anticipated this line of thought roughly four centuries ago when he said that God achieves a new self-awareness by interacting with a creation that is simultaneously part of and distinct from Himself. We find the same concept in the Cayce reading used as the epigraph to this chapter, when it says that "The Spirit of God *is aware through activity* and we see it in those things celestial, terrestrial, of the air, of all forms." Ironically, we may find the most poetic expression concerning the birth of consciousness in the cosmos from Carl Sagan, one of America's best-known scientists: "We are the local embodiment of a Cosmos grown to self-awareness. We have begun to contemplate our origins—star stuff pondering the stars!"[24]

Each of these thought leaders identifies consciousness as the developing edge of evolution, the quality toward which all is moving. Henri Bergson, in his enormously popular *Creative Evolution*, (English translation, 1910) went so far as to call consciousness not only the product of evolution but its "motive principle," suggesting that the increase of consciousness may be the ultimate *raison d'être* for the evolution of the cosmos and all living things within it. The words of Teilhard de Chardin speak to the inseparability of greater consciousness from unfolding evolution when he says, "the history of the living world can be summarized as the elaboration of ever more perfect eyes within a cosmos in which there is always something more to be seen."[25]

While it may be axiomatic to any student of metaphysics that consciousness of a sort pervades all that exists, there is, nonetheless, a developmental aspect to consciousness as it manifests in the world of matter. Leading contemporary evolutionary thinker Ken Wilber puts the issue succinctly when he says, "Both humans and rocks are equally Spirit, but only humans can consciously realize that fact, and between the rock and the human lies evolution."[26] Thus we often see language suggesting consciousness "waking up," as if the vast, underlying ground

[23]Barbara Marx Hubbard, "Conscious Evolution Defined," Foundation for Conscious Evolution, retrieved from barbaramarxhubbard.com.
[24]Carl Sagan, *Cosmos* (New York: Random House, 1980), 345.
[25]Teilhard de Chardin, *The Phenomenon of Man*, 31.
[26]Ken Wilber, *Eye of Spirit: An Integral Vision for a World Gone Slightly Mad* (Boston: Shambhala, 1997), 279.

of all that is (known alternatively as "life" or even "Spirit") has been a sleeping, unconscious force only now coming into the fullness of its capacity for awareness. Not surprisingly, perhaps, the Cayce readings would concur with the view that sees Spirit-consciousness metaphorically waking up in this world of time and space. For example, one reading suggests that God "gave of Himself" such that "Spirit moving in space becomes matter" and "that in time and in the evolution matter becomes *aware* of its oneness with the source that gave it energy and activity" in the first place.[27] Another reading even seems to have anticipated Sagan's comment about us being "star stuff" when it says that in analyzing our purposes, ideals, and latent urges, we should keep in mind that being part and parcel of the universal consciousness makes us part and parcel of the stars, the planets, the sun, and the moon. " . . . Do ye rule them or they rule thee? . . . For ye are as a corpuscle in the body of God; thus a co-creator with Him, in what ye think, in what ye do. . . . "[28] Here we come face to face with our responsibility as the carriers of awakened consciousness into the world of matter.

Consciousness: The Current Frontier of the Evolutionary Advance

We stand at a crucial point in a process that has brought matter from its most unconscious to its most conscious manifestation to date. It's not that matter is inert, with consciousness as an overlay or addition that comes only with the more advanced life forms, but rather that consciousness develops in complexity just as the forms of nature, both organic and inorganic, do. "To produce life from inert matter would result in the discovery that there is no 'inert' matter, because no life can be produced where life does not exist," wrote theosophist Harold W. Percival early in the twentieth century. "The forms of manifestation of life may be infinite," he continues, "but life is present in all forms. If life were not co-incident with matter, matter could not change in form."[29]

---

[27] 873-1, emphasis added
[28] 2794-3
[29] Harold W. Percival, "Life," *The Word* (Winter 2001): 5.

This view is consistent with that of the Cayce readings, which speak of each cell containing the essence of life in what he often calls the "cell force" or "cellular forces." While most often the context for such comments is the human body, it is interesting to note that in at least one place it extends to a substance normally thought to be inanimate. When asked about a vision showing a loaf of bread where every cell was illuminated with an aura, the Cayce source answered that this represented "the essence of life itself" *in the cell force of the bread.*[30] Interestingly, it's not only Cayce and the theosophists who had early insights concerning the life force in all of matter. In *Natural Law in the Spiritual World* we find nineteenth century Christian spokesman Henry Drummond (from whom we heard in the last chapter as well) saying essentially the same thing when he writes, "There being no passage from one Kingdom to another, whether from inorganic to organic, or from organic to spiritual, the intervention of Life is a scientific necessity if a stone or a plant or an animal or a man is to pass from a lower to a higher sphere."[31]

Cayce ups the ante when he suggests that not only life, but even mind of a sort is to be found in all of matter. This is especially true when it comes to the matter in our bodies, for at least one reading claims that each cell in the body can "know" its purpose.[32] Surprisingly, he was in good company in making this assertion; Thomas Edison was quoted in an interview for *Harper's Magazine* as saying,

I do not believe that matter is inert, acted upon by an outside force. To me it seems that every atom is possessed by a certain amount of primitive intelligence. Look at the thousands of ways in which atoms of hydrogen combine with those of other elements, forming the most diverse substances. Do you mean to say that they do this without intelligence? Atoms in harmonious and useful relation assume beautiful or interesting shapes and colors, or in certain forms, the atoms constitute animals of the lower order. Finally they combine in man, who represents the total intelligence of all the atoms.[33]

[30]281-4, emphasis added
[31]Drummond, *Natural Law in the Spiritual World*, 41.
[32]1158-5
[33]Thomas Edison, *Harper's Magazine* (February, 1890).

The idea that cells and even atoms can have a rudimentary form of "knowing" is commonly found in the theosophical literature of the early twentieth century. For example, Alice Bailey's 1922 publication, *The Consciousness of the Atom*, offers a comprehensive mapping of the development of consciousness, where beginning with the atom there is a rudimentary intelligence in the "selectivity" with which atoms are drawn to other atoms. With the combining of atoms to form a variety of minerals, a quality of "elasticity" is added to selectivity, she says. Then, with the vegetable kingdom, rudimentary sensation is added to the first two, while in the animal kingdom we find the further increment of instinct. It is in humans, she continues, that the rudimentary qualities of the lower kingdom reach more advanced form. The rudimentary elastic selectivity of the mineral kingdom manifest as intelligent activity in human beings; the sensation of the vegetable kingdom develops to emotion and ultimately love, and the instinct of the animal kingdom develops into full "mentality," which manifests in the human species as "intelligent will."[34]

This same incremental building toward intelligent will is described in the Cayce material, where it is clear that each cell has the full "life principle" (rudimentary consciousness) within it and that some form of selectivity or direction from the "One Spiritual Infinite Mind" is at work when cells combine to form a body.[35] Eventually, the cells become "subservient" to the "will force" of the person whose body they comprise,[36] with countless readings mentioning the impact that the consciousness of the individual has on the functioning of the cells within his or her body. With this will force or intelligent will, humanity rises to its highest evolutionary potential.

In one particularly fascinating reading, the Cayce source frames the "projection of psychic forces into material forces" in terms of purpose, calling plant or vegetable life a "one purpose life;" the animal kingdom a "two purpose life;" and human beings a "three purpose life." It continues then "with the entrance into the spiritual, the fourfold or purpose life." In this progressive addition of purpose upon purpose,

[34]Alice Bailey, (1922, pp. 42-3), *The Consciousness of the Atom*, e-book.
[35]900-237
[36]108-2

we see intimations of consciousness increasing toward full expression of spirit in matter. "Hence the necessity of each living, as it were, upon the other."[37] Sri Aurobindo speaks similarly of a necessary ascent up through the life forms to the great potential for divinization now before the human race:

> As the impulse toward Mind ranges from the more sensitive reactions of life in the metal and the plant up to its full organization in man, so in man himself there is the same ascending series, the preparation, if nothing more, of a higher and divine life.[38]

There is something all-encompassing here—a complex, integrated, and organic view of the way in which spirit's purposes are unfolded throughout the layers and levels of the manifest world. The foundational levels of spirit's expression in the mineral, plant, and animal kingdoms are as necessary to our spiritual awakening as anything else in our experience. Yet with us lies the supreme responsibility of bringing self-aware spirit into matter. Just to be born human means we are participating in the "three purpose life," but "only again in the soul development, wherein man takes on that from the creative forces as supplied by creator, do we find the fourfold life as is manifested in man."[39] We, as an expression of soul development, have the distinctive potential to be the embodiment of the next purpose-level of spirit's infusion of matter. For this reason, Cayce calls man " . . . God's highest creation in the earth's plane . . . "[40] In Bailey's words, "He [man] is the deity of his own little system; he is not only conscious, but he is self-conscious."[41]

[37]900–47
[38]Sri Aurobindo, (1939–40, p. 78), *The Life Divine*, e-book.
[39]900–47
[40]900–14
[41]Bailey, *The Consciousness of the Atom*, 49.

Self-Reflective Awareness:
Evolutionary Breakthrough

It's not just that we are conscious, but that we can be *aware* of our consciousness; that is the crucial characteristic that puts human beings at the apex of the evolutionary ascent. That ascent, as we have been seeing, involves incremental increase in awareness rather than an all-or-nothing, conscious-or-not-conscious division. Anyone who has ever had a responsive pet or seen a documentary on animal intelligence will attest to the fact that animals are capable of both complex and sophisticated levels of thought and feeling. From elephants who mourn their dead to zoo gorillas who pick the locks of their cages and crows who've learned to use bread as fishing bait, the evidence is abundant that we are not the only ones who feel, think, reason, and problem-solve. Add to that the demonstrated language ability of primates and dolphins, and it would seem that very little that was once considered the sole domain of humans turns out to be uniquely ours. But even those whose close relationship with a loving pet has taught them the full depth of what animals can think and feel would probably agree that your dog or cat does not ponder such questions as "Where did everything come from?" or "What will happen to me when I die?" or "Is this fair?" To be conscious at all is a great evolutionary advance. We share that advancement with the higher forms of animal life. But to be able to *reflect* on your thoughts is an even higher attainment, one that took more than thirteen billion years to occur and is unique to humanity.

The consensus of evolutionary thought, from purely scientific perspectives, such as that of Carl Sagan when he speaks of "starstuff pondering the stars," to the more spiritually oriented perspectives of those who see self-conscious awareness as a milestone in spiritual awakening, points to the pivotal significance of this attainment. The German philosopher Hegel zeroed in on the consciousness-elevating potential of reflective thought when he said, "It is thinking that turns the soul, with which the animals are also endowed, into spirit."[42] Similarly, Rich-

---

[42]As quoted by Rudolf Steiner in *The Philosophy of Spiritual Activity*, (1894, p. 154), e-book.

ard Bucke distinguishes "simple consciousness," which we share with the more advanced animals, from the "self-consciousness" that is a significant step toward cosmic consciousness. As Bucke puts it, self-consciousness makes us not only conscious of trees, rocks, water, our own limbs and body, but allows us to be conscious of our self "as a distinct entity apart from all the rest of the universe." "Further," he goes on to say, "by means of self-consciousness man (who knows as the animal knows) becomes capable of treating his own mental states as objects of consciousness."[43] The theosophical school would concur: "The human level is the point where consciousness has become completely individualized and is capable of turning back upon itself and studying its own inner processes," wrote L.W. Rogers.[44]

Evolutionary thinkers point to the Axial Age from 800 to 200 BCE as the time when this enormous breakthrough to self-reflective awareness dawned among the human race. This was a time of great spiritual awakening, where the spiritual traditions of China, India, Persia, Judea, and Greece arose spontaneously. Figures like Plato, Buddha, Lao Tzu, Zarathustra, Confucius, and the major Hebrew prophets were spokesmen of this awakening. Scholars believe that this period of great spiritual awakening was also the time when the ability to be aware of and contemplate our own inner state, including things like our motives, feelings, and thoughts first arose in humans. This reflective self-awareness was the breakthrough of a whole new level of consciousness, one that would make it possible one day for evolution to awaken to itself and which would pave the way for the next-higher development: conscious participation in evolution.

Heretofore, the mysterious impulse within the cosmological and biological worlds to evolve has been operating beneath the surface of awareness. A powerful drive within the very fabric of things has reached onward toward a proliferation of forms and the development of complexity. Now, with the coming of self-reflective consciousness within the human species, evolution has awakened to itself. And we have a choice to make: will we continue to be carried along on the currents of the unconscious evolutionary drive, or will we use our

---

[43]Bucke, *Cosmic Consciousness*, 1.
[44]L.W. Rogers, (1917, p. 206), *Elementary Theosophy*, e-book.

capacity for self-reflective awareness to move into conscious participation in the evolutionary advance? The call is stated eloquently by
Barbara Marx Hubbard:

> Conscious evolution is the evolution of evolution, from unconscious
> to conscious choice. While consciousness has been evolving for
> billions of years, conscious evolution is new. It is part of the
> trajectory of human evolution, the canvas of choice before us now
> as we recognize that we have come to possess the powers that we
> used to attribute to the gods.[45]

Now, in our own day and time, we are on the brink of the next
emerging consciousness, where a fully matured, self-reflective awareness holds the potential to lead us onward to its natural expression:
universal or unity consciousness.

Unity Consciousness: Our Evolutionary Future

Students of the Cayce readings will recognize that destiny often
spoken of wherein we can know ourselves to be ourselves yet be one
with God. Such a paradoxical state is hard to comprehend, as most of
us for most of human history have experienced unity and selfhood as
an either/or proposition: *Either* I can blend with the group *or* I can be
a rugged individualist; either I can meet my own needs first *or* those of
others first; I can be either one with God *or* a unique consciousness.
Our very notion of being a self is predicated upon recognizing what is
not self, and it's hard to escape the dualistic implications of that. Yet
surely we have also known those moments when, in the midst of an
especially compatible group, we have felt more like ourselves than
when in a discordant setting. Or perhaps there have been shining
moments when we experience our very selfhood fulfilled in an act of
sacrifice or service for another. Anyone who has ever become engulfed,
even for a brief moment, in the beauties of a natural scene has known
a deeper sense of selfhood in those moments than is "normal" in a

---

[45]Barbara Marx Hubbard, "Conscious Evolution Defined" Foundation for Conscious
Evolution, retrieved from barbaramarxhubbard.com.

daily life cut off from such oneness with nature. These are but just a few foretastes of how we will someday find our deepest selves within the full consciousness of oneness.

We shouldn't be surprised, really. It is the pattern of nature. Only cells that are healthy and functional as individual cells can make up a healthy organ. Should we expect, then, that cosmic oneness would erase individuality? Cooperation, rather than loss of the individual components, is the key to higher orders of functioning. Similarly, it is individuals who are psychologically healthy in themselves who can form healthy relationships. Wherever we care to look, collective bonds become stronger and more resilient when component members bring their individual strengths and resiliency to the collective. British evolutionary biologist J.B.S. Haldane may not have been a theist, but even he pointed out the natural extension of the pattern. Referring to the humanist religion of Auguste Comte, which posits a "Great Being," (that is, the human race seen as one) instead of a traditional notion of God, Haldane wrote, "Now, if the co-operation of some thousands of millions of cells in our brain can produce consciousness, the idea becomes vastly more plausible that the co-operation of humanity, or some sections of it, may determine what Comte calls a 'Great Being.'"[46]

This "something" that brings and holds such collective bonds together is that mysterious drive underlying all of evolution. "Latent infinity" is what one Cayce reading[47] calls it when describing the primal drive toward connection that brings two cells together in conception. Teilhard de Chardin, in talking about how the component parts of any material substance are held together, says that they are not independent of each other. "Something holds them together. Far from behaving as a mere inert receptacle, the space filled by their multitudes operates on it like an active centre of direction and transmission in which their plurality is organized," he wrote. As this applies to future human evolution, he says that at each developmental step "we shall find ourselves faced by the unimaginable reality of collective bonds."[48] To know ourselves to be *ourselves* and yet be one with God—

[46]J.B.S. Haldane, *The Inequality of Man*, (London: Chatto, 1932), 113.

[47]136-37

[48]Teilhard de Chardin, *The Phenomenon of Man*, 41.

which is to say "to be one with the All"—that is our evolutionary future; and it is predicated upon a matured and healthy selfhood. Or, as we may also describe it, unity consciousness is the blossoming of the bud which first emerged in self-reflective awareness.

It may seem like a snail's pace for it to take 2,000 to 2,800 years for self-reflective awareness to blossom into widespread awakening to cosmic, universal or unity consciousness. And such consciousness may appear to be on the most distant of horizons for us even now. Neither state is exactly commonplace among the mass of humanity, even though the pioneers of both these attainments have been sprinkled through the world's religions for more than 2,000 years now. But when we stop to consider this in the context of what is often called "deep time," we realize that 2,000 to 3,000 years is a very short time span indeed. Scaling the entire 13.7 billion years since the Big Bang to the amount of time in a single year, the time elapsed between the Axial Age and now would amount to a matter of a few seconds! As illustrated in Figure 1, "A Deep Time Perspective," the earth would not have formed until mid–September, with the dinosaurs not arriving until Christmas Eve. Humans would have just shown up within the last ten minutes of December 31, and the Axial Age would have been less than seven seconds ago if now is a nanosecond before midnight at the conclusion of our one-year scale.

A Deep Time Perspective

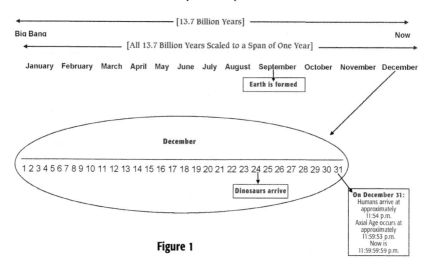

Figure 1

This long view is important if we are to have the patience and per-
sistence it will take to nurture the evolution of consciousness within
ourselves, for it is no overnight accomplishment. Even a lifetime devoted to this cause is not an unreasonable undertaking, when we make
the pace of cosmic evolution our context. Within the brief time period
of our lifetimes and even the hundreds of years before our time, evolutionary advance may appear to be so slow as to be virtually non-
existent—which is often the dynamic at work when people will say,
"Things getting better? You've got to be kidding! Things are steadily
getting worse!" Yet more careful observation will tell us that this is not
so. Although humanity is a long way from completely exorcising the
demons of cruelty, greed, and domination over others, we live in a
time when the majority of the world reacts with horror to public ex-
ecutions, blood sports, and tyrants who ruthlessly subjugate others.
This was not so a mere few centuries ago, when families would gather
to watch a hanging, the seats of Roman coliseums were filled with
those who came to watch gladiators fight to the death and people
generally accepted the inevitability of tyranny. Teilhard de Chardin
puts human progress in the context of deep history when he says that,
"compared with the zoological layers which preceded [self-aware hu-
manity] . . . mankind is so young that it could almost be called newborn." Elsewhere he says that "we cannot expect to see the earth
transform itself under our eyes in the space of a generation. Let us
keep calm and take heart."[49]

Let us heed this advice and take heart as we, too, prepare to take up
the evolutionary cause. For while the history of the world's wisdom
traditions will tell us that spiritual adepts have had access to unity
consciousness for more than 2,000 years, remember that there will
always be outliers—those who are ahead of the pack and those who
are behind the pack. Each evolutionary advance is only consolidated
when it becomes the norm within the vast middle of a population.
That is the work before us today: to bring a new norm to reality as we
cultivate our self-reflective awareness and foster its maturation into
unity consciousness in our thoughts, words, and deeds.

---

[49]Teilhard de Chardin, *The Phenomenon of Man*, 276–77.

Chapter 4:
The Evolutionary Perspective of the Cayce Readings

Much has been written respecting that represented in the Great Pyramid, and the record that may be read by those who would seek to know more concerning the relationships that have existed, that may exist, that do exist, between those of the Creative Forces that are manifest in the material world. As indicated, there were periods when a much closer relationship existed, or rather should it be said, there was a much better understanding *of* the relationship that *exists* between the creature and the Creator.   5748-6

Rediscovery is one of the methods of progress. Very much that we believe to be original with us at the time of its discovery or invention proves in time to have been known to earlier civilizations.

L.W. Rogers, *Elementary Theosophy**

*B*efore going on to explore the promise of awakened consciousness as the product of evolution, it's important to address something that may be a sticking point for students of the Edgar Cayce material. Were we really so unconscious until a few thousand years ago? What about ancient civilizations like Atlantis and Egypt, which Cayce places well before the Axial Age? Is higher consciousness a new attainment for the human race or the re-attainment of something that has been lost? Another way to put the question would be to ask whether evolution has had one steady forward direction, or whether there have been backtracks and retrogressions along the way.

While few would claim that evolution has been one steady forward movement with no setbacks or repetitive loops, it is true that most contemporary lines of evolutionary thought are predicated upon a

---

*Rogers, *Elementary Theosophy*, 7.

single forward trajectory. Under this assumption, the great wisdom
traditions of the world are typically cast as less complete apprehen-
sions of truth than what is currently accessible to human
consciousness. But Cayce—along with the theosophical exponents of
evolution—presents a more complex story, claiming that " . . . Many
times has the evolution of the earth reached the stage of development
it has today and then sank again, to rise again in the next development . . . "[50] How does this jibe with the idea that contemporary humanity faces a unique opportunity that is the product of 13.7 billion
years of evolution?

Furthermore, what of the idea that an increase in consciousness
follows an evolutionary trajectory? If the attainment of self-reflective
awareness is the product of a 13.7 billion year process that began with
the Big Bang, how does that fit with the Cayce story of conscious, free-
willed souls whose existence preceded the earth plane? It would seem
that we have two incommensurate paradigms. One involves self-aware
beings who descended into matter and one involves protozoa emerging from the primordial soup to follow a very long evolutionary path
toward sentience. Many a thoughtful reader, when confronted with
the Cayce story of souls in the earth, has encountered the crux of the
issue in wondering "Where do cavemen fit into this picture?"

Where, indeed, do we put an anthropological record which shows
primitive *homo sapiens* still chiseling out spearheads long after Cayce
and other esoteric sources claim Atlanteans had mastered air travel? Is
the fit too artificial for us to properly class the Cayce legacy as part of
the evolutionary canon? It would be disingenuous to ignore these
significant differences between the Cayce evolutionary view and the
prevailing view in today's evolutionary spirituality movement. But I
think we will see, after a closer examination, that these are differences
in detail rather than substance.

Matter to Life to Mind to Spirit

Most of the evolutionary spirituality movement, in presenting the
big picture of cosmic evolution and humankind's place in it, suggests

a progression from matter to life to mind to spirit. We might illustrate it like this:

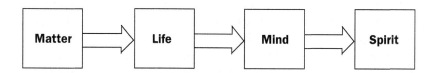

We might think, from this diagram, that spirit is a product of mind and life is the product of matter, each simply being further developments of an earlier state. In fact, for purely scientific evolutionists, that might not be too far off. Witness the excitement over the "God gene," a seemingly biological foundation for the capacity for spirituality and those neuroscientists who take the position that mind is an epiphenomenon of the brain. It is true that for thoroughgoing materialists matter has combined itself in such a way as to produce life in each of its successive manifestations. But for evolutionaries of a spiritual bent the developmental chain is not about the absolute beginnings of life or mind or spirit but rather their breaking through in this three-dimensional world of form. As we will be seeing, this point is crucial in our attempt to place Cayce in the context of mainstream evolutionary thought.

In its existence beyond the realm of manifest form, Spirit, God, Ground of Being, Consciousness Itself (by whatever name we call it) is complete and needs no development. But within manifestation, there is growth and evolution of spirit. In the eastern and platonic traditions, this distinction has been described as that of "Being" vs. "Becoming." As Being, the Absolute is changeless and formless. As Becoming, it is both the world of form and the consciousness that is awakening within it. As cosmological and biological evolution provide an ever more sophisticated means by which it can manifest, Becoming becomes more conscious. The non-dual nature of the Absolute—in the language of the Cayce readings its oneness—includes *both* Being and Becoming. To exclude the manifest realm as "other" than the Absolute is to slip into dualism.

Of course, there is always a problem in describing the Absolute that is within yet beyond all time and space. Because it is beyond all limits, the minute we attempt to describe it with words, we limit it and therefore introduce incorrect concepts. As it is said in the Tao Te Ching, "The Tao that can be spoken of is not the everlasting Tao." Verbal attempts to describe that which gives rise to the world of form often use such words as "unmanifest," "ground of being," "formless," "emptiness," "the void," or the "implicate order." While all of these in various ways communicate some of the unqualified, non-tangible, and ultimately incomprehensible nature of this all-encompassing Something that is no thing, they seem to fall short of conveying the wonder and magnitude of this ultimate Reality. No wonder people gave it a name and just called it God! But let us always be careful, when we use that convenient handle for the Absolute that encompasses both form and formlessness, that we do not reduce it to anything less than its incomprehensible majesty. As eighteenth century German reformed Christian writer Gerhard Tersteegen said, "A comprehended God is no God at all."

From the standpoint of evolutionary spirituality our existence, like that of the Absolute, is both unmanifest and manifest. And because our unmanifest existence is pure formlessness, there is nothing to evolve "there" (recognizing that "there" is no place). But that's not the whole story. As the formless ground gives rise to manifestation of the cosmos, we also have existence in *that* place—which *is* a place, real and concrete, within the limitless field of the unmanifest. Even as the use of words that are time bound and space conditioned impairs our ability to describe these things, diagrams limit us because we attempt to show in two-dimensional form that which is multi-dimensional and beyond all dimensions. Nonetheless, the diagram shown in Figure 2 may help clarify these points, as long as its limitations are kept in mind.

In the words of Sri Aurobindo:

> Thus the eternal paradox and eternal truth of a divine life in an animal body, an immortal aspiration or reality inhabiting a mortal tenement, a single and universal consciousness representing itself in limited minds and divided egos, a transcendent, indefinable timeless and spaceless Being who alone renders time and space and cosmos possible.[51]

---

[51]Aurobindo, *The Life Divine*, 78

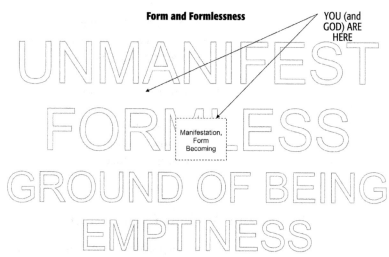

Please note that just as descriptive words place limits on a reality that is, in fact, limitless, this model attempts to put into visual form that which is beyond all depiction. With that in mind, imagine that the page on which this is printed represents timeless, spaceless, unlimited reality and that the 3-dimensional world of form is one small aspect of ultimate, limitless Reality.

Figure 2

We find the same idea expressed in the language that is so characteristic of the Cayce readings:

> . . . For as the entity finds, we are body, we are mind, we are soul. The soul is in the image of God, thus eternal, everlasting. Life in its expression, then, in a mental and in a material world, is only a mental and material manifestation of the soul-entity; that which was brought into being as a part of Creative Forces. Thus it is eternal.[52]

The same paradox of form and formlessness is expressed in the Cayce material in terms of a God who grows and yet is changeless:

> If there be any virtue or truth in those things given in the spiritual or Christian or Jehovah-God faith, His laws are immutable. What laws are immutable, if truth and God Himself is a growing thing— yet an ever changeable, and yet ever the same, yesterday and today and forever? These things, these words, to many minds become

---

[52]3459-1

contradictory, but they are in their inception *not* contradictory; for Truth, Life, Light, Immortality, are only words that give expression to or convey a concept of one and the same thing.[53]

Thus far, then, we can see that there is no real contradiction between the position that consciousness is increasing with evolution of the world and the Cayce story of conscious souls preceding the world. What becomes more sticky, however, is how this awakening of spirit in matter correlates with the Cayce story of the history of our planet and the human race.

Evolution and Ancient Civilizations

On the surface, we have an enormous problem. Contemporary evolutionary spirituality heralds the arrival of self–reflective awareness a few thousand years ago at most, while the Cayce readings—like much New Age thought as well as the theosophical traditions—speak of advanced civilizations in the past which held deep spiritual knowledge that has since been lost to the masses. Atlantis and Egypt figure heavily in such lore. Take, for example, this very representative reading which suggests that the pyramids of Egypt hold the records of ancient wisdom:

. . . The entity also aided in the laying of, and should be an interpreter of that given to the world as a lasting memorial of the relationships between man and man, man and the Creative Forces; and that [which] it brings through being at an at-oneness with, instead of at an at-variance with, Creative Energy in a material world.[54]

Another reading (part of which is quoted as an epigraph to this chapter) states that during this same period "there were many who sought to bring to man a better understanding of the close relationship between the Creative Forces and that created, between man and man, and man and his Maker."

[53]276–7
[54]539–2

Notice particularly how prominent is the theme of "Creative Forces" and "Creative Energy" when the Cayce source speaks of ancient wisdom. If Cayce is correct, earlier civilizations did indeed understand that our role is a co-creative one. In accordance with much esoteric tradition, the Cayce readings tell us that this ancient knowledge was carefully preserved so that it could be passed on to future generations. In speaking of lost civilizations such as Atlantis, the readings suggest that much of the record-keeping in ancient Egypt was centered upon preserving the history and knowledge of a civilization already submerged in both time and the ocean, knowledge that was to be " . . . manifested again and again in the earth as that manner or way for the gods of the high heavens to make themselves felt and known among the children of the earth plane."[55]

To the modern evolutionary, whose views are formed by both science and post-mythic spirituality, such claims may well sound preposterous. It is understandable if they are cast aside as mythic beliefs carried over from more naïve, less scientifically informed times. Seen in that light, they create an enormous gulf between the evolutionary path described in the Cayce legacy and that of the contemporary evolutionary. Yet there is meeting ground. If we are to understand how these assertions of ancient sagacity may in fact be compatible with modern evolutionary thinking, we must step back, re-consider that paradox of manifest/unmanifest reality, and realize that it is even more finely shaded than we have yet acknowledged.

The Many Levels of Manifestation

So far, we have considered only a broad and rather crude dividing point between what is manifest and what is non-manifest, what is form and what is formlessness. But of course dividing lines are human inventions, something that makes the oneness of all graspable to a human mind. On the color spectrum we go from red to orange to yellow, for example, while in reality there is an unbroken gradation between what we call red and what we call orange and again between what we call orange and what we call yellow. At what point has the

[55]2402-2

color stopped being red and started being orange? Where along the spectrum do we leave orange and first meet yellow? We can divide sound frequencies into musical notes, but what about the infinitesimal stages of slowing or speeding up that fall between every note? Furthermore, beyond the infinite gradations in every type of spectrum we can perceive, there are those ranges above and below what our human senses are equipped to pick up. More amazing still, who, from the evidence of their senses, would have guessed that color and sound are segments of one continuous spectrum?

When we realize how artificial are the lines we draw, it becomes less likely that what we perceive in three-dimensional matter is the whole of manifestation. It is far more likely that all of manifestation is a graded spectrum from the most dense to the most ephemeral. As theosophist C.W. Rogers explains it,

> The mental world, or sphere, or plane, of theosophy, is a world of matter, not merely thought. It is matter, however, of such remarkable tenuosity that it may properly be called mind-stuff, and in its rarest levels it is said to be "formless" so far as the existence of what the physical senses know as form is concerned.[56]

These higher levels of the spectrum of manifestation may not be easily apparent even to those who have experienced advanced meditative states of consciousness, which may at least partially explain why there is virtually no mention of them in the discussions and literature of contemporary evolutionary spirituality. Yet the esteemed Sri Aurobindo admits that "I had experience of Nirvana and Silence in Brahman long before I had any knowledge of the overhead spiritual planes."[57] Spiritual though these planes may be, the very fact that they are layered expressions of spirit makes them, by definition, part of form rather than formlessness. By analogy, the formless ground of being would be that from which and in which the entire spectrum has its being. It would lead us into a digression far outside our field of concern in this book to go into descriptions of the many planes of non-material

---

[56] Rogers, *Elementary Theosophy*, 45.
[57] Sri Aurobindo, *On Yoga II, Tome One* (Pondercherry: Sri Aurobindo Ashram, 1958),

and yet manifest existence described in the esoteric literature. For our purposes, let's just say that these unseen worlds are said to exist the same way that frequencies of light or sound exist beyond the range of human eyes and ears. They form an orderly progression, with those just beyond the material plane being its progressively less dense replicas.

It is on these planes that souls' earliest entanglements began and on these planes the earliest threads of so-called ancient wisdom began as well. (As a refinement to the simple manifest/unmanifest scheme depicted in Figure 2, please refer to Figure 3 for a graphic, albeit limited, depiction of this point.) For the path of evolution is only part of the story. As told in the Cayce readings and much of the esoteric tradition, before we can have *e*volution, *in*volution first must take place—that is, a descent of spirit through a graded spectrum of ever-more-dense levels of manifestation (involution) precedes that process wherein that spirit awakens to itself in matter (evolution). The beginnings of ancient wisdom can be traced to knowledge held *before* spirit became completely engulfed in matter. It is quite a story.

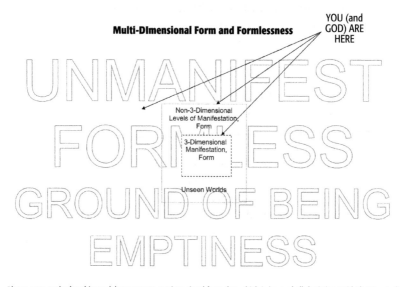

Please note again that this model attempts to put into visual form that which is beyond all depiction. With that in mind, imagine that the page on which this is printed represents timeless, spaceless, unlimited reality and that not only the 3-dimensional world of form, but every dimension beyond the 3rd as well, is just another aspect of the Absolute's manifestation in form.

Figure 3

Involution Precedes Evolution

The cosmology of the Cayce readings is amazingly in accord with the scientific theory of the Big Bang, even though these readings pre-date that theory by decades. They describe God moving and bringing the Spirit into activity, which brought light and then chaos. Then the physical cosmos, including this Earth, arose out of the light–and–chaos movement of the Spirit. Materiality was born through spirit pushing itself into matter. Then, " . . . Spirit was individualized, and then be-came what we recognize in one another as individual entities . . . "[58] This is a description of two distinct aspects of the creative act: the inception of the material realm and spirit giving rise to facets of itself in the form of individual entities. Therefore we now have three factors at play: 1) the all–encompassing, formless Ground of Being; 2) its mani-festation in the world of form, and 3) individual spirit–entities.

For our understanding of involution, it is important to note that we had our origin as individual projections of God *beyond* time and space. From there, according to the readings, the point was for us, as spirit-beings, to "use matter" and everything in the earth's environment for the glory of the Creative Forces.[59] From this we get that we were al-ways intended to be a part of that creative unfoldment. In fact, we seem to have a starring role: " . . . For the universe was brought into being for the purpose of being the dwelling place of the souls of God's children—of which birthright this entity is a part."[60] Yet long before taking on the role of earthlings, we showed an inclination to disregard our stage directions.

When the earth became a dwelling place for matter, when gases formed into those things that man sees in nature and in activity about him, then matter began its ascent in the various forms of physical evolution—in the *mind* of God! The spirit chose to enter (celestial, not an earth spirit—he hadn't come into the earth yet!), chose to put on, to become a part of that which was as a

---

[58] 3508-1
[59] 3508-1
[60] 2396-2

command not to be done![61]

Let's pause here for a moment to unbundle that. Notice that this reading is describing conditions at the time when gases were first coalescing into the bodies of the physical cosmos. Based on current scientific dating, that could have been anywhere from about from 200 million years after the Big Bang until our sun and its planets formed around five billion years ago. (Note again that in this passing reference to gases forming Cayce is in step with modern scientific thinking concerning the origins of the cosmos.) During that time, the beginnings of the evolutionary ascent of matter is described in this reading and others (#s 262-78, 900-227, for example) as occurring in the *mind* of God.

Once again, we find essential agreement with this idea from a most unexpected source, the Christian writings of Henry Drummond:

> The lines of the Spiritual existed first, and it was natural to expect that when the "Intelligence resident in the 'Unseen'" proceeded to frame the material universe He should go upon the lines already laid down. He would, in short, simply project the higher Laws downward, so that the Natural World would become an incarnation, a visible representation, a working model of the spiritual.[62]

To today's reader, this may smack of an anthropomorphic God executing an "Intelligent Design" version of evolution, a position that is held in disdain by most modern evolutionaries. Indeed, anyone who looks deeply at the dead ends and backtracks—as well as the carnage and destruction—inherent in the natural world, past and present, would find it hard to imagine that it is all part of a perfect, pre-set plan. As Ken Wilber points out, if this universe was engineered by a designer, "that Engineer is an idiot."[63] So let me be clear that, whatever Drummond's underlying theology may have been, in this excerpt he is talking about the scaffolding of laws upon which the evolutionary advance is built. He is describing the involutionary process whereby

---

[61] 262-99

[62] Drummond, *Natural Law in the Spiritual World*, 32.

[63] Wilber, *Integral Spirituality* (Boston: Shambhala, 2006), 241-2n.

the evolutionary drive within all matter is taking form at the less dense level of the divine mind. According to Cayce, this is happening even as a physical cosmos is first beginning to form out of the coalescing gases of the primordial past. Think of the gradations of the spectrum. Events can be occurring simultaneously at different levels.

As these events are taking place, we find spirit-entities at a celestial level involving themselves in a way that is not aligned with the divine intention. The Cayce readings tell us that their intrusion was into " . . . fields of thought that pertain to a developing or evolving world of matter . . . "[64] Thus, this was *not* a coming into flesh, but an interference with the creative unfoldment then taking place at the level of thought. Picture this, if you will: Creative Force has pushed itself out into matter, birthing a physical cosmos. An evolutionary ascent of consciousness through matter is formulating in the mind of this Creative Force/God. Remember, in the involutionary trajectory, creations at the level of mind precede three-dimensional manifestation. Then, in blind or willful disregard of the process still unfolding, the entities Creative Force has spun off begin to involve* themselves in it. In so doing, they take upon themselves involutionary descent.

It's not that souls were not intended to have a role in the manifest realm. Rather it seems to have been a matter of jumping the gun by prematurely interfering while the great evolution was still unfolding in the mind of the Creator. For, as we'll be seeing, when the earth plane reached the stage capable of sustaining souls' experience here, humankind appeared as " . . . Lord over all that was created . . . "[65] Elsewhere in the readings we are told that this unfolding world of form had been created "in all its splendor to supply every want or desire" souls might have and that the cosmos had been prepared for souls' "indwelling" " . . . even unto the four hundred thousandth generation from the first creation . . . " To this very day, these same creative forces are at our disposal to use for our regeneration, our pleasure, or our undoing.[66] The choice remains open, for we're also told that for " . . .

---

[64]364-10

*Note that *involve* is to involution as *evolve* is to evolution.

[65]3744-5

[66]364-10

hundreds and thousands of years to come," evolution will bring forth that which will meet our needs.[67] We will return to this point in Chapter 7, when we take a closer look at the value of incarnation. For now, we are only interested in the implications of this idea for the light it sheds on the puzzle of an esoteric ancient history that precedes the prehistoric period of the anthropologist.

In most esoteric thought, the involutionary process whereby spirit manifests in the world of form has been one of successive degrees, the earliest forms associated with earth-life being far less dense or concrete than we experience today. The theosophist C.W. Leadbeater describes it this way:

> The forms built in the first round were very different from any of which we know anything now. Properly speaking, those which were made on our physical earth can scarcely be called forms at all, for they were constructed of etheric matter only, and resembled vague, drifting and almost shapeless clouds. In the second round they were definitely physical, but still shapeless and light enough to float about in currents of wind.[68]

The Cayce story falls in with these ideas, placing most of the fantastical, mythic-sounding lore concerning Atlantis at a non-physical stage of involution, when our bodies and even our personalities did not have the fixed, human form that we see today. At this level, we had a much more immediate interaction with the laws of the universe, creating form with thought, for example, and transporting objects through the air. It was at this time, prior to the deeper stages of involution, that the spiritual knowledge still with us was put into forms that could be passed along. Subsequently, direct access to that knowledge was lost because involution was a process of "continual hardening" that resulted in less and less ability to remember our source (i.e., a loss of consciousness).[69] Thus we find reference to an esoteric tradition that over the ages has passed along knowledge forgotten by most. It complicates our story beyond what is strictly necessary here to go

---

[67]3744-5
[68]Leadbeater, *A Textbook of Theosophy*, 77.
[69]364-10

into detail concerning the claim that there were those souls who did *not* lose themselves in involution and were the preservers of spiritual knowledge in the non-material planes. Some of these eventually lost their consciousness in earthly life and some remained at levels beyond the three dimensions to serve as helpers and teachers.

The Beginnings of Human History

For the souls who had first left the orderly progression of involution-evolution by doing "that which was commanded not to be done," a fresh beginning was made possible in an opportunity to join the physical evolution already underway on earth. This was the start of the Adamic races. According to Cayce, the evolutionary refinements that gave rise to humanity as we know it today took place in response to the need that arose when souls lost their way in the involutionary process:

> (Q) Was it originally intended that souls remain out of earthly forms, and were the races originated as a necessity resulting from error?
> (A) The earth and its manifestations were only the expression of God and not necessarily as a place of tenancy for the souls of men, until man was created—to meet the needs of existing conditions.[70]

Those "existing conditions" were that spirit entities had become entranced by their own creations on the thought plane and entrapped by the lures of raw physicality in the earth. Independent of this glitch, however, evolution was already taking place here as the natural expression of Creative Force progressively awakening in a material world. Reading 900-340 describes that natural pattern of evolution as " . . . the mineral kingdom, the plant kingdom, the animal kingdom, each developing towards its own source . . . ," yet all being part of a unified purpose of becoming one with Creative Energy or God. This is yet another articulation of the developmental pattern we looked at in the last chapter. Continuing with this same excerpt, we see the co-creative role that was given to us in this natural progression. Each of these

---

[70]5749-14

kingdoms of the earth was to have its day, " . . . yet man given that to be lord over all, and the ONLY survivor of that creation." The human body was developed as a means by which entrapped souls could regain their sovereignty and take their place in the evolutionary advance.

According to Cayce the elements of the body were " . . . of the earth-earthy. For, it was made from that which was already a part of God's evolution. Thus the physical body is oft subject to those things and influences, those related things . . . "[71] In Chapter 10, when we consider both the blessings and the complications presented by our biology, this will take on special significance. For now, let us just note that this idea meshes with what evolutionary biologists tell us about the evolutionary past that saddles us with propensities which are often challenging.

According to the Cayce source, the evolution of an early hominid into a fit dwelling place for souls resulted in the advent of the human race in five places simultaneously. The yellow race appeared on that part of the globe that is now the Gobi desert, the white race in the area now known as the Caucasus Mountains, the red race on the now-lost Atlantean continent (but with remnants of that race surviving in North America), the brown race in the Andes, and the black race in the African plains.[72] This is especially interesting in the light of an observation made by Teilhard de Chardin:

> Man came silently into the world. As a matter of fact he trod so softly that, when we first catch sight of him as revealed by those indestructible stone instruments, we find him sprawling all over the old world from the Cape of Good Hope to Peking. . . . Thus *in the eyes of science*, which at long range can only see things in bulk, the "first man" is, and can only be, *a crowd*, and his infancy is made up of thousands and thousands of years.[73]

Teilhard de Chardin further corroborates the idea that the human

---

[71]3189-2

[72]364-13

[73]Teilhard de Chardin, *The Phenomenon of Man*, 185.

form is especially suited to expansion in consciousness when he points out how a better brain was a requirement for greater consciousness, but that to get to that better brain, it was important for the creature to be able to stand on two feet, thus freeing the hands to do things that the jaw would have done for a creature on all fours. Why was that important? Because the resultant loosening of the jaw muscles allowed the cranium to grow beyond what it could have done when it was wrapped tight by the tighter jaw muscles! He also points out that the use of hands resulted in the eyes coming closer together on a smaller face to converge on what the hands were doing—this was a precursor to reflection. Truly, we can exclaim with the Psalmist that we are wonderfully made![74] As the Cayce source put it, this time it was *God's* projection rather than our own that put us here in the earth.[75]

Now that we are here in the human condition, the path outlined in the Cayce story once again converges with that described in modern evolutionary thought. Evolution in the flesh, as one reading puts it, involves passing through the various experiences of being in the earth, from primitive man seeking the attributes of fleshly experience, to consciousness of the higher laws. Then when we apply those laws we evolve spiritually " . . . until man becomes in the spiritual sense the one-ness with the Creator's forces . . . This we find then is evolution . . . "[76] How do we accomplish this? The same reading goes on to say that it is by acquiring understanding of both spiritual law and physical law—both characterized as God's laws—and applying them here in earthly life. "Then truly is it given, 'The righteous shall inherit the earth.'" Missteps aside, from the time we entered the earth plane in the human bodies suited to our developmental needs, we were given the opportunity to reclaim our evolutionary calling as co-creators: " . . . The soul of each individual is a portion then of the Whole, *with* the birthright of Creative Forces to become a co-creator with the Father, a co-laborer with Him . . . "[77]

To summarize, then, the main points thus far in this chapter: The

---

[74]Psalm 139:14
[75]262-115
[76]900-70
[77]1549-1

growth of consciousness over the course of evolution on this planet is an evolution of the manifest aspect of the Absolute rather than an evolution of the Absolute in its non-dual totality. Within the manifest aspect of the Absolute, there is a deep history from which ancient wisdom springs. It tells a tale that predates the advent of humanity as we know it and that begins at non-material levels of manifestation. Even today, a thread of that wisdom as passed on in the esoteric traditions stretches back to earlier human civilizations. But for the mass of humanity the evolutionary trajectory has led upwards from the most primitive of human states. More important still, no matter how great the ancient wisdom may be, there is an even deeper realization that lies in our present and future planetary history.

The point of the foregoing is not to convince the non-Cayce-oriented evolutionary that the readings' story is true. Rather, it is to convince the reader who is steeped in the Cayce readings' version of history that the evolutionary path does, indeed, call us to plow new ground rather than simply return to an earlier golden era and do it right this time. Contemporary evolutionaries may still consider the fantastic stories of advanced civilizations to be mythic thinking. That's okay. We've already seen that there is a distinction between the purely materialist evolutionary and the spiritually oriented evolutionary. Yet both can work together at the leading edge of evolution, for they agree that consciousness and an ethic informed by that consciousness is their field of operation. So too can those who believe the ancient stories join evolutionary forces with those who see such stories as mythic carryovers.

Ancient Wisdom, Modern Breakthrough

The current evolutionary opportunity is not a mere turn of the wheel back to knowledge gained and then lost in the dim past, for never before have souls *indwelling the human form* been at the particular threshold we now face. " . . . our modern souls see and feel today a world such as (in size, interconnections and potentialities) escaped all the great men of antiquity," declared Teilhard de Chardin.[78] How could it be otherwise? Mysteries of the cosmos once addressed only in myth

[78]Teilhard de Chardin, *The Phenomenon of Man*, 286n.

that spoke the language of the soul but did little to elucidate the three-dimensional universe are now also unveiled with the Hubble Telescope, the electron microscope, and the Hadron Collider. Old hierarchies of tribe and temple are rapidly collapsing in an information age that makes the collective knowledge of humankind readily available to average people. A global communications network gives spiritual seekers a bird's-eye view of the world's religious systems, giving those with eyes to see an opportunity to recognize what their religion has in common with that of people whom previous generations tended to loathe and fear as "heathen," "pagan," or "infidels." (This is not to make the naïve claim that such prejudice is anywhere near eradicated, but for the first time in human history the means of such eradication is at hand.) The sciences of biochemistry and genetics are rapidly accelerating our understanding of the control systems of the amazing piece of biological equipment we've been issued to navigate our way through this world.

It seems that on every front, knowledge is growing and the world is getting smaller. Meanwhile we struggle to solve the age-old problems of greed and aggression and our blindness to our own shadow. The very limitations of our knowledge, information, and technology force us to turn to awakened consciousness as the hope of our age. All of this makes for unprecedented evolutionary opportunity, and it will call for a new application of spiritual truth, beyond what was called for in days of spear and chariot.

Spiritual truth, if it really *be* truth, is timeless. We can expect to find it in every human epoch. But to give that truth flesh-and-blood expression is a growing thing. It requires consciousness to keep pace with both our knowledge and the challenges of a changing world. On the foundations of ancient wisdom, we need modern breakthrough to new levels of spiritual realization. What really matters in the end is how many of us are truly ready and willing to accept the evolutionary call.

Chapter 5:
Responding to the Call

Then, the entity finds himself as a co-creator with the divine that is manifested in self. Thus, if the choice leads the entity into the exalting of self, it becomes as naught in the end. If the choice is that self is to be used in whatever manner—as in the talents, the attributes, the associations with its fellowmen—to *glorify* the Creative Force, then the body, the mind, finds that peace, that harmony, that *purpose* for which it chose to enter a material experience.   622-6

Selfish occupation with one's own salvation, when the world is burning, is not a sign of spiritual regeneration.
                Gopi Krishna, *Kundalini: Empowering Human Evolution**

*P*robably everyone has had the experience of lying in bed, half asleep, after the alarm clock has gone off. You know it's time to wake up and get on with the day's responsibilities, but in that moment, nothing seems more desirable than to stay in bed and drift off to sleep. Maybe you hit the snooze button and fall asleep again, only to awaken yet again when the next alarm sounds. The need to get up is stronger now; there's less time to do the necessary rituals of the morning, and still the desire to drift back to sleep is overwhelming. And so it goes, the battle between wakefulness and sleep, until the will to wake up and get on with the day overcomes the will to sleep.

It's much like that with humanity's sleeping consciousness. We have seen how evolution has come to a critical juncture and landed us on the transition point between unconscious and conscious evolution. It's time now for us to wake up and get on with the work of conscious evolution. Some of us are so soundly asleep that much time will pass before the struggle to awaken even begins. Others are already up and about, and the bustling sounds of their activity in the world call to

---

*Gopi Krishna, *Kundalini: Empowering Human Evolution* (St. Paul: Paragon House, 1996), 46.

those of us who still inhabit that twilight zone between sleep and
wakefulness. It remains for each of us to choose whether to arouse
ourselves from our passive slumber or succumb to it and hit the
snooze button; but the call is nonetheless upon us. As one man was
told in his Cayce reading, " . . . To make the will one with the Creative
Energy should be the desire of *every* being . . . "[79]

The call to offer ourselves in service to Creative Energy is not an
easy one to answer, for it beckons us to a new level of engagement
with the unseen laws of the universe and a lifting of human nature
beyond the point to which biological evolution has brought us. Consider both the grandeur and the sobering challenge in this statement
from Rudolf Steiner concerning the evolutionary work at hand:

> We must unite ourselves and become as one with the higher truths.
> We must not only know them, but be able, quite as a matter of
> course, to manifest and administer them in living actions, even as
> we ordinarily eat and drink. They must become our practice, our
> habit, our inclination. There must be no need to keep thinking about
> them in the ordinary sense; they must come to living expression
> through man himself; they must flow through him as the functions
> of life through his organism. Thus doth man ever raise himself, in
> a spiritual sense, to that same stature to which nature raised him
> in a physical sense.[80]

Make no mistake; this call stretches us beyond the commitment to
"personal spirituality" that most of us steeped in New Age sensibilities
hold sacred. It is a spirituality based not primarily on our own attainment of peace, enlightened states of consciousness, or a happy, harmonious life (although those things may well be its bi-products), but
rather on dedication to evolution as something greater than ourselves.
As we'll be seeing, this is a path that will often call us to do what we
least desire to do or that which is least comfortable to ourselves. Indeed, almost as if to remind me of just how tenaciously we hold to
what is personally comfortable, I found myself struggling, plodding,

[79]78-3
[80]Rudolf Steiner, (2008), *Knowledge of Higher Worlds and Its Attainment*, e-book.

and procrastinating my way through the writing of this section. There was always something more "necessary" to do—hadn't I better organize my house and paperwork first so that I could really *concentrate* on my writing without the distraction of undone tasks? There was always something more fun to do—surely I would find it easier to get into the flow after I'd relaxed with a cup of coffee and just one chapter of that great novel I was in the middle of. Then one evening I awoke in the middle of the night with a clear sense that this whole section, calling readers to give their all to the evolutionary cause, sounded just plain preachy.

You see, the truth is, I (like so many who will be reading these words) secretly want a spirituality that showers me with its benefits while making relatively few demands on me. To meditate because it makes me feel good means that when I skip it, I hurt no one but myself. Yet the evolutionary view reproaches me that to be faithful in meditation—which means doing it when I don't feel like it or sticking with a meditation session even when my mind is wildly uncooperative—is the very least I can do if I'm serious about this evolution of humanity's consciousness bit. To address my personal failings or areas of blindness because I have a more contented life when I am growing means that when I get lazy or allow myself to be engulfed by unconscious patterns, I am simply delaying the "soul growth" that sooner or later, one day—or one lifetime—or another, I will have to get around to. Yet the evolutionary perspective chides me that it is the epitome of self-centeredness to think that my soul growth is a private affair, only about me.

How many of us are out there, dilly-dallying and thinking we'll get around to it someday while in the meantime that need for awakened, committed evolutionaries becomes more and more apparent with each day's news? If every person who has felt that stir of excitement about the potentials of conscious evolution would truly get on with it, what kind of changes might we see even now in our world? Yet still, is it not the height of egotistical self-importance to think that we hold such responsibility?

Why Me?

If you find yourself less than fully comfortable with the role suggested for you by the evolutionary world view, you are not alone. There is no denying that it can sound rather grandiose to say, "We are the leading edge of evolution in the manifest realm; in us and through us comes the evolutionary advance of all that is." And grandiose it is, if by that we mean that we are the self-appointed deciders of how the world should go or that we alone are spiritually advanced enough to carry this special responsibility. But taking responsibility for furthering the evolutionary advance becomes far less grandiose and far more a humble duty to perform when we base our commitment on two principles:

1. We are responsible to apply what we know.
2. When we are given much, much is expected of us.

However long you may have been on the spiritual path, stop to consider how much knowledge you have amassed as you've read books or attended workshops or searched the web or joined in discussion groups. How much more do you know than you have so far been willing to actually *live* in your life? You are a rare individual if you can honestly say that you are regularly applying everything you know about the application of spiritual principles in the affairs of your life. Take just one key concept, "we are all one." Do you practice oneness every time you jockey for a place in the best line at the bank or the grocery store? Is oneness uppermost in your awareness when someone expresses a bigoted religious belief or a political opinion that you disagree with? Yet if the evolutionary advance would move us toward unity consciousness, how will that happen unless those who intellectually accept the premise of oneness will take responsibility for making oneness real in their own consciousness? We are responsible for the evolutionary advance because we know too much not to be!

We are also responsible for the evolutionary advance because we have the opportunity to do so. If you are reading this book, you are someone who has more opportunities of time and freedom than the great majority of the world's inhabitants. Most likely, you have a computer (or could have one if you wanted one). You have enough education to be able to read and think about complex concepts. You have been exposed to cultural influences that allow you to chart a fairly self-determined course through your life. In a universe that is going somewhere, is it possible that some people would be so highly favored strictly for their own satisfaction? And how satisfied are we anyway, when we are living only for ourselves? We are responsible for the evolutionary advance because we have been blessed with the means to fill that role.

You may still be saying, "Why me?" not because you are unmindful of your knowledge and opportunities, but because you do not feel adequate or worthy to accept the responsibility placed in your hands. But here is the marvelous thing about the evolutionary advance: It takes us where we are, as representatives of an imperfect humanity, and uses us to leverage that humanity beyond its current weaknesses. So you have fears and anxieties despite all you know about spiritual truth. Fine. Great numbers of other human beings also fear. As you surrender yours even just every now and then to the expansiveness of consciousness itself, humanity is that much closer to being freed of its fears and anxieties. So you fail to consistently treat people as spiritual law would have you do. That's no bar to your conscious participation in evolution. Humanity as a whole is still in its infancy of learning to get along with one another according to spiritual law. Each time you *do* practice spiritual law in your relationships, you move us closer to a new age when spiritual law will govern the affairs of humanity. And meanwhile, the knowledge that you are trying to apply spiritual law in your relationships for the sake of our collective evolution is bound to be a powerful motivator to help you do better!

No matter what weakness or failing may seem to disqualify you from the path of the conscious evolutionary, see yourself as representative of a human race where that weakness or failing is commonplace. The thing about you is that you *know something* about that weakness or failing from a spiritual perspective and you have *opportunity* to do something about it. Many others with that same weakness or failing may not have the same knowledge or opportunity that you have. If you don't answer the call to evolutionary action, who will?

In the final analysis, it may be no more and no less than our natural place as human beings to take up the evolutionary agenda as our own. Reminiscent of the Cayce readings' assertion that we are part of the plan of salvation in the earth and Teilhard de Chardin's vision of a spiritual renovation of the earth, we find this stirring evolutionary call to all humanity from a figure no less illustrious than Jonas Salk:

> The most meaningful activity in which a human being can be engaged is one that is directly related to human evolution. This is true because human beings now play an active and critical role not only in the process of their own evolution but in the survival and evolution of all living beings. Awareness of this places upon human beings a responsibility for their participation in and contribution to the process of evolution. If humankind would accept and acknowledge this responsibility and become creatively engaged in the process of metabiological evolution consciously, as well as unconsciously, a new reality would emerge, and a new age would be born.[81]

Salk, the medical researcher best known for the development of a polio vaccine, held what he called a "biophilosophy," which dealt with the implications of biological evolution for our cultural, social, and psychological issues. "We are to be co-authors with nature of our destiny," he said. Semantic differences aside, we can recognize that the Cayce readings said pretty much the same thing in " . . . man is the co-creator with the builder and the maker of the universe . . . "[82]

Some Thoughts to Ponder

From the standpoint of evolutionary spirituality, we can see the fingerprint of an irrepressible drive to create in both the exterior world of stars, planets, plants, and animals, and the interior world, where consciousness itself is evolving on a cosmic scale, influencing every atom of manifest creation as it does so. How ready and willing are we to engage fully in that co-creative process? The Cayce readings are

---

[81]Howard Taubman, "Father of Biophilosophy," *The New York Times*, November 11, 1966.
[82]3351-1

pretty clear that our purpose in being here transcends our own agenda, insisting that the purpose of our material manifestation " . . . is not then that there may be the satisfying of the mental or material body, or mind. It is not to the indulgence of, nor to the glory of self alone, but that—through the very activities of the body and mind—the fruits of the spirit of truth may be manifested in the material experience."[83] Our spiritual quest is not to "graduate" from this earth, as if it were a mere school to get through, but to participate as incarnate, awakened souls who can serve as pacers for what may be the greatest evolutionary advance this world has ever known—to be agents of transformation.

What is your response to this call?

Examining Your Response to the Evolutionary Call

Points for Personal Reflection

The lists below encompass the main premises and commitments of evolutionary spirituality. Reflect on both what you think and how you feel about each one. Some may be more naturally acceptable to you than others. You may experience some as exciting calls to action and experience others with more trepidation. Which premises or commitments are you already working with? Which ones would be the biggest stretch for you to really live out in your life? If you sense disagreement or hesitation anywhere, get in touch with just what it is that you object to. If you are inclined to journal, consider journaling about some of these premises and commitments and how they do or do not apply to your experience. Return to these reflections periodically as you continue your internal dialog with the ideas presented in this book.

1. **Premises:** Evolutionary spirituality is a world view, an interpretation of the facts at hand, that suggests:

---

[83]1722-1

- The manifest universe is evolving: not just the cosmos, not just plants and animals, but consciousness itself is evolving on a cosmic scale, influencing every atom of manifest creation.

- The manifest realm has intrinsic meaning and purpose; it is far more than just an illusion to be rolled away or a dream to be awakened from.

- Our purpose in the manifest realm goes beyond "soul growth." We are called to nothing less than co-creatorship.

- We are the leading edge of evolution in the manifest realm; in us and through us comes the evolutionary advance of all that is.

- Death and dissolution is a necessary component of life and evolution.

- The outcome of the evolutionary trajectory is in our hands.

2. **Commitments:** Evolutionary spirituality is a commitment to:

- Take responsibility for bringing consciousness into our thoughts, our bodies, the world, and creation itself.

- Embrace the unique opportunity of incarnation.

- Transcend our personal agendas in service to the whole.

Applying Evolutionary Purpose and Priorities to Your Life

1. With your most normal habits in mind, think about some of these life areas:

- Time you spend attending to inner work. That would include meditating and/or praying, reading or listening to materials that feed your spirit, inspire you, or spiritually strengthen you in some way.

- Time you spend with other people—family, friends, partner, neighbors, co-workers, intentional group bonds. How satisfactory are these aspects of your life? What are you doing (or not doing) to care for the relationship dimension of your life?

- Your relationship with your body. Include things like eating habits, exercise, and any other activities or habits that support or detract from physical health and well-being.

- Your work (whether through formal employment or other structures). What about it do you enjoy most, what fills you? What do you enjoy least, what drains you?

- Creative pursuits and interests, whether you are the one doing the creating or the one enjoying the creations of others. Consider music, art, literature, dance, or inventions— whatever may come to mind as an interesting aspect of creativity to you. Notice those feelings and senses that are gratified by creative expression.

- Contact with nature. How much is nature a part of your "normal" life? Be aware of your places of impact on the environment and what you do (or neglect to do) to take care of it.

- Ways in which you are serving or helping others. In whose life are you making a positive difference?

- How you tend to spend unstructured time; for example, TV-watching, the Internet, hobbies and sports, gaming, talking on the phone.

- Anything else not touched on here that is a part of your

normal course of experience on a somewhat regular basis. Just notice the presence of those elements in your life.

2. Now turn your awareness to your emotional life and your thought life. Most people will find that certain thoughts and feelings run through their minds on a fairly recurring basis. Just get a feeling for your mental-emotional climate. It may have wide variations from day to day, or it may be rather static; in either case, just notice what it is.

3. Now conduct a little imaginative experiment.

- Think of all of these habits, priorities, and conditions radiating outward from you, as waves of creation, affecting your life, your family, your social circle, any spiritual groups you may be a part of, either in the live or digital world.

- Imagine the influence your choices, behaviors, and priorities have as they ripple out to your community, the nation, the world. Think of them as an energy that you are sending out into the world, your creative force field.

- Imagine your creative force field combining with that of others, wherever there may be a matching of habits, priorities, or conditions. In this way your creative power multiplies.

- Notice the ways you are contributing to the renovation of the earth, as well as the ways your influence is withheld due to things you know to do but do not do, the ways or times when you are a drag on the evolutionary advance.

4. Ponder any insights that may have come from your imaginative experience. Without congratulating yourself on those places where you find yourself doing well or condemning yourself for those places where you fall short of your ideals, just be aware that you

represent the human race—in all of its potential and in all of its shortcomings. And let that creative force of God within you suggest just one place where you can put in more consistent effort and attention, for the sake of us all.

Chapter 6:
Cultivating Evolutionary Consciousness

... The *I AM* that seeks may gain, then, that access to the *I AM* that brought, brings, holds, the worlds in their place.   254-85

Never mind what lies beyond Death, Mr. Bast, but be sure that the poet and the musician and the tramp will be happier in it than the man who has never learnt to say "I am I."   E.M. Forster, *Howard's End**

*T*here is a great paradox at the center of the evolutionary path: The more we awaken to the consciousness of who we are *beyond* the forms of time, space, and matter, the better equipped we become to act effectively and creatively *within* time, space, and matter. This is why meditation, though not the sole practice of the evolutionary lifestyle, is nonetheless foundational to it. It connects us with the source of all creative energies. " . . . But when ye say Creative Force, God, Jehovah, Yahweh, Abba, what meanest thou? . . . " asks a Cayce reading somewhat rhetorically. Answering its own question, the reading goes on to say that they are " . . . one and the same thing . . . " reflecting various phases of our own consciousness. By whatever name we call this Source of all creation, we may seek " . . . to be one with Him yet to *know* self to *be* self, *I AM*, in and with the *great I AM*."[84]

The Great "I Am"

We are each, at core, a being who is an "I am" within the "Great I Am." Repeatedly within the Cayce material our oneness with God or Creative Force is described in these terms, reminding us that the "I am" within the heart and soul of each person is an ever-present connection to the universal "I am." It follows, then, that learning to be conscious of the "I am" within us is key to developing consciousness of

---

*E.M. Forster, *Howard's End* (New York: Vintage Books, 1954), 238.
[84]262-86

our essential unity with the Source of all creation. " . . . There is no way to be pointed out save the *'I AM . . . ,'*" said a reading given for the spiritual lesson, "Know Thyself." " . . . It is a birth of the spirit . . . "[85]

As we will be seeing, self-reflective awareness, in its characteristic capacity for thinking about thought itself, is an enormous step toward consciousness of the "I am." Indeed, sustained consciousness of "I am" is the ripened fruit of self-reflective awareness, and it holds the seeds of unity consciousness as well. To see how this is so, we can follow a progression that Teilhard de Chardin traces through three principles of consciousness. First, he says, every consciousness centers everything partially on itself. We might describe this as seeing everything as it appears through our own eyes. It's not that we can't imagine how those same things would look from another's perspective; in fact, the ability to do so is one of the characteristics of maturity and psychological health. But even when we are able to truly see something from another's perspective, we are still doing it *as ourselves*. We take a sense of "I" or "me" with us. For example, maybe as a child you had times when you wished you were someone else who was better looking, more popular, more athletic, or smarter than you were. But even when you fantasized being that other person, who were you really? Didn't you simply import *your* self-sense—your "I am"—into another person's body and life? Really, it's impossible for you to imagine anything without *you* being there to do the imagining. So to re-state Teilhard de Chardin's first proposition: It is an unavoidable characteristic of consciousness to experience *as* a consciousness whatever is *in* our consciousness. The consciousness you experience yourself *as* is the "I am" within you.

Teilhard de Chardin's second proposition is that consciousness also has the ability to center on itself constantly and increasingly. To understand what he means by this, we might think of self-reflective awareness as a continuum. At the threshold of self-reflective awareness, we become aware that an inner world of a "self" exists and we can reflect on what that self thinks and feels, what it values, etc. As self-reflection turns increasingly from the contents of the mind to the processes of the mind, it intensifies. For example, we may become

---

[85]262-10

increasingly focused on how our minds work and this turns the eye of self-reflection more concertedly on interior aspects of mind. Ultimately, self-reflection can take the form of consciousness centered on consciousness itself—or as we might also state it, awareness centered on awareness itself. At this point, we are no longer reflecting on what we think or even how we think; consciousness is oriented around the immediate experiencing of consciousness itself.

The exercising of this ability to center consciousness on itself "constantly and increasingly" leads to Teilhard de Chardin's third proposition: When a consciousness is so intensely centered on consciousness, it is drawn into "association" with all other centers of consciousness surrounding it. Why? Because ultimately all consciousness is one. When we know ourselves as consciousness, we are tapping the same reality that everyone else who knows self as consciousness is also tapping. Notice that this is exactly what the Cayce readings were describing in saying that we can know our selves to be an "I am" in and with the "Great I am." In this way, say the readings, we know our oneness with God. In Teilhard de Chardin's description, unity consciousness is born of intensely centered consciousness being drawn into association with other intensely centered consciousness. It would seem crucial, then, for us to understand what it is for consciousness to increasingly and constantly center on itself.

Consciousness Centered On Itself

Most of the time our consciousness—including the ever-present "I am"—is the instrument through which we experience whatever is going on in our thoughts, feelings, and perceptions. As such, it is invisible to us. Just as we don't see the eyeball with which we are seeing, we are not aware of the consciousness that makes every thought, feeling, and perception possible. Of course we can look at an image of our seeing eyeballs in a mirror, but as we gaze into the mirror, we are looking at an image of the organs of seeing, rather than the eyes themselves. We are still looking *through* our actual eyes to see the image of our eyes in the mirror. In the same way, we can certainly think about consciousness (indeed, such thoughts are the foundation of self-reflective awareness), but those thoughts are representations of the *con-*

tent of consciousness, rather than the *function* of consciousness itself. We can never bring consciousness to center on itself by thinking about anything taking place within consciousness—even thoughts about consciousness itself. Consciousness can only center on itself by *being* consciousness. Note that I did not say consciousness centers on itself "by being conscious," but "by being conscious*ness*." There is a very significant difference.

Admittedly, the instruction to "be consciousness" is a slippery one to get a hold of. Just how, exactly, does one go about that? There is no one single best approach—although all effective approaches are really just different ways of articulating the same process. One approach is to persistently explore what it's like to know that you are you. We did a little of that in speculating about the self-sense that we take with us no matter who we may imagine being or what we may imagine changing about our perceptions. Another approach is to practice "catching" awareness in the act of being aware. This involves shifting awareness from the content in our mind to the consciousness that makes it possible for there to be content. Neither of these is easily described in words, because both are internal *practices* that simply must be experienced rather than conceptualized intellectually. They are exercises in being consciousness rather than thinking about consciousness. This is why in meditative traditions we find "pointing out" instructions that serve as guiding commentaries. Such commentaries attempt to lead the participant to a direct, inner apprehension by simply calling attention to various internal, subjective conditions and events.

There is no substitute for this direct inner realization which no words can adequately convey. And yet I am communicating here in a word-based medium, and there is value in describing what can't be learned via words if only so that it may be recognized when one finds it. From such descriptions, those who may be new to the practice of "being consciousness" may also better grasp how to go about it. With this in mind, I offer descriptions and a framework for practicing each of two ways that one might go about "being consciousness" and thereby knowing the inner "I am."

Placing Awareness On Consciousness

As we've already seen, consciousness focused on itself is an intensified focus of self-reflective awareness. It is far along the continuum from the ordinary variety of thought that occupies awareness for most of us. Most of the time we never even think about our thoughts. They propel us along, creating the inner landscape of our world, forming our reactions and emotions, triggering our choices and behaviors. To self-reflect is to pause long enough to turn our attention inside and think about the thoughts, feelings, perceptions, and values that dominate our innerscape. This is the witness consciousness used most effectively in many spiritual and psychological disciplines that are designed to give insight and free us from the autopilot of a largely unconscious inner life. But the awareness we are concerned with here is interior to even the witness consciousness. When we are in witness consciousness, we observe our inner world from a detached and therefore more resourceful perspective; but what is the function that allows us to even witness whatever it is that we witness? It is consciousness itself that makes witnessing possible, just as it makes every other thought, feeling, and perception possible.

Awareness of awareness, consciousness of consciousness—both of these are descriptions of a meditative discipline that involves patiently, repetitively shifting awareness *from* whatever may be going on in our heads *to* the process or function of awareness itself. It is not an attempt to cease thinking or even quiet all thoughts. It can be done even when the mind is racing with thoughts, because it is a search for the element of consciousness that is the base or context or field underlying every thought. Those doing this practice for the first time may find it quite challenging to even recognize consciousness or awareness as distinct from the *contents* of thought. And even once recognized, such awareness can be frustratingly ephemeral as it is repeatedly engulfed by the thought or perception it makes possible. Each time that happens, awareness becomes once again the unperceived conduit of perception. But for those who are willing to repeatedly, patiently redirect their awareness back toward awareness itself as soon as they realize it has become engulfed in thoughts, feelings, or perceptions, the impact is profound.

If you are among those who have practiced this discipline, you will know that to sustain that awareness is to find yourself resting in Consciousness Itself. This encounter with unadorned consciousness is simultaneously the most natural, ordinary thing in the world and an exquisitely restorative elixir. Like the proverbial fish that is not aware of the water, we spend most of our lives unconscious of the consciousness that illuminates every moment of our existence. When we do become conscious of it—even if it is only for a string of disconnected moments—that illumination becomes a more prominent factor in our lives.

A framework for the practice of placing awareness on consciousness appears below.

Placing Awareness on Consciousness
A Framework for Meditative Practice

Take a moment to get comfortable and then allow your gaze to move around the room. As you notice what you happen to notice, see if you can also notice the awareness inside of you that says, in essence, "I am conscious of what I'm seeing." In similar fashion, notice any sounds that you may hear. With each sound that you become aware of, notice the consciousness that makes it possible for you to even know "I am aware of what I hear." Continue your observation of what you can hear and see, always moving from the observation to the consciousness or awareness that makes the observation possible.

After a few minutes of practicing this way, close your eyes and continue to notice what you are aware of. You may start with awareness of your breath . . . the feel of it as it flows in and out . . . or the movement of your abdomen or chest cavity as the breath rises and falls. And notice also that the part of you which thinks inside of you can not only notice these things, but also reflect, can be aware *that* you're aware of these things. Your attention may go to a hand or a foot, and while there is a part of the inner thought process that is simply conveying to you an inner thought of the hand or the foot, notice also that part of you which can notice that you're aware of these things. In the same way, you may be able to scan your body and notice feelings of comfort or feelings of discomfort—it doesn't matter which—just notice that along with the direct perception of comfort or discomfort, there is a component of mental awareness where a part of you can know "I am being aware of this."

Stay with this simple practice regarding what you can see, hear, and feel for a few minutes, and when you have been able to notice awareness as distinct from the thing you are aware of, move to something a bit more abstract. Think about a memory. It doesn't have to be a big, significant memory. It could be some small event from earlier in the day. Just think about it for a moment, and notice that here, too, there is that component of your thought which might be described as the *capability of being aware* of that memory. Or you can think about something you may want, some object of desire. It doesn't have to be anything big. Maybe it will just be something nice to enjoy later on, and you can be aware that this is something which you would like to do or experience or have—whatever it may be. Notice your internal awareness of the wanting of whatever it is.

You're also capable of another level of awareness when you ask yourself, "Why do I want that?" You can begin to examine your own motivation, your own internal reasons, the interior rationale for whatever it may be that you want. But even as you examine your own internal process of wanting something, notice that you can only do this examining because you are using the faculty of awareness. You may even have thoughts of approval or disapproval of whatever it may be that you find yourself wanting. Notice that underneath your approval or disapproval, there is a completely neutral function of awareness.

Now, in the midst of all of this self-reflection, you may have already noticed that you can also place your awareness on the simple act of being conscious. Rather than having your thought on the hand or the foot or the thing that you want or the thing that you hear, or the feelings of approval or the analysis of your motivation—whatever may have been the *content* of your awareness, notice the *function* of awareness as it operates inside of you.

There are so many analogies we might use. For example, imagine that the thoughts and feelings and sensations tend to just drift through the mind are like the clouds that drift across the sky and consciousness is the sky itself. But of course the minute you think about a sky, it becomes an object that you, the awareness, are perceiving. Or we might say that awareness is like the screen upon which every internal event is projected. But again, the minute you start making a mental image of a screen with things projected on it, the awareness has become an object . . . and there is a deeper you being aware of that image of the screen that you've just created.

What you'll find, as you repeatedly but gently train awareness on the process of being aware, is that something will begin to shift. But don't be dismayed at how quickly you once again become engaged with the thoughts themselves. Whatever the thoughts may be—big thoughts, little thoughts, significant thoughts, insignificant thoughts—all of the flotsam and jetsam that flows through the mind very quickly captures our attention, and we lose our awareness in it. The point of this practice is to develop the mental discipline it takes to repeatedly pull your center of awareness away from the thought and place it instead on awareness itself. Chances are that even in a short meditation period your awareness will be captured again and again by the content of your thoughts and the feeling of your feelings. No matter how many times you lose your center on awareness and instead get lost in the mental content that has captured your attention, patiently re-orient yourself on the simple state of paying attention to awareness. Like any skill that requires training, your ability to rest in awareness will steadily improve with practice.

Recognizing the Changeless "I Am" Underneath All of Our Changing Experience

If awareness of awareness is the ultimate self-reflective consciousness, then the interior consciousness of "I am" is the ultimate consciousness of the true Self, the one that has never left its boundless Source. "I am that I am," the Almighty is reported to have responded when Moses asked him who he should say sent him to lead the Israelites out of Egypt. "Tell them that I am sent you."[86] When we practice recognizing and resting in the "I am" consciousness, we truly experience our oneness with God rather than simply affirming it as an article of faith. Then we too are "sent" into the world of form with a purpose.

When we imagine that state of realized oneness with God, often we assume it to be a most non-ordinary state of consciousness, something replete with mystical delights only to be imagined. And although it may have those qualities at times, we seldom realize that we can, through the "I am" that each one of us is, touch that oneness at any time. We know that our oneness has not been lost but merely submerged beneath our awareness. Yet for most of us, how elusive this awakened consciousness seems to be! The secret of "I am" is that the very awareness that is our oneness with God is present in every waking and dreaming moment of our lives. It has been hiding in plain sight.

Think about it for a moment. No matter what is going on in your thoughts, feelings, or perceptions, there is a hard-to-describe "I am" who is also present. It is the constant sense within us that we are ourselves, the self-sense that causes us to call ourselves "I" or "me." This "I am" is the bedrock of your identity, for it is present underneath every chameleon-like identity change of ego and every fluctuation in how you feel, what you think and believe and even what you know. When ego is pleased with itself, "I am" is there. When ego is frightened or defensive, "I am" is there. No matter what identity ego may be spinning at the moment, "I am" is still there. There is a changeless sense of "I am myself" no matter what it *feels* like at that moment to be "me."

---

[86]Exodus 3:14

Emotions shift and change, depending on countless factors, both internal and external to your experience, yet "I am" is equally present in joy and sorrow, love and loathing, passion and apathy. You had the "I am" sense that you were you when you learned your alphabet, and it is the same "I am" sense that is silently present with you as you read these words.

Everything in your life changes. Your physical form and function, your activities, interests, beliefs, relationships, moods, aspirations, and opinions shift and change over time—but throughout all of it, you are one, continuous you. Even when you dream, no matter how bizarre the experiences may be and no matter how out of character you may act compared to your waking life, you still experience yourself to be you in the midst of these dream events. Not even the abrupt transition of waking up from the dream disrupts the unbroken flow of "I am," for you continue to experience yourself as yourself despite the fact that you have just changed worlds! But, you may be asking, what about those times when sleep has been so deep that you wake up wondering "Where am I?" or even "Who am I?" If you'll think about it, you'll realize that even then you know yourself as an "I" or a "me;" it is just the moorings of time and place and the markers of identity that are missing.

It's true that most of the time we are not thinking about "I am." It's just there as the underlay of all awareness. To be aware of anything at all is to function with "I am" consciousness. And as we've seen, the "I am" is the very consciousness that is the Ground of Being. It is the consciousness we share with our Source. It stands to reason, then, that a meditative practice that moves "I am" from background to foreground of awareness cultivates our connection with the universal "I am." "Keep then that mental force of the *"I AM"* within, that is all sufficient to bring the correct vibrations to this body," one woman was told in her Cayce reading.[87] The practice, like focusing awareness on awareness, is very simple but demanding. First, we recognize the "I am" as distinct from, but always present with, every other thing going on in our awareness. In the description of the meditation practice which focuses on awareness, I contrasted awareness itself with the also use-

---

[87]147-16

ful witness consciousness by asking, What is the function that allows us to even witness whatever it is that we witness? Here, in meditation that recognizes and then rests in "I am," the question is just slightly different: Even when you have stepped back from your internal stream of thought enough to be merely witnessing it, ask yourself, "Who is the watcher when I am being the witness?" The rub, of course, is that as soon as you answer that question conceptually you must ask, "And who is aware of *that?*"

In my childhood, I had a "Kaboodle Kit," a vinyl-covered box for the storage and transport of miscellaneous trinkets. Printed on its cover was a picture of a girl holding a Kaboodle Kit just like mine. So of course it had a picture of a girl holding a Kaboodle Kit on *it*–and *her* Kaboodle Kit had a picture of a girl with a Kaboodle Kit on *it*. I remember staring at my Kaboodle Kit, pondering the infinite progression of pictures of girls holding Kaboodle Kits that depicted a girl holding a Kaboodle Kit . . . Recognizing the "I am" who is witnessing the thought of the moment can be much like that. The moment you start *thinking about* the "I am" who is aware of the thought, there is a deeper "I am" aware of *that* awareness. The minute your *awareness* of that deeper "I am" becomes *a thought about it,* you can notice the "I am" underneath *that* awareness. And so it goes. The practice requires patiently, repeatedly *being* "I am" every time you revert to *thinking about* "I am" or saying things to yourself like, "There it is! That's the 'I am' awareness!" Yet each time you touch the "I am" beneath the thought, even for a moment, you are opening the connection a bit wider.

For a guiding framework for this practice, see "Meditating as 'I am'" below.

Meditating As "I Am"
A Framework for Meditative Practice

Make yourself comfortable in a seated position, take a few slow and easy breaths, and then close your eyes. Slowly orient yourself to the you who thinks inside your head. You will probably experience your thinking self as residing somewhere in behind your eyes, or maybe

---

in the very center of your head. Notice how you experience your feet to be below your center of thought, your neck more immediately beneath your thinking center, and your ears off to the sides of where you find yourself as a center of thought.

Now, starting from that place where you find yourself inside your head, thinking, imagine a line that extends out in front of you. Let that imaginary line extend all the way to the edges of the known universe. Create another imaginary line that extends backward from your location inside your head and continues all the way to the limits of the known universe. Make another line that extends to your right, and one that extends to your left, each stretching to the bounds of the known universe. Trace an imaginary line that extends beneath you, right through the floor, on through the center of the earth, out the opposite side of the earth and on through space to the edge of the known universe. From that point inside your head, imagine lines extending at every conceivable angle out to the reaches of the universe until you find yourself to be a thinking center in a sphere that extends to the edges of the known universe.

Rest for a few moments with the awareness that you are a focal point of awareness in the vastness of space which extends all around you to infinity. Take time to really feel yourself *as* a self, a thinking awareness. You will recognize an indefinable quality whereby you know yourself to be you. That presiding sense within you that causes you to use the pronouns "I" and "me" is very difficult to describe, but you can sense it as a familiar component of your awareness. It is the "I am" within you, deeper than any thought. It is the one constant of your existence, for "I am" has always been present, in every moment of your life. Although you may have recognized it by locating it as a focal point of awareness within infinity, you will now recognize that this awareness has no location as such. It *is* wherever you *are*.

Now think back to when you were very young and small. Go to any early memory you choose and notice that the "I am me" awareness was present then too. No matter how much your body or your circumstance or your knowledge and beliefs may have changed, your sense that you were you has been there through all of it. Notice the great continuity of "I am." Let your mind continue to flip through memories and experiences at random—things you did, places you lived, people you were with—and in each case note that the same sense that you were yourself was present. "I am" never changes, no matter how much everything else about you or your circumstances might change.

Let your mind go to the world of feelings and think of times when your feelings were strong. Include times of great worry, fear, anger, or grief as well as times of joy, excitement, love, or peace. Look for the awareness that, at your most miserable and most buoyant moments of life, was the one constant. Even though you felt wildly different at different times, the sense of "I am me" was equally present in all of them. Try to "feel into" that.

Now ask yourself: Who is engaging in these various exercises of thought? Notice that the same inner sense that lets you know you are you has been behind or underneath every thought. Continue to notice this "I am" component to every thought, feeling, and perception that drifts through your awareness. Try to simply rest in *being* "I am." In your attempts to do this, if "I am" morphs into a sentence that you are saying to yourself, the moment you notice this ask "Who is present while I am saying 'I am' to myself?" Each time that you find that "I am" has receded to its usual place as transparent conveyor of awareness, turn your awareness back to that inner sense that you are an "I." In this way, you come to rest more and more in "I am."

The Many Facets of the One Consciousness

Meditation is often described as listening to God. The Cayce readings adopt this definition, contrasting it to prayer as talking to God. The approaches we've been looking at here would fully support this understanding, for they make listening to God practicable. Think of it this way: Our internal thought stream is analogous to talking to God;

it is a filling of our inner field of awareness with the thoughts that we endlessly generate. But when we learn to consistently place awareness on the consciousness–context in which all thought–talk arises, we discover a profound quiet; our incessant inner speaking pauses long enough for us to truly hear. Since there is ultimately only one Consciousness focalized into many points of awareness, when we pay attention to consciousness itself, we are, in effect, listening to God. In the same way, when our awareness rests in "I am," we are in a profound state of silent openness to "the Great I am." Such complete receptiveness is the epitome of a listening orientation.

There are other equally effective ways of framing the internal orientation that places us receptively in the presence of our Source-Consciousness. Attending only to now while turning attention away from all thoughts of the past or future is one such approach. We need only remember that the Ground of Being rests beyond the confines of time to realize that as we continually rest our awareness in now, we, too, begin to awaken to the reality we inhabit beyond time and space. Letting everything just be as it is, without needing to react to it in any way, is another means of awakening to the aspect of our being that is consciousness itself. In this approach, the practice is to simply allow— but not actively pursue—any feelings or thoughts that may come up in the inner field of awareness. The objective is to keep a purely neutral stance toward every thought that may arise, without the need to give it an overlay of liking or not liking, approving or not approving, welcoming or pushing away. It just is and you (the meditator) just are; there is no necessary link between those two facts.

What will be obvious to all who practice these various approaches is that in the end they are just different word descriptions that approach the same process from slightly different angles. When we are only paying attention to now, we are also automatically letting everything be just as it is, paying attention to consciousness itself, and resting in the "I am." When we rest in the "I am," we are automatically in the now and allowing everything in our innerscape to just be as it is. And when we practice letting our internal world just be as it is, we are in the now and we are consciousness itself, resting in "I am." These are all simply facets of the same gem which is consciousness, different lenses that all illumine the same Eye.

The Many-Lensed Eye

Oddly enough, immediately after I had written an early draft of this chapter—including the last line above—I had one of those amazing experiences that seem to come as confirmation that we are on the right track. Having spent the morning writing, I was ready to take a break and so I went out to my patio with a book. I had been reading only a couple of minutes when a dragonfly lighted on the top edge of my book. Now dragonflies have always been interesting insects to me, definitely unlike the creepy kind of flying bug that makes me want to get as far away as possible. A few years ago I found a large dead one and kept it for months on the sill of my porch, often looking at it to marvel at its alien-like, globed eyes and intricate, delicate wing structure. And now here was a live dragonfly, inches from my face, and it seemed to be as interested in observing me as I was it. It cocked its head to one side and then the other, as if to view me from different angles. I examined the details of its face, eyes, wings, its sticky-haired legs and could only tell it softly how glad I was that it was there and what a magnificent creature it was. It flew off after a while, but before I'd had time to stop pondering what had just happened and get back to my reading, it returned and resumed its examination of me.

I tried to send energy toward it as we continued our contemplation of one another and to feel the kinship of oneness with it. I tried to apply some of what I'd just been writing about and hold "I am" consciousness as this fellow-creature rested in my awareness. Then it occurred to me that, to this creature, I might be in the position that God is in with respect to me. I tried to be the kind of benign, loving, affirming presence that I seek myself when approaching my own concept of God. I began what I fancied was a sort of universal form of communication with it. Each time it moved its head, I would move mine the same way. Cocked to the right side, cocked to the left, moving up and down just like a human nod, the dragonfly went through an assorted series of these movements, with me mirroring each one. Who knows what was really there and what I imagined out of wishful thinking, but it seemed to me that my little friend was actively engaged in our game. When it began to rub its lower mandible with its front leg, I raised my hand to brush my own chin. That was a bit too much, apparently, and it flew away. I was sorry to have ended our little tête-à-tête with a movement that frightened it. But my disappointment didn't last for long; in a flash it was back yet again and we resumed our game. All told, my visitor and I spent nearly a half hour together before it flew away for good.

Writing all of this, I'm aware that it may sound a bit silly to some. Yet I know that many who read this will understand just how profound such face-to-face contact with a non-domesticated creature can be. I must admit that the now-obvious synchronicity of this insect with the large, many-faceted eyes landing on the edge of my book did not occur to me then; I was too absorbed in the magnificence of the insect and the closeness bordering on communion that I was experiencing with it. But when I went into the house, filled with curiosity and Googling "dragonfly" to find out more about my mysterious winged friend, one of the search suggestions that autofilled was "dragonfly symbolism." Of course I had to bite on that bait! Imagine my inner state when I learned that the dragonfly is said to symbolize change in the perspective of self-realization, especially that which comes from maturation and looking into the deeper significance of things. It is also said to represent moving beyond self-created limitations to truer experience of the self who is able to live in the now. And, of course, there are those incredible eyes which enable the dragonfly to see 360 degrees around itself, symbolizing the unfettered vision of a mind that sees beyond the limited slice of self-awareness in which we tend to live our lives.

Surely the arrival of this dragonfly was synchronistic, coming as it did on the heels of my writing about the underlying force of evolution and its linkage to universal consciousness, the "I am" as the core identity and the many lenses that illumine the same Eye. To me it felt like the underlining of an important point, a signature, if you will, of the Great I Am. Then, as if to be sure the point was properly emphasized, there was a post script later on that day. Just before turning off my computer for the night, I opened my Facebook page to see what new posts had arrived that evening. There at the very top of my page was a large picture of a dragonfly sitting on a boy's finger, inches from his face! The text that accompanied it said, "As Mother Gaia is shifting, Her vibration is accelerating as She offers a portal for our consciousness to experience our multidimensional essence through our earth-teachers." The language may not be the same language that I have been using, but the take-home message is the same: We are at a time of great evolutionary breakthrough in consciousness; and yes, our fellow earth creatures can convey to us the reminders we need. May we each be led in our own way to an awakening as multi-faceted as the eyes of the dragonfly.

PART TWO:
THE PRECIOUS OPPORTUNITY
OF INCARNATION

(Q) As created by God in the first, are souls perfect, and if so, why any need of development?

(A) In this we find only the answer in this: The evolution of life as may be understood by the finite mind. In the first cause, or principle, all is perfect. In the creation of soul, we find the portion may become a living soul and equal with the Creator. To reach that position, when separated, must pass through all stages of development, that it may be one with the Creator . . .   900-10

If pianos slowly grew to maturity then only when the instrument was mature could the master musician give a practical demonstration of his skill; and only when the physical body has reached its maturity can the soul that is using it fully express itself.

L.W. Rogers, Elementary Theosophy*

---

*L.W. Rogers, (1917, p. 109), *Elementary Theosophy*, e-book.

Chapter 7:
Embracing the Incarnation
in Reincarnation

Hence as we find, when souls sought or found manifestation in materiality by the projection of themselves into matter—as became thought forms—and when this had so enticed the companions or souls of the Creator, first we had then the creation in which "God breathed into man (God-made) the breath of life and he became a living soul," with the abilities to become godlike.   257-201

It is only a character which is itself developing that can aid the Evolution of the world and so fulfill the end of life.
            Henry Drummond, *Natural Law in the Spiritual World**

*F*or many years I specialized in teaching and writing about reincarnation and past lives. I became a hypnotherapist primarily because I wanted to conduct past–life regressions with clients (only coming to fully appreciate much broader applications of hypnosis after I had entered the field). In my own life, reincarnation–related concepts have been so helpful that I can't imagine what my spiritual path would have been like if it hadn't included a view that takes our entire experience in the earth into consideration. Nonetheless, the reincarnation lens, like any favored world view, can be limiting if we don't look through other lenses from time to time. Looking through the lens of evolution, something very important happens when we let thoughts of reincarnation recede into the background and instead place our focus on *in*carnation.

In one sense, the distinction is semantic. The very notion of reincarnation hinges on incarnation, the coming into flesh. But that simple prefix *re-* rivets our attention on the multiplicity of lives and

---

*Drummond, *Natural Law in the Spiritual World*, 63.

naturally directs us to emphasis on questions like: When and where did I live before? What happened to me? What was I like? How is my past affecting me now? What will my future lives be like? In other words, like the magician's sleight of hand that directs your attention to everything but where the real action is taking place, the very word reincarnation can divert our thoughts, energies, and priorities away from the most important aspect of all: incarnation—being here in the world of manifest form, fully embracing the unique opportunities of this time, this place, this body.

The Buddhists make this point concerning the value of incarnation with teachings about "precious human birth." Nowhere is human birth considered more precious than in the evolutionary world view. So in this chapter we're going to let thinking about reincarnation recede into the background while we focus on the gifts of incarnation. We might think of this as a figure–ground reversal. Everyone is probably familiar with pictures that demonstrate how our perception determines what is the figure (or main object of perception) in a picture, and what we perceive to be mere background. For example:

Is it a chalice or is it the profiles of two people? It depends on what you lock in on as the main object of perception and what fades into the background. Or how about this one:

Which do you see–a pretty young girl or a haggard old woman? If you've never seen this picture before, it may be a bit more challenging at first to see more than one image. Whichever one you first perceive tends to take over and make it more difficult to see the other. But once you do see the image that initially eluded your perceptions, you can easily switch back and forth between the two images and accept that both are equally present in the totality of the picture.

The application to our emphasis here is pretty basic. While there is great truth and value in the viewpoint that emphasizes the process of reincarnation in all of its dynamics, when we let that fall into the background and focus for a while on the importance of incarnation itself, we get a broader perspective that gives us a deepened appreciation of the *whole* picture, both incarnation and reincarnation.

Taking the Expansive View of Incarnation

What is so valuable about incarnation that we would do it again and again, despite the obvious hardships of life here as compared to what we are told it is like in the spirit realms? Of course it is axiomatic to the reincarnation doctrine that each life gives us an opportunity to learn from our past mistakes. We are not the victims of random events in a universe that seems to shower blessings on some while withholding even a modicum of life's necessities from others. That's usually why the philosophy of rebirth first appeals to us. It puts the struggles and inequities of life into a meaningful context. We are always meeting the results of our own past choices. Yet many of the clients with whom I've done regression therapy get in touch with feelings that would suggest that their presence here is only quasi voluntary at best. They give the impression of being strong–armed into physical birth by spiritual beings or forces beyond their control. Even those who regress to an experience of choice before birth often report a *"What was I thinking??"* reaction once they got here. And among participants in reincarnation–themed workshops, it's not uncommon to find people focused primarily on finishing their karmic business so that they never have to come back.

All of this would suggest that to many of the most spiritually minded, incarnation is little more than a necessary evil. But–imagining for a moment that we hadn't made any mistakes–would there be any purpose for incarnation other than its corrective opportunities? In other words, does incarnation have intrinsic value? The evolutionary view would answer with a resounding *yes*!

It all goes back to the reason we exist at all, the purpose for which the Absolute spun off individual entities. In the narrative drawn from the Edgar Cayce material, our existence has a strong connotation of companionable partnership about it. According to these readings, in addition to being a part of the universe and the Creative Energy that brought the universe into manifestation, we have each been gifted by the Creator to " . . . be His companion, one with Him in each of the activities."[88] And it is here on earth that we are enabled to prepare for this "companionship" with God.[89] To be a co-creator is an awesome thing in itself, when we stop to really think about it. But to be on the intimate footing of companion to that which comes before the Big Bang, companion to the source and essence of all that is, companion to the power behind every law of the universe and the answer to every mystery–now *that* is really something!

Most students of the Cayce material can easily recite the catchphrase that we were made to be companions and co-creators with God and accept the concept as foundational to their spiritual philosophy. But do we really get it? Is it a part of our day-by-day consciousness or the self-concept that forms our daily choices, behaviors, and priorities? Do we stop to really think of what this means, in terms of our having a positive, creative purpose that infuses the so-called daily grind? When we do stop to really let it sink in, when we orient our thinking around that identity and calling, the story that frames our existence is the story of creation and becoming–the story of evolution–rather than the story of wayward

[88]1549-1
[89]5284-1

souls working their way back to the halcyon days before we got involved here.

In broadest terms, we could say that the evolutionary viewpoint calls us to an expansive rather than a remedial view of incarnation. The remedial view says that we are here only to undo some very big mistakes we made at the dawn of time and that when we've paid back all our debts, we can get out. The expansive view says that our presence here is an opportunity to realize God in the earth. The remedial view says that when "bad" things happen in our lives, it's because we did something to deserve it in another life. The expansive view says that every experience is an opportunity to develop a new spiritual muscle. For example, sometimes our adversities make us wiser. Sometimes they call from us strengths we did not know we had or force us to develop abilities or do things that we would not have otherwise taken the time and effort to accomplish. Sometimes they enlarge our capacity for compassion or enrich our sense of oneness with others who suffer as we do. Sometimes they challenge us to learn forgiveness or selfless love. And sometimes they give us no choice but to develop our faith.

Think of it this way: Every tough experience or situation that comes our way is a dumbbell in the gym where our souls have taken out a membership! The remedial view looks at incarnation as compulsory school. The expansive view embraces incarnation as the academy to which we've been granted the honor of admission. The remedial view reduces the earth to a penal colony for wayward souls. The expansive view delights in the opportunities we have to grow our appreciation for the good, the true, and the beautiful in the earth's rich soil.

The Cayce reading excerpted in this chapter's epigraph enlarges on the already-astounding idea of companionship with God when it says that incarnation holds the potential for us to become godlike. The reading goes on to amplify that idea by saying that through material manifestation—through our "living and being"—we can acclaim and align ourselves with the purposes of creation itself. Now that's expansive!

When we respond to the evolutionary call, we begin to re-orient our thinking about incarnation around the expansive view. Adopting an expansive philosophy of life is straightforward enough; changing the way we view our personal circumstances and the specific experiences we have each day can be a bit more challenging. Such change usually does not happen overnight, but is rather the product of our habits of thought. First we become aware that we could hold a different perspective. Then we train ourselves to notice specific assumptions and thoughts as they arise in our mental thought-stream. Only then can we make the choice to gently re-direct our thoughts and assumptions to the expansive view. (For those who wish to develop this more expansive view of life, the personal reflection exercise below, "Changing the Filters on Your Lens," is offered as a guide.)

Changing the Filters on Your Lens

How much of your life do you view through the lens that says life is remedial and how much of your life do you view through the lens that sees life in primarily expansive terms? It is a choice, because the same experience can be viewed as remedial or expansive, depending on your viewpoint and depending on how you subsequently respond to the experience. If you wish to develop a more expansive view, consider the points below:

First, let us consider again these principles that differentiate the expansive and remedial views of why we are here, experiencing incarnate life:

1. The remedial view says that we are here only to undo some very big mistakes we made at the dawn of time and that when we've paid back all our debts, we can get out. The expansive view says that our presence here is an opportunity to realize God in the earth.

2. The remedial view says that when "bad" things happen in our lives, it's because we did something to deserve it—either earlier in this life or in another life. The expansive view says

---

that every experience is an opportunity to develop a new spiritual muscle. Think of it this way: every tough experience or situation that comes our way is a dumbbell in the gym where our souls have taken out a membership!

3. The remedial view looks at incarnation as compulsory school. The expansive view embraces incarnation as the academy to which we've been granted the honor of admission.

4. The remedial view reduces the earth to a penal colony for wayward souls. The expansive view delights in the opportunities we have to grow our appreciation for the good, the true, and the beautiful in the earth's rich soil.

With the points above in mind, consider places in your life where you have adopted—either consciously or unconsciously—a remedial or an expansive view. In cases where your view tends toward the remedial, spend some quiet moments deeply considering the expansive alternative.

1. If someone were to ask you, "What is the purpose of life?" what is the first thing you would say? Quick, before you have time to self-edit—is the **first** part of your answer about getting out or finishing or making up for past mistakes? If you find that your first response to a question about the purpose of life is primarily framed in these remedial terms, take a moment to formulate an expansive response that feels appropriate to you. Anything that deals with expansive themes such as growth, becoming, exploration, the expression of God and divine attributes like love, or the things you can do or create while you're here would provide an expansive frame to the purpose of life.

2. Think about places where "bad" things have happened to you in your life. These could be health problems; financial setbacks; difficult or unfair things that happened at your job, in

your family of origin, or in your social life; or interpersonal calamities such as failed relationships. Not to diminish the very real human suffering that you may have experienced in these situations (and that you may still be experiencing), how did (or could) this situation help you develop desirable spiritual attributes? Notice where in your life you have allowed difficulties to develop your spiritual muscles and where you have fallen into victimhood or self-blame. In those latter instances, think about how the situations have grown you or still have the potential to grow you.

As you start each day, prime your awareness to be on the lookout for opportunities for expansive perspective.

1. Think of the day ahead as a day of training at a premier academy for souls, one that you were lucky enough to get into, one that is equipping you to be better and better at manifesting God's love and creative impulse in all that you think, do, and say.

2. Look for opportunities to both see and create things that are good, true, and beautiful as they arise in your daily experience.

3. When you find your thoughts gravitating toward the remedial perspective, gently suggest an expansive alternative to yourself.

Why is it important to do this? Because in aligning ourselves more and more with the expansive view of life in the earth, our view of ourselves can't help but expand as well. And that means everything to the evolutionary advance. For our first, our primary co-creative assignment is to *become* what we, as individual expressions of the divine, have the potential to be—individuals in full partnership with God. This destiny ascribed to us in the Cayce readings is one that is in the making rather than one that was fully developed at the start, and it is through incarnation that the essential identity that makes us ourselves comes into full blossom.

In a series of readings on the topic of "Destiny," we find a powerful reference to our role in co-creating ourselves:

> . . . As it has already been given, the Destiny of the Soul is to return to the Giver, the Maker. To man, in the body, does there remain the destiny of whether it, that soul, shall return (as of the creation) empty, or bearing the name . . .[90]

What a fascinating idea! Of course the soul must return to God. The Absolute encompasses all, and there is nowhere and no way for a soul to exist that is not part of the Ground of Being. But it may return "empty" as it was when first spun off as an individual aspect of the divine or it may return "bearing the name." What does it mean to bear a name? If this is the spiritual high road, the destiny for which we are to expend our will and our effort and our very life's blood, it's probably a good idea for us to explore just what that phrase means.

What's in a Name?

In spiritual traditions as diverse as the Native American to the Hindu to the Judeo-Christian, we find great significance placed on names. The first biblical indication of their importance comes in the creation story, when Adam is given the task of naming the animals. In Native American culture, the people are often named after animals and other elements of the natural world to acquire their attributes. All of the old Hebrew names had meaning, and some of the most memorable characters in the Bible had name changes to accompany changes in the direction of their lives. Abram was changed to Abraham after he responded to a call from God. Jacob, "one who supplants," became Israel, "one who strives with God," after his transformative nocturnal wrestle with an unknown visitor. Jesus changed the name of Simon, "hearing," to Peter, "rock,"

---

[90]262-82

after Simon recognized the Christ in Jesus. Even in the twenty–first
century, a scholar writes in *Hinduism Today* magazine, "It is unfortu-
nate that, not realizing the significance of the name, many Hindu
parents thrust Western names on their beloved children." The article goes on to explain that this significance, which can be traced
back to the framing stories of the Hindu gods, is an important
marker of cultural and religious identity.[91]

Names are descriptive labels that can carry great evocative
power. Contemporary society seems to understand this, thanks to
studies that have shown a widespread tendency to associate particular names with certain traits such as attractiveness, intelligence,
sociability–or their less–desirable opposites. Predictably, the new
specialty of "name consultant" has arisen to address the anxiety of
some parents lest they saddle their offspring with an albatross-
name or deprive them of the advantages inherent in a name that
creates a positive image.

There was a time when surnames were occupational labels, such
as Smith, Miller, Cartwright, or Cooper. Or they may have indicated
filial connection, as in Peterson, Jameson, and Jackson, or geo-
graphic links like Rivers. Even though these names may have lost
much of their significance to their current bearers, according to the
Cayce readings they give us a good symbolic picture of how the
spiritual name reflects the soul's cumulative experience in the entire manifest realm. Just as our earthly names relate us to our fore-
bears and other conditions of our collective experience in time,
place, and culture, the spiritual name is ultimately " . . . the sum
total of what the soul–entity in all of its vibratory forces has borne
toward the Creative Force itself."[92] In other words, as the correlate of
our unique interaction with Creative Force over the eons, the name
carries a vibratory quality that is our unique creative stamp. It is
our core identity, the "I am" in unique expression:

(Q) Who comes to me when my consciousness is partially

[91]Amrit Pal Binda, "The Importance of Hindu Names," *Hinduism Today*, Web Edition,
(July, August, September 2005): www.hinduismtoday.com.
[92]281-30

submerged, and how can I be receptive to, or understand their message?

(A) Who better than thy better self, or that thou hast been or hast taught or thought in thine inner self? It is the remembering, as it were, the vision of thine inner self. What more wonderful can there be than to know that self's own ego, self's own *I AM* with the spirit of truth and life, has made aware within self that thou hast been called by name? . . . [93]

We would do well to heed this conjoined power of the name and the core "I am" identity, for we often give ourselves names and labels that go far beyond what may appear on our birth certificates or drivers licenses. "I am" is perhaps the most potent phrase in the English language, for whatever we put after "I am" becomes a name, a part of our identity, and therefore a powerful shaper of our destiny. "I am a procrastinator." "I am addictive." "I am weak." "I am flawed." What words do you put after the phrase "I am?"

In a reading that offers a lengthy discourse on the significance of the name (281–30, referenced above), the Cayce source concludes by saying that we may use our creative faculty in accord with, or in opposition to "constructive force." " . . . For ye *are* gods! But you are becoming devils or real gods!" There's that god–in–the–making promise again. It is reminiscent of the final lines in Emerson's poem "Give All to Love" that say, "When the half–gods go, the gods arrive." The expansive agenda of the soul in the earth is to outgrow the half–gods that cloud our identity so that we may grow into our fullness as companions and co–creators with God. Or, to use the language of the Cayce readings, to fill the emptiness of our first state with character-building experiences that formulate our unique identity, our "name."

Let's be very clear about something: This is not a *return* to our true Selves*, but a *creation* of our true Selves. We saw in Chapter 4 that there is an *aspect* of that Self that has never left the timeless,

---

[93]707-2

*"Self" and its derivatives are capitalized whenever the ultimate, fully spiritualized entity is meant.

spaceless Ground of Being, and we saw in Chapter 6 how the core "I am" identity is always present, even in the most mundane or distracted states of awareness. But the fully formed individuated Self will not appear until we are finished making it! To do this, we apparently need incarnation, for we are told that it is in the body that this destiny is worked out.

Full Spiritual Realization Requires Materiality

In the yogic teachings which say that *Perusha* (spirit) finds its manifest form in *Prakriti* (matter) as well as in Cayce, matter is that which enables the essence of Being to Become. That principle applies to us, too, in that we cannot grow into our full Selfhood without the physical bodies we inhabit. It's tempting to think that if we could just shake loose of these pesky bodies (with their voracious appetites) and all of the nonsense that earth life seems to generate, we would become wise, enlightened, and free. Unfortunately, it's not that simple. With a purpose and destiny that is tied to the ongoing evolution of creation, we seem to have a long-term stake in this admittedly troubled marriage of spirit and matter. As C.S. Lewis once quipped, "God likes matter; He invented it." When we step back and examine the big picture, we may get a better understanding of why.

We have already encountered Cayce readings that say " . . . The spirit of God is aware through activity, and we see it in those things celestial, terrestrial, of the air, of all forms . . . "[94] and that time and space are the means by which the "forces of the divine" bring the evolutionary changes for souls " . . . who seek to become one with Creative Energies."[95] From this we can see two interlocking purposes for our presence here in materiality. First, we have purpose here through the general principle that spirit is awakening to itself in and through matter. The Cayce readings often refer to conditions in the three-dimensional world as the "phenomenized" state of

[94]262-99
[95]254-95

mental and spiritual forces and suggest that there is a unique opportunity for Spirit to "phenomenize" (manifest) in the world through our bodies. The second purpose, our personal development, is closely linked to the first. If spirit is awakening to itself in matter, we are the most complexly organized instance of that awakening.

Who, we may ask, among all the varieties of biological life on this earth, has the capacity of mind developed enough to make it an instrument of matter's *conscious* evolution? Clearly we are involved in an evolutionary agenda that makes our personal soul evolution and the evolution of the material world have interdependent outcomes. The experiences that the soul amasses in the earth are " . . . towards its own development, and [toward the] development of the creation or world . . . ," says one Cayce reading.[96] There is no tending to the evolution of the world without tending to our own developmental process. And that process requires us to be here. Consider this question as well as the answer given by the Cayce source:

> "(Q) As created by God in the first, are souls perfect, and if so, why any need of development?
> (A) In this we find only the answer in this: The evolution of life as may be understood by the finite mind. In the first cause, or principle, all is perfect. In the creation of soul, we find the portion may become a living soul and equal with the Creator. To reach that position, when separated, must pass through all stages of development, that it may be one with the Creator. . . . "[97]

Notice that this reading makes a distinction between all being perfect "in the first cause" (what we have been calling the Ground of Being) and the need for development once "portions" have been given the potential to be equal with the Creator. Just as a newborn baby has a relatively unformed sense of self and exists in a kind of oceanic oneness, so too does the primordial entity at the dawn of

---

[96]3744–5
[97]900–10

its existence have an undeveloped self–sense. Through experiences
of life a child grows up into an individual. In the same way, the
soul matures into its fully fledged destiny as a companion and co–
creator with God.

The Great Paradox of Existence

In many places the readings describe this state of spiritual maturity as "knowing ourselves to be ourselves and yet one with God."
This, of course, is yet another expression of the same paradox we
have already encountered: The oneness of unmanifest and manifest, formlessness and form, being and becoming, the universal "I
am" and the "I am" within each one of us. Two things that seem
mutually exclusive, irreconcilable to the three–dimensional mind,
and yet they are not. Nowhere is this mystery more enticing than
in the implication that only when we are our true Selves we will
also be one with God. From Chapter 6 you will be familiar with
Teilhard de Chardin's ideas of how concentration of consciousness
leads to unity consciousness when intensified consciousness is
drawn into close association with other intensified consciousness.
Yet he makes the point that a concentration of consciousness in a
conscious universe (what he calls the Omega Point) would be "unthinkable" without "each particular consciousness remaining conscious of itself at the end of the operation, and even (this must be
absolutely understood) each particular consciousness becoming
still more itself and thus more clearly distinct from others the closer
it gets to them in Omega."[98]

Each and every one of us is in the process of individuating,
evolving through the medium of experience into unique identities
that are simultaneously one with God. As we actively cultivate *both*
our unique identities *and* a sense of oneness with God, we allow this
paradox to stretch us. In this way, we mature into beings capable
of filling the august position of companion and co–creator with
God. Theosophist writer Annie Besant describes this paradoxical

[98]Teilhard de Chardin, *The Phenomenon of Man*, 261.

state as "a living, fiery Centre in the divine Flame."[99]

It's as if the Creator called us into being and then sent us out into the universe saying, "Go out and become who you will be and then come back and delight me with your uniqueness. Grow into the full expression of your individuality so that I can delight in who you are." This idea first really took on personal meaning for me during my early years of motherhood. At that time, my son was little and loved to play with Legos. He always wanted to get the latest extravaganza Lego kit, even though he was far too young to follow the complex steps for building the item. Consequently, my husband or I would spend hours painstakingly assembling the kit according to the step-by-step instructions—only to have him take it apart within minutes, it often seemed. Then he would use the pieces to make his own creations. One night when I went into his room to check on him, there beside his bed was a little Lego vehicle that he had made. It had five wheels, two windshields, antennas sticking out at jaunty angles, and a little Lego man sitting up on top of it all with a little Lego smile on his face. As I looked at that creation, I saw the essence of my son's quirky little personality in that little vehicle. And from somewhere within me, pure delight bubbled up, a deep delight in this representation of my son's essence. In that moment awareness dropped over me with a sense that I had hit a piece of bedrock truth. It said, "This is how God desires to experience us. Not what we put together with step-by-step instructions, but what we do with our own creativity."

Harold Percival wrote truly when he said that "one's real identity, one's own individual great Self, among other individual immortal Selves" is "the most precious thing that anyone can have" and that it is a mistake to think the spiritual path is about losing oneself entirely in universal consciousness.[100] Cayce would concur, going even a step further to suggest that such loss of identity is the fate of the soul that continually denies its birthright.

---

[99]Annie Besant, (1905, p. 97), *Esoteric Christianity, or The Lesser Mysteries*, e-book.
[100]Harold Percival, *Thinking and Destiny* (Dallas: The Word Foundation, 1987), 15.

The Unthinkable Alternative

So intrinsic is our purpose to be fully developed co-creative companions with God, that we simply *have* no purpose if not that. " . . . An individual entity's experience must be finished before the entity may either be blotted out or come into full brotherhood with the greater abilities, or the greater applications of self in the creating or finishing of that begun."[101] Somehow, as we go through the daily choices we make as to whether we will or will not rise to our calling, it doesn't seem to occur to us that the two ultimate options before us are: "full brotherhood" with everything our potential implies or being "blotted out!"

Apparently, opting out of the creative advance is not a decision to be made lightly. What is at stake is the very opportunity to know ourselves to be ourselves. In other words, our essence can never be lost, but if we wish to retain our God–given capacity to know that we *are*, to have self–reflective awareness, we must engage in the growth that is ours to do in the earth. If we repeatedly choose not to do so, we may end up losing our consciousness of existence. Or, as the following reading puts it, to be "lost" as a soul means to lose the sense of a being *part* of the whole and instead become *submerged* in the whole:

> (Q) Must each soul continue to be reincarnated in the earth until it reaches perfection, or are some souls lost?
> (A) Can God lose itself, if God be God—or is it submerged, or is it as has been given, carried into the universal soul or consciousness? The *soul* is not lost; the *individuality* of the soul that separates itself is lost. The reincarnation or the opportunities are continuous until the soul has of itself become an *entity* in its whole or has submerged itself.[102]

It follows from this that our place in creation must be freely chosen. The Cayce readings assert that it is through the use of will

---

[101] 3003–1
[102] 826–8

that we form our individuality. " . . . Know that what is in the heavens, even, did not produce a single characteristic in the individual soul; but that the individual soul, as a part of God . . . wrought the changes that are signified . . . at the time of materialization into a three-dimensional consciousness . . . "[103]

Beyond Personal Development

As this chapter draws near its close, I find myself uneasy on a certain score: amidst all of this trumpeting of the glories of incarnation and its absolute necessity for our attainment of true Selfhood, what can be said about the in-the-trenches struggles of life? Few who have really grappled with life would say that it is easy to be here. The earth's allurements and goodies notwithstanding, it is a rare person who has not faced much in the way of disappointment, sickness, or sorrow. Even those who seem to have it all must wrestle with the fear of losing it. There are times when we might well ask whether, in proclaiming the precious opportunity of incarnation, we are whistling in the dark. At those times we can't help but wonder whether those who preach freedom from the bondage of incarnation are that far offtrack.

While we will address this question in greater depth in Part Three, the issue is worth a preliminary look here. I recently came across a passage in the writings of C.W. Leadbeater that seems very much to the point. During the involutionary descent into matter, he says, spirit increasingly involves itself in matter so that it can learn to receive impressions through it. With the beginning of the evolutionary ascent, the drive to both spiritualize and escape from matter comes into play. This is a phase of development when spirit is learning to dominate matter and see it as an expression of itself. As evolution continues, the twin developments of differentiation (what we have been calling individuation) and unity lead to even greater spirituality. The process culminates in spirit that has learned perfectly how to both receive impressions and express

---

[103]2408-1

through matter. Then, "having awakened its dormant powers, [it] learns to use these powers rightly in the service of the Deity."[104]

No wonder we may feel at times, as we learn the ropes of expressing through–yet dominating over–our material form, that the struggle is more than we are up to! This is truly an undertaking of epic proportions, and I would never want to give the impression that the embrace of evolutionary purpose frees us from the messiness of life. Rather, it gives us a meaningful framework for staying the course and keeping our eyes on the deeper significance of those things we face over the course of incarnate life.

In this book's introduction I mentioned the inspirational writing practice that was the arena in which the evolutionary perspective first broke through into my awareness. I continued to touch on this topic from time to time as this interior dialog delved into issues that were of concern to me at the time of writing. One day, when I was feeling somewhat discouraged at how slow and plodding this journey through incarnation seems to be, I complained that the path through the earth plane seemed like the long way around. The response that shot back at me put my impatience in perspective: "The entire earth cycle *is* the long way around–from a time-bound perspective. Yet those who realize their divine co-creative selves through the earth plane carry a fullness of creation within themselves that is unique in the universe."

Now of course I don't know if it is literally true that the earth-path is unique in the universe. It's a pretty big place, after all! On the other hand, God's signature move is to create endless variety. Why not a universe full of unique expressions of creative fulfillment? In any case, the sense of possibility that arises from the thought of us carrying the fullness of creation within ourselves puts the largest frame I can imagine around what it means to be incarnate. More than a mere classroom for souls' instruction, this earth and our fleshly existence here are also the workshop and art studio provided for the nurture of our creative capacity. All of the tools and materials we need are here. The drive toward creation is

[104]Leadbeater, *A Textbook of Theosophy*, 64.

there in our spiritual DNA, for we were made in the image and likeness of a God whose primal act is to create. Our core purpose is to be companions and co-creators with that God. The fruit of our becoming is burgeoning creation.

Chapter 8:
Unmasking Ego

... There has been in the experience of the entity the necessity of the pruning of much of the own ego, that the *I AM* may find the greater expression ...   657-3

Whenever I climb I am followed by a dog called 'Ego'.

Friedrich Nietzsche*

*I*n the last chapter, we looked at the essential importance of our unique identities that are both the product of our evolution and the means by which we continue to serve the evolutionary advance. Consider this chapter to be a major caveat: The age-old pitfall for the soul has been to mistake a false ego-based self for this god-in-the-making true Self. To set out on a course of spiritual development without a healthy knowledge of ego's ways is like going in to put out a forest fire with a can of lighter fluid in your back pocket. It's only a matter of time before you crash and burn. Or, to use a metaphor given a Cayce reading: " ... The abilities that are indicated are excellent. The ego of self may destroy that which may come to fruition, just as a character of parasite of the mind may destroy the character and abilities of the entity ... "[105]

It sounds like we overlook the lurking dangers of ego to our own hazard. Yet, separating ego from the true Self can be a daunting task, for ego is endlessly inventive in its ability to develop cunning disguises. The greatest of great imposters, ego can easily fool us when it takes on identities like The Wounded One, The Selfless Servant, or—and this is one of its most brilliant disguises—The Serious Spiritual Seeker. The process of growing into our ripened identity as individual Selves requires a willingness to unmask ego time after time, stripping away the false notions of self like so many weeds that suck nutrients

---

*Friedrich Nietzsche, retrieved from brainyquote.com.
[105]2987-1

away from the true Self and block its light. But before we can do anything with ego, we have to first know what it is and learn to recognize it.

Just What *Is* Ego, Anyway?

There are many definitions and understandings of ego. The dictionary will tell us that it is: 1) the "I" or the self of a person, that which distinguishes one thinking self from other selves or objects; 2) (in psychoanalysis) the part of the psyche that experiences and reacts to the outside world and is responsible for modifying the antisocial instincts of the id according to the demands of the conscience or superego; 3) one's image of oneself; 4) conceit or self-importance and 5) (in philosophy) the enduring and conscious element that knows experience or the complete person comprising both body and soul.[106] No wonder we can find it hard to pin down just what we mean when we talk of ego.

Nor will I be able to offer a concise treatment of how the term is used in the Cayce readings. One hundred and thirty-nine readings refer to the ego, with every one of the five definitions above implied at different times. Often the ego is equated with the "I am" and just as often the ego is pitted against the "I am." For every reading that ties ego to traits like self-indulgence, self-aggrandizement, or self-glorification, we can find opposite examples, like the reading that says " . . . ego turned in the other direction may be and is the constructive force in each soul; expressed in the *I AM* being one with the *I AM* presence.[107] So let's sort out just what I do and do not mean when I speak of ego as something to be unmasked.

On the one hand, ego can mean nothing more than the functional self that keeps us whole in navigating through this world. This is akin to the first and second dictionary definitions. In this sense, without a "healthy ego," we are beset by various neuroses that only interfere with our spiritual progress. As Buddhist teacher Jack Engler once said, "You have to be somebody before you can be nobody." The ego that

---

[106] www.thefreedictionary.com.

[107] 261-15

glues us together as healthy personalities is not what I mean when I say that we are to unmask ego—although it may also be true that the ego that performs a valid function at one stage of our development may be the very ego that must be cast aside at a later stage. More on this later.

It is also important to note that I do not use the term *ego* as it is used in most of the older literature coming from the various streams of New Thought and theosophy. In those writings, *ego* is used in a way that is almost opposite to how it is most commonly used today, for we find the term used to describe what we have been calling here the "true Self"—that is, the enduring entity that makes its way through the cycles of incarnation to ultimate fulfillment as a unique being aligned with divine purpose. This understanding of ego is most like the fifth dictionary definition above. In theosophical cosmologies describing our sojourns through the non-three-dimensional levels of form, ego is the core self that transcends not only physical existence, but the etheric and astral as well. So that is most certainly not the ego that we are concerned with here.

For our purposes here, ego is most closely tied to definitions three and four above. As I will be using the term, it is any version of self that is misaligned with our divine origin and destiny. With this under-standing as our operating definition, ego is therefore any and all false identities that limit our capacity to identify with who and what we really are. As such, ego is primarily a construct of self-image. By this definition, ego is not necessarily tied with the kind of self-inflation that is often implied when we say someone is "egotistical"—although it can be. The ego can just as often be an identity of self-deprecation. The ego can manifest as a desire for indulgence and ease, but it can also manifest as an identity wrapped up in a self-image of being hard-working and self-denying. The ego can be outrageously interested in being the center of attention or it can be deeply fortified against being seen and known. The ego can be greedy and put self first, but it can also be invested in a self-image of being "the kind of person" who never takes too much and who always steps aside for the other guy.

The Subtle Disguises of Ego

From these examples, you will see that traits or behaviors are not reliable indicators of a limiting ego identity. Those familiar with the New Testament scriptures will recall a warning that Satan himself can be transformed into an angel of light.[108] From this statement, many of the orthodox faithful have reasoned that there is a "counterfeit" version of every spiritual gift and that the devil uses these counterfeits to lure people away from the true faith. I would suggest that, rather than a diabolical being who corrupts people's faith with counterfeit "works of righteousness," the Satan transformed into an angel represents some of ego's subtlest and most convincing disguises: things that look like spirituality but are really motivated by the preservation of a self-image. Chew on this Cayce reading for a moment:

> . . . Let the body-mind, the body-consciousness, gain this lesson: That "I must be made one with the *I AM*," rather than the I made to appear as the representative of the *I AM*, see?[109]

Do you catch the distinction between *being* one with the "I am" and making oneself *appear* to be the "I am's" representative? It usually comes down to our deepest—and often unconscious—motivation. Are we doing what we are doing to preserve an image that is somehow important to our identity or are we doing it for less self-protective reasons? For if we look closely, we will usually find that far more significant than ego's role of Great Pretender is its role of Great Defender. Its role is to create aspects of self-image that protect us from perceived threats (and change of any kind is usually perceived by ego as a threat) and then hang on to those identities for dear life. Sometimes ego is defending something no more complex than a penchant for short-term gratification. The temporary comfort or pleasure of doing something that feels good in the moment, whether it be indulgence in a cutting comment or cutting one too many slices of cake, is satisfaction enough for the ego-self, and it will tend to cling to that

---

[108] II Corinthians 11:14
[109] 257-20

satisfaction despite undesirable long-term outcomes. Other times, ego's behavior is more deeply motivated to preserve an aspect of what the small self clings to as right or even necessary for its own survival.

We are usually much better at spotting ego in someone else than in ourselves. Why do we find popular television characters like Larry David in *Curb Your Enthusiasm* or Britain's curmudgeonly Doc Martin or classic American sitcom figures like Frasier or Ray Barone so amusing? I think we find something endearing in characters that put the ego-self, in all its blindness, its arrogance, and most of all its vulnerability right out there for us to see. These are people who, if we actually had to deal with them in real life, we might find more than a little difficult. Yet when we get to follow them through their fictional experiences, we feel a certain indulgent affection for them because we recognize in their foibles the familiar face of ego. We don't need to be just like them to recognize our shared human blindness to ego.

Because the unfolding of the true Self is an evolutionary process, our realization of what is ego and what is indeed true Self will be a progressive experience. Ego that manifests as blatant self-indulgence and blatant self-glorification is fairly easy to spot. But as we progress in our awakening to the true Self, it gets more tricky. What seems to be the true Self at one stage of our development may reveal its underlying egoic nature at a later stage. This is especially true for spiritual seekers who will often discover that ego can very quickly co-opt even our best intentions and make them a part of its well-crafted self-identity. Such discoveries are both painful to ego and bracing to the soul. Let me offer a very personal example.

I embarked on the spiritual path at the relatively young age of nine, when I experienced a distinct spiritual calling. The spiritual element has been a dominant theme in my life ever since. I got serious about the Cayce material at the tender age of sixteen, attending a Cayce *Search for God* Study Group every Friday night of my late teens and college years. Unbeknownst to me, ego was all the while crafting the identity of Spiritual Prodigy. Not that people who knew me would have been likely to see that; I wasn't the least bit aware of it myself. It was just a quiet little comforter, hanging out somewhere in the recesses of self. It was especially useful if I happened to be feeling insecure about my progress on the spiritual path.

Then one day the lid blew off the whole thing when I suddenly realized that there had been an ulterior motive mixed in with all that youthful yearning after things spiritual. I was a fat kid (back when fat kids were still rare) who felt like damaged goods—the one not picked for teams, the one who had to face the humiliation of the "chubby" rack in clothing stores, the one assigned the role of "Sally Sweets" in the fourth grade class play about good nutrition (I kid you not!). But from the moment the spirit within me stirred and started to awaken, I had found my world. It was a world where I could feel good about myself and forge an identity not sullied by the shame of my physical form. It was ego to the rescue!

Don't get me wrong. I'm not saying that ego did a bad thing in thus shielding me. Neither am I saying that my entire spiritual path was founded on egoic deception. The genuine aspects of that spiritual unfoldment early in life far outweigh the egoic overlay. But nonetheless the day had to come when I recognized and stepped away from that very subtle flutter of self-satisfaction to think of how young I was when I first stepped on the path and to recognize it for what it was: an egoic co-opting of my spiritual awakening.

The realization shook me to my core. The most frightening thing about owning up to a manifestation of ego in your life is that it leaves you feeling temporarily like an utter fraud or a terrible failure or a horrible person—depending on the nature of the egoic identity you are unraveling. Had more than forty years on the spiritual path been nothing but a garden variety defense mechanism? There comes a split second of decision in any unmasking of ego where truth has to be more important than one's psychological comfort. Otherwise, we quickly find a rationalization that restores us to at least some measure of the complacency we had before we were rudely confronted with such a disturbing idea. The last words of each egoic manifestation are, "Don't let me go! You'll never survive without me!" Yet most often we find that truth is only painful briefly. Like antiseptic applied to a dirty wound, it very quickly morphs into a healing balm if we will be willing just to endure the initial sting. In the situation I've been recounting, the unmasking of ego allowed me to love that fat child rather than hide her in spiritual pride. My life's experience with spiritual unfoldment was not nullified, but instead liberated from yet one more aspect of egoic overlay. There will be many more such liberations necessary before I've grown completely into my true identity, but each one does its part to release me from an aspect of the small self and take me a step closer to my true Self.

Liberating the True Self

Repeatedly in the Cayce material, "self" is identified as that which stands between us and the deeper realization of spirit. "There is naught that may separate thee from the knowledge of the eternal save self," says reading 3184-1 and countless others like it. Perhaps equating ego with self (small *s*) is the simplest way of all to recognize the endless variety of faces that ego assumes. The "self" may at times manifest those traits we easily spot as selfishness—putting one's own wants and needs ahead of others—or self-centeredness—the classic "it's all about me" syndrome. In those cases, it's easy to see how such attitudes separate us from the deeper consciousness of a true self that thrives on oneness. We can be far more easily deceived by some of the other tactics devised by a small and limited self that constantly strives for ownership of the "I am." When we are embarrassed or humiliated, who is that but self? The "I am" is not subject to such assaults on pride. When we are fearful, who is that but self? The "I am" rests in those eternal realities where fear has no meaning. When we condemn ourselves or judge others, who is that but self? The "I am" abides in a state of divine grace, where every experience is an opportunity to learn or grow or bring more love into material conditions. Whenever in the face of change we cling to what has been, who is that but self? The "I am" flows through the world of form, recognizing change as one of the engines of creation.

From these examples, it should be obvious that the ego–self is not some great villain to be stamped out, but simply a tendency to misplace our identity on self-images that hide us from and rob us of our true heritage as divine offspring of the Absolute. Ego is the small, frightened, unknowing one who tends to shrink into the world of its own creation and hide behind a fortress of walls made of masks. The ego–self really believes that to surrender to the larger Self is to die, and so it holds on tenaciously to each mask, as if holding on to life itself.

Blind to the glory of the true Self waiting to take over a bit more of the psychic real estate, the ego–self asks, as each of its mask–walls is threatened, "If I am no longer this mask, then who will I be?" With the instincts of a clever animal avoiding a trap, ego adopts its wily ways as an act of self–preservation. But if the true Self is to emerge, these ways must be ferreted out and disavowed.

But, you may be asking, how can we ever be completely free of the ego–self? This sounds like an enormous project, a transcending of our very humanity. It is indeed just that. But let's remember that that is the work of our becoming, the essential co–creative project with which we are tasked. We should not expect it to be a single, simple operation to move from ego–self to true Self. We are not looking for a single, "Aha! *There's* my ego!" revelation that shoots us into enlightenment, but are rather committing to an ongoing practice. That practice requires a layer–by–layer lifting of the veils that separate us from our deepest Selves. The more we awaken to our true Selves, the better we can discern the more subtle disguises that ego has spun. Conversely, the more we collude with the ego–self by neglecting the spirit, the more lost we become in ego's hall of mirrors:

> But when [the soul] has lost sight of its *spiritual* force, its spiritual nucleus, and the body–mental begins to build toward the self, the ego—not the *I AM* of *I AM THAT I AM*, that is the center, the source of all forces or influences, but toward the self—it loses its hold.[110]

For those who are willing to make the commitment to grow beyond ego's confining walls, a three–pronged approach will usually be most effective. Such an approach includes awakening to the true Self, acting from true Self–generated motivations and turning a discerning eye toward the wily ways of ego. Because it's hardly fair or even do–able to ask the false self to vanquish the false self, it stands to reason that the more we awaken to the true Self within, the more we build our capacity to recognize what is not consistent with our deeper identity.

So far, we have encountered the true Self largely in its appearance as the "I am." This will be a reliable pathway to awakened conscious-

---

[110]416-10

ness of the authentic Self—so long as we meditate on the essential "I am" consciousness in such a way as to strip it of any and all overlays that we typically affix to "I am." We can find yet another avenue to the authentic Self in what is perhaps a surprising place—the Cayce readings on the guardian angel.

The Self Before the Throne

You will recall that, just as the Absolute has its states of Being and Becoming, so too do we. The part of us that takes on flesh (and so easily allows consciousness to become engulfed in it) is engaged in becoming, while another aspect of us remains beyond the world of form, resting in pure being. The Cayce readings describe this state as "standing ever before the throne." The imagery here, drawn from the Christian scriptures Cayce was steeped in, is a poetical way of saying "in God's presence." This aspect of the Self that remains in the presence of the All is variously called a guide, guard, guardian, or guardian angel. For example, "Each and every soul, as we have given, has that guardian influence that is ever before the throne"[111] and " . . . The face of the self's *own* angel is ever before the Throne. Commune oft with Him."[112]

Lest we think that the guardian angel is someone or something other than our Selves, when another person asked, "How may one be constantly guided by the accompanying entity on guard at the Throne?" the reading's answer clearly identified the guardian influence with the deeper consciousness or the " . . . subliminal self that is on guard ever with the Throne itself . . . "[113] In another case, the sleeping Cayce was queried, "Is it through the guardian angel that God speaks to the individual?" The answer is somewhat detailed but ultimately concludes with the statement, "Yes—through thy angel, through thy *self* that *is* the angel—does the self speak with thy Ideal!"[114]

In our quest to move beyond the false identities of ego and nurture

---

[111]275–31

[112]1917–1

[113]5754–3

[114]1646–1

the development of the true Self, that part of us here imaged as the guardian angel is a powerful ally. To meditate on that within us that has never broken its communion with its Source is to awaken the true Self. So often when we meditate, we come with the sense that there is something we have to do or stop doing before our consciousness can reach the desired state of attunement. But here we simply direct awareness to an inner sense of the guardian influence that is "ever before the throne." There's nothing you have to change or create or better understand in order to make that Self appear. Instead, you just contemplate that it *is* and that it is already face to face with the divine.

Whether we approach the true Self in its appearance as the "I am" that is present in every moment of consciousness or as the guardian angel that is ever before the throne, our success in growing beyond ego will be both ratified and augmented by our ability to patiently cultivate that consciousness in our daily lives. The more we commune with Spirit, the more natural it becomes to express the traits of Spirit. So if we want to know whether we are making progress in our growth beyond ego, the way we treat ourselves and others will be a good indicator. Conversely, as we increasingly follow impulses toward love, wisdom, compassion, generosity, creativity, courage, kindness, and forgiveness, we also grow in our ability to recognize their egoic opposites and counterfeits. Then, we are better equipped to more consciously and consistently remove ego's many masks. For as Annie Besant has said, "You do not control your Self; that is a misconception; you control your Not-Self."[115]

Noticing the Wily Ways of Ego

While I cannot tell you what is and is not a manifestation of ego in your own thoughts, feelings, and behaviors, it does have some characteristics that we can become alert to in ourselves. However far our level of sensitivity to the distinction between ego and the "I am" has developed, we will always be capable of noticing the difference if we watch ourselves unflinchingly. If you are ready to have some fun with this, please see the experiential exercise for this chapter, "Stalking the Wild Ego," on page 111.

[115]Annie Besant, (1907, p. 34), *An Introduction to Yoga*, e-book.

Stalking the Wild Ego

Become aware of your capacity to catch the ego "in the wild"—that is, operating stealthily underneath the radar of your normal conscious awareness. When you notice ego in action, do not blame or internally criticize yourself. Instead, maintain a neutral attitude—or possibly even one of mild amusement. Think of this as a game of "Gotcha!" that your awareness can play with the wily ego that likes nothing better than to run the show without being detected.

To give you a few ideas of what to look for, the inventory below is a partial list of some of ego's common characteristics. Ego is usually the one who:

- Is separate from others and/or God.
- Is not good enough.
- Avoids unpleasant disciplines of mind or body.
- Avoids unpleasant realizations.
- Has to be right/is embarrassed about being wrong.
- Is motivated to preserve a cherished image of self.
- Is motivated to preserve a hated image of self.
- Finds fault with self and/or others.
- Focuses on self—whether critically or in self-congratulation.
- Needs to feel okay about self, no matter what.
- Belittles self or others.
- Thinks "I'm the kind of person who _____."
- Resists change.
- Resists new ideas.
- Feels better about self when another person is worse off (or fatter or poorer or less successful) than you are.

In reading this list, you may come up with some of your own additions. The point of this exercise is not to beat up on the ego and banish it as the "bad guy" in your makeup. Rather, simple awareness of ego's many masks is a good way to build your identifica-

tion with your true Self. The awareness that can notice ego in action is not the ego, but a deeper, more authentic part of the self
that, with use, will gain prominence in your consciousness. But
beware. Just as you start getting really good at spotting ego, ego
may come up with a new disguise—The One Who Is Virtuously and
Consistently Spotting and Putting Down Ego! Just smile to yourself
when you notice it.

If the awareness of an aspect of ego in your life suggests a modifi-
cation you can make in your reactions of thought or your words or
your behaviors, that's great. Just be sure you don't let ego co-opt
the process by becoming the critical taskmaster. Meanwhile, keep
your connection with the true Self as strong as possible by tuning
in through meditation and acting on impulses of love, generosity,
kindness, and forgiveness—toward yourself as well as other
people.

The Evolutionary Imperative

It's important, in this focus on growing beyond the limitations of
ego, that we continue to keep our eyes on the overriding purpose for
our doing so. Of course it is necessary to our own spiritual development; but far more to the point, it is not optional to the evolutionary
advance. Only awakened consciousness can be clarified and directed
along lines that are in keeping with the first impulse of the divine in
bringing something out of nothing. If we have any aspirations to fill
the co-creative role we have been honored with, it is incumbent on us
to face the larger implications of egoic blindness as a force that stalls
our collective progress. One young woman was told in her Cayce reading that she needed to know her limitations as well as her abilities so
that she could correct certain weakness of her ego. "For, the purpose of
an entity's entrance into the earth (and this might apply to all) is to
manifest the personality of God in the own individuality and personality. For each soul is as a corpuscle—yea, as a thought—in the mind
and the heart of God.[116]

---
[116]3351-1

If we are corpuscles within God, then the choice we face is whether to be cells that bring life, growth, and vitality or death, destruction, and disease to the body of humanity and its host-globe. This may sound melodramatic—until we look at the world around us. There the contrast between the two choices is all too evident.

Chapter 9:
Corpuscles in the Body of God

... for each cell of the blood stream, each corpuscle, is a *whole* universe in itself...   341-31

After all, what nobler thought can one cherish than that the universe lives within us all?   Neil deGrasse Tyson[*]

*A*t the conclusion of the last chapter we saw a Cayce reading likening us to corpuscles in the heart and mind of God. This corpuscle concept is actually one that comes up with great frequency in the Cayce material, with most of the statements making the even more startling assertion that we are corpuscles in the *body* of God. I can think of no concept that better frames the evolutionary purpose in life. And if we want a blueprint for the evolutionary lifestyle, we need look no further than this:

> Each entity, then, is as a corpuscle in the body of that force called God. Those activities in which there has been the presentation, the manifestation of His love, His activity in the earth, are as the blood stream; while the spirit of consciousness is as the nerves of the body itself. Hence self, as an individual, is a manifestation of Creative Forces in action in the earth.[117]

Who can entertain the possibility suggested by this reading without experiencing a more precise sense of what it means to say that we humans are at the leading edge of the evolutionary trajectory? Whenever we speak of evolution as having a divine purpose, there is always the danger of someone thinking that we mean there is an external God "out there" who made this thing we call the universe. When we speak of humans as having a divinely appointed co–creative role, we

---

[*]Neil deGrasse Tyson, *Death by Black Hole: And Other Cosmic Quandaries* (New York: W.W. Norton and Company, 2007).
[117]2174-2

can inadvertently create the impression that we're like the little construction workers that God has sent into His project to get the job done. But here, in this astounding and humbling and glorious image, we see the universe as God's body. This is no detached God implementing an intelligent design. This is the Absolute, vesting itself in matter, taking form as a living, breathing, developing universe. We are not disconnected emissaries. We are the organic material of God's body. What we do matters as much to God as what our cells do matters to us.

Corpuscle is the diminutive form of *corpus*, the Latin word for "body," and we are little bodies within God's big body. What an interesting way to describe us. Once again a trip to the dictionary proves very enlightening. In biological usage, a corpuscle is an unattached cell, especially the kind that floats freely, such as a blood or lymph cell. Our acts of love are the very bloodstream in God's body. In anatomy, a corpuscle is a small mass or body forming a more or less distinct part, such as the sensory receptors at nerve terminals. The spirit of consciousness that we hold is the nervous system of God's body. In physical chemistry, a corpuscle is any minute particle of matter, such as an atom or a proton within the atom.[118] This is really fascinating, when you consider that atoms and protons are perfect physical examples of things that are whole unto themselves, while simultaneously being part of something else. They are also the wholes of which smaller components are parts. For example, an atom is whole unto itself, yet it is also part of any substance which it is used to compose. At the same time, there are smaller components of the atom, such as protons, that are also whole unto themselves yet part of the greater body. We can go on to quarks and neutrinos and other sub-atomic particles that I don't pretend to really understand, and the pattern still holds. Who knows how far it goes? Here we are looking at the microscopic level of the great paradox of our existence, knowing ourselves to be ourselves and yet be one with God. Or, as Cayce put it in one reading, " . . . awareness of the entity's being as an individual entity, and capable of being part of or being the whole, yet *not* the whole."[119]

---

[118]www.thefreedictionary.com.

[119]1602-3

We are component corpuscles of God's body, yet whole unto ourselves. At the same time, the component corpuscles of our bodies are part of us and yet individual unto *themselves*. As Bruce Lipton says in his breakthrough book *The Biology of Belief*, "You may consider yourself an individual, but as a cell biologist I can tell you that you are in truth a cooperative community of approximately 50 trillion single-celled citizens."[120] When we remember that the life force—which carries the rudiments of consciousness in its very essence—is present in every cell, molecule, and atom of our bodies (see Chapter 3), it is easier to see how our consciousness is the organizing principle for the consciousness in the cells, molecules, and atoms of our bodies. As we awaken to the greater Consciousness in which we live and move and have our being, we exist within the fullness of God and the fullness of God exists within us.

We Are in the Universe and the Universe Is in Us

Within us—within this flesh body—the entire cosmic order is playing out. This is an oft-repeated concept in the readings. "For remember, even within each atomic force of a corpuscle, or the very *humor* of the blood stream, is the pattern not only of the body but of the universe . . ."[121] This is nothing short of astounding. First, that the Cayce source could have known that a corpuscle in the blood contains the pattern of the body is truly remarkable. Today, with reports from the Human Genome Project regularly making their way into mainstream media, we take it as a given that our physical template can be found within the DNA of a single cell. Although the existence of DNA was known in the late 1800s, it was not until well after this reading was given in 1938 that DNA's role in heredity was confirmed. And only with the Human Genome Project, begun in 1990, could we begin to see just how detailed the blueprint that patterns our body actually is. Second, in saying that these same cells contain the pattern of the universe, Cayce was particularly prescient. It is only with the benefit of

---

[120]Bruce Lipton, *The Biology of Belief* (Santa Rosa: Mountain of Love/Elite Books, 2005), 27.
[121]1770-1

modern biology and physics—as well as their finely tuned instruments of observation—that we can begin to realize just how literally true this statement is. Microscopic images of brain neurons and their connections look shockingly like computer-simulated images of a galaxy cluster with smaller galaxies, stars, and dark matter surrounding it. Images showing the birth of a cell closely correspond to images depicting the death of a star. You may have seen some of these pictures, as they circulate widely on the Internet, but if you have not, a simple web search will easily bring them up.* When we gaze at such images, these words from Cayce (which recapitulate the raptures of the psalmist 3,000 years ago) take on a deepened significance:

> . . . For first there should be the realization by all that matter in any form is of the spirit, whether from the atom in a corpuscle in the body, or the sphere or orb of any of those systems seen about the earth and described by the psalmist, "The heavens declare the glory of God, the firmament showeth His handiwork; day unto day uttereth speech, night unto night sheweth knowledge."[122]

In terms of proportion, we are approximately halfway between the size of the known universe and the size of the smallest known subatomic particle. Let's take a minute to let that really sink in. Scientists tell us it's approximately fifteen billion light years to the edge of the known universe. I can't even begin to comprehend a distance like that. One light year is almost six trillion miles. If we were to travel at one mile per second, it would take more than 180,000 years to reach the six trillion-mile mark. But wait; we're not there yet. Multiply that distance by fifteen billion if you want to get to the edge of the known

---

*I continue to delight in the synchronicities that have accompanied my immersion in writing this book. The very morning that my work was set out for me to begin this chapter on "Corpuscles in the Body of God," the images I have just described, plus one that puts a close-up of the human iris and pupil side-by-side with a Hubble telescope picture of the "eye nebula," appeared on my Facebook newsfeed. I had already included this point in the material previously gathered for this chapter, so these pictures were not new to me; but to see them show up in front of my face moments before I was to go to work on writing this chapter was yet another reminder of the mysterious *responsiveness* of the universe to our efforts.

[122] 818-1

universe. Yet that's only half of the astounding fact before us. As much distance, as much largeness, so to speak, as there is outside of us, there is proportionately just as much smallness *inside* of us. The impossibly small atoms that make up one molecule of one of those corpuscles in your body are gigantic compared to level after level after level of smaller subatomic particles, each one inconceivably smaller than the one above it.

If you could take the perspective of the smallest subatomic particle within, let's say, your heart, your skin boundaries would be as far away as the edge of the known universe is to you! You contain something as vast as what you think of the universe as being—inside of you! Here we stand—an endless expanse beyond us, an endless expanse within us. As we experience that state called incarnation, we are suspended halfway between two directions of infinity. These lines from Emerson's poem, "Nature," say it well:

> Atom from atom yawns as far
> As earth from moon, or star from star.

We bear the full imprint of both heaven and earth. Perhaps that's why the Cayce readings also say that " . . . Each element, each corpuscle of the body is a universe in itself, or a universe on the beginning of power and force . . . "[123] Wow! "A universe on the beginning of power and force." It sounds like something pretty important is happening within us! We are corpuscles in the body of God, and the corpuscles in our bodies are universes awakening to their power. Could it be that within the very cells of our bodies, consciousness is awakening, just as we, in our capacity of corpuscle in the body of God, awaken God consciousness in God's "body" (that is, the manifest realm)? Is this how we, as we awaken to God-consciousness, also bring consciousness into matter?

The readings would seem to suggest that this is the case, that our awakening consciousness is the means by which consciousness can awaken in all matter. " . . . Out of Time, Space, Patience [it is] possible for . . . the finite to *know* the infinite," we find in a reading given for the

---

[123]262-56

lesson "Spirit."[124] And make no mistake; the readings are talking about matter itself waking up as we become more conscious: " . . . there is the evolution of the soul, evolution of the mind, but not evolution of matter—*save through mind, and that which builds same.*"[125] Just as all matter is ultimately spirit, all consciousness partakes of spirit as well—but it is under our guidance while it is in our bodies, say the readings, patterning the very elements that comprise us.[126] With this the theosophical thinkers agree, suggesting that by the time an atom reaches its apex as part of the makeup of a human body it has passed through a succession of forms in the mineral, plant, and animal kingdoms.

Life-promoting Cells

When we take seriously the idea that our consciousness shapes the consciousness within the matter of our bodies, we realize the full force of our co-creative power as well as the responsibility attendant upon that. The biblical admonition, "Do you not know that your bodies are temples of the Holy Spirit, who is in you, whom you have received from God? You are not your own."[127] takes on new meaning. Under the symmetry of the universe within us/the universe beyond us, as we take responsibility for shaping the consciousness in our own cells, we ourselves become life-enhancing cells in the body of God.

And so we return to the deep significance of the reading that began this section. Please read it again, holding in mind everything you've just been considering:

> Each entity, then, is as a corpuscle in the body of that force called God. Those activities in which there has been the presentation, the manifestation of His love, His activity in the earth, are as the blood stream; while the spirit of consciousness is as the nerves of the body itself. Hence self, as an individual, is a manifestation of Creative Forces in action in the earth. [128]

[124] 262-115
[125] 262-56, emphasis added
[126] 5756-4
[127] I Corinthians 6:19
[128] 2174-2

The bloodstream is the body's means of delivering nutrients and life-sustaining oxygen, while simultaneously purifying itself of toxins and the waste products of cellular metabolism. In the same way, our acts of love keep God's body nourished, enlivened, and pure. The nervous system is the body's primary communications system. By it information necessary to proper internal function is passed along from part to part and by it action is made possible. Without nerve function, there is paralysis. In the same way, our development of consciousness makes possible effective action in this world of form.

Echoing Jesus' teaching that "Inasmuch as ye have done it unto one of the least of these my brethren, ye have done it unto me," Cayce shifts the idea from metaphor to literal truth when he says that because we are all corpuscles in God's body, whatever we do to one another we are in fact doing to our Maker.[129] Which raises another point: so far, I have dealt only with the enormous evolutionary potential of our corpuscle status and said nothing about rogue cells like cancer cells or cells that are diseased in some other way. Is there really any need to? The implications for the whole body when we are corpuscles that pollute the bloodstream or disrupt the nerve forces should be obvious:

> For, each soul is as a corpuscle in the heart of the Maker, and either makes for development or retardment within its relationships and dealings with others; it either becomes as a creative force or a disturbing influence that brings in the material plane inharmony or disturbance, dissatisfaction, and those things that make an individual or soul afraid.[130]

Here, as always, a choice rests with each one of us. It is not a once-and-for-all choice, but one that we make with each human interaction; each time we decide whether to bother meditating; and with each attitude and emotion we throw out there into the consciousness-nervous system of God's body. Fortunately, we can move toward "creative force" and away from "disturbing influence" (to use the two

---

[129]2401-1
[130]2082-1

alternatives in the Cayce excerpt above) by increasing our mindfulness that we are, indeed, corpuscles in the body of God.

Practicing Being a Corpuscle in the Body of God

The same person who was given the reading stating that we, as
corpuscles, affect the bloodstream and nervous system of God was
told in a subsequent reading to: " ... visualize ... the spirit of life as it
manifests itself through a material body ... Each atom or corpuscle *of*
the body is an whole universe within itself, with *all* the attendant
elements or sources *of* life about same," he said. " ... hence we may see
how those in a material plane may so raise that consciousness to coor-
dinate same with life in its various forms in the earth, as to *magnify*
Him the more . . . [131] Taking this suggestion, a meditative practice centered on awareness of your role as the guardian of consciousness
within one of God's corpuscles can be a very powerful transformer of
consciousness. Some suggestions for a "Meditation on Being a Corpuscle in the Body of God" are given below for those who wish to
work with this awareness.

Meditation
On Being a Corpuscle in the Body of God

The instructions below are written in a somewhat meditative style. It
is not expected that you will memorize each part of this imagery, but
rather read it to get a feel for how you might flesh out the basic
structure suggested here:

1. Meditatively ponder what it means to be a corpuscle in the body
   of God.

2. Picture and imagine corpuscles in specific parts of your own
   body. Think of the consciousness within those corpuscles and

---

[131] 1742-4

imagine each corpuscle to be an entity unto itself, working in cooperation with other corpuscle-entities to help your body function. Then imaginatively shift perspectives so that you are God, aware of the corpuscle that is you.

3. Return to imagining your own corpuscles, this time taking the perspective of a corpuscle in your own bloodstream. Then shift context to let that bloodstream be God's bloodstream. Let awareness of what that means grow.

4. Return awareness to your own nervous system and imagine its intricate form and function. Take the imaginative perspective of being a nerve cell accomplishing its role in your body. Then shift the context to be God's nervous system. Let awareness of what that means develop.

5. Return to a deepened meditation on "I am a corpuscle in the body of God."

6. Zero in on a corpuscle in your own heart and delve successively deeper in, until you are imagining the subatomic level within that cell in your heart. Feel that universe within you and fill it with light.

7. Send that light out through the successive levels until your entire circulatory system is flowing with light. Extend that light through the nervous system.

8. Return to a deepened meditation on "I am a corpuscle in the body of God."

9. As you conclude, let possible actions which would reflect the consciousness you've raised come to mind.

It all might go something like this:

Make yourself comfortable, turn your attention within, and ponder what you have been reading in this chapter. Using whatever images might come to you, imagine what it is to be a corpuscle in the body of God. Stay with those images for a few moments.

Then think about the corpuscles inside your own body, as you rest there, thinking quietly inside yourself. Imagine a cell that's part of the bloodstream. Or a cell that's part of the nervous system. Maybe it is a receptor in the tip of your finger that allows you to feel. Or any of those cells that make up your physical body ... And notice how, from your perspective, they're a part of you. You claim them. Your cells. Your blood. Your nervous system. Feel how everything that makes up your body feels like you. And then imaginatively shift perspectives for a moment. Imaginatively take the perspective of God, feeling **you** being a part of God's own self ... **You** are a part of God's own being ... as God's being expresses itself in materiality. You are a corpuscle in the body of God.

Return once again to think about the corpuscles in your own body. Imaginatively enter into your own blood stream. Think about the intricate network of your circulatory system, and think about how blood flow is indispensable to life in the body. As you think about yourself there, flowing through your bloodstream, you are in a virtual soup of nutrients ... as you allow yourself to imagine that flow within you ... vitalizing oxygen is being carried to the cells ... waste is being removed from the cells, allowing the cells to develop and do their job and even to pass on in due course. Imagine yourself to be one cell in that bloodstream.

Now shift the imagery so that it's no longer your own bloodstream but God's bloodstream that you are floating through. You are a cell, a corpuscle, in the body of God ... feel into the significance of that ... and as you continue to imagine that blood flow ... and its significance for you on a symbolic level, feel what it is to need that continuous spirit-flow of nourishment, spiritual vitality, and cleansing that is the blood-flow of the world. Stay with that for a few moments.

Now think of how the nervous system, the carrier of every nerve impulse, is required for you to think, to move, to maintain every autonomic function in the body. Imagine that intricate web of neural connections, from brain to spinal cord, to all the branches of the nervous system, as they become ever finer in order to reach every portion of the body ... like a root system that begins large and eventually turns into tiny little hairs. Imaginatively go inside your body so that you can fully appreciate what happens when an impulse is sent from the brain down into the hand to cause you to grasp something ... the communication that has to travel all the way to the muscles, the tendons, the ligaments in the hands and the fingers, the arms ... And take a moment to imaginatively experience the communication that flows the other way ... when a perception is sent from the tips of the fingers or from the eyes or the nose or the ears or the tongue, carrying the communication back to the brain for your sense perception ... And while you're in that body, your thoughts themselves have correlates in your nervous system activity ...

Now bring your thoughts to awareness that your consciousness is like God's nervous system in the earth ... Contemplate how the thoughts you hold, the things you do, and the very way your being connects with a network of other beings just like you maintains God's nervous system in the earth ... You are a corpuscle in the body of God ... Rest with that awareness for a while.

Now visualize the spirit of life manifesting in the earth through your body. Send your awareness to your heart ... and from that place of focus on the heart, imagine that you have a microscope that can be ever more finely tuned ... look through that microscope to one cell within the heart ... And imagine yourself at the very center of the nucleus of that cell, the walls of the cell are around you ... and then turn up the magnification of your microscope again ... to see a molecule that makes up that cell ... However you do this is just fine ... the power is in the imagination. And place your awareness, your consciousness inside that molecule that is within the cell ... and then turn up the magnification of the microscope yet again ... to one of the elements within the molecule ... And further still ... to one of the atoms within the element ... that's within the molecule that's within the cell of your heart ... and imaginatively place yourself at the very center of that atom ... feel into the wide spaces ... the distance to your farthest electrons ... And then turn up the magnification yet again ... to that vast mysterious subatomic level ... where it's as if you are viewing the stars in outermost space ... place yourself there ... within the subatomic within the atom that's within the element that's within the molecule that's within the cell that's within your own living, beating heart ... and visualize the spirit of life ... as you raise the consciousness in that subatomic world ... to magnify the presence of the divine ... let that presence illumine that universe within that one subatomic world ... Fill it with light.

Now let that light extend outward ... to the atom ... and to all of the atoms that make up that element ... and to the elements that make up the molecule ... and to all of the molecules of that cell ... until that cell within your heart ... is a radiant point of light ... a light that spreads out into all the other cells of the heart ... your entire heart, now, illumined with the light of spirit ... so that as the blood courses through your heart, it, too, is flooded with light ... and the light that streams through your bloodstream is carried to every cell of the body ... every corpuscle in the body now ... is a carrier of light ... every cell that makes up your nervous system ... is alive with light ...

Return to the awareness that you are a corpuscle in the body of God ... and your acts of love are God's bloodstream ... and that consciousness is God's nervous system in this world ... just feel yourself as a corpuscle in the body of God ... and build that feeling through those images of light ... through those imaginative images of just what it is to be a corpuscle ... through those images of the interconnectedness ... in the circulatory system ... in the nervous system ... let all of that just come together ... in the thoughts and feelings and images that for you bring meaning to knowing you are a corpuscle in the body of God. And just rest with that ...

As you conclude your meditation, having raised that consciousness ... and having strengthened the awareness that you are indeed a corpuscle in the body of God, let that now give rise to activity in your life ... activity that presents and manifests the love of God in the earth ... hold the intention to be one whose activities make God's love active ... And perhaps you may think of some specific ways that you may do this in the hours and days ahead ... or possibly you can carry it with you as an awareness and intention ... allowing you to be aware, in every human interaction, of how you may better manifest the love of God, be God's activity in the earth ... Take that intention with you, as you prepare to rise from this time of quiet contemplation ...

This is a nice foundation upon which to develop further engagement with spirit's evolving expression through the matter in our bodies. In this regard, perhaps nowhere is the interplay of spirit and biology more developed than in the chakra system. We begin our exploration of the chakras in the next chapter.

Chapter 10:
Biology, Spirituality, and Chakras

... there is innate in each physical individual that channel through which the psychic or the spiritual forces, that are manifest in material world, *may* function. They are known as glands and affect the organs of the system.   294-141

In the final analysis, religions, then, are one. All spring from the evolutionary impulse in the human body.

Gopi Krishna, *A Kundalini Catechism**

*O*ur very biology is pulling us along the evolutionary trajectory. This is quite apparent in the phenomena known as convergent evolution, parallel evolution, and evolutionary relay, which all point to recurring patterns in the traits that evolution has produced in living things.* For example, we find wings in birds, insects, bats, and even prehistoric flying dinosaurs. A pill bug and an armadillo have similarly structured armor bodies that allow them to roll up in a defensive position, despite belonging to phyla with separate developmental lines that stretch back to the beginning of the animal kingdom. The same is true for bees and hummingbirds, which use the same hovering "technology" to get at nectar. There are photo receptor cells not only in the eyes of humans, mammals, and other advanced animals but also in insects and invertebrates like snails. In the repeated appearance of very distinctive traits as well as in the basic forms seen everywhere in nature to sustain life, we find what appears to be a virtual thrust toward a greater complexity that pulls evolution onward. As Teilhard de Chardin observed,

The more complex organisms become, the more evident becomes their inherent kinship. It manifests itself in the absolute and

---

'Gopi Krishna, *A Kundalini Catechism* (Darien: The Kundalini Research Foundation, 1995).
*The distinctions among these three terms, while significant to the evolutionary scientist, are not relevant to the point here.

universal uniformity of the basic cellular pattern, and it manifests itself, particularly in animals, in the identical solutions found for various problems of perception, nutrition, and reproduction— everywhere we find vascular and nervous systems, everywhere some form of blood, everywhere gonads and everywhere eyes.[132]

Observing this amazing pattern, British evolutionary biologist Richard Dawkins comments, "It seems that life, at least as we know it on this planet, was almost indecently eager to evolve eyes."[133] Dawkins may be a very vocal atheist, but we can see in that eagerness to evolve eyes the irrepressible urge of creation toward expanded perception— and, by extension, awareness. This is a brilliant metaphor for biological life waking up to consciousness itself.

Despite the age-old war between flesh and spirit, the deeper truth is that the body is marvelously equipped—with its intricate system of channels and conduits and collection points for subtle energies—to mediate spirit into matter. Seen in this light, the chakras, as the interface whereby the unseen energies of the spiritual are transmuted into physical manifestation, become integral to the evolutionary advance; for it is in the energy fields of the chakra system that we find the template for ongoing evolution as well as the record of our evolutionary past. They are like the internal GPS that identifies our current position and maps out the course ahead. Yet this analogy has severe limitations, because unlike the computer-generated feedback and directions that come to us via the GPSs in our cars, the forces that speak to us through the chakras are living, breathing spirit. The map our chakra energies provide us is alive with the force of creation itself. And nowhere is our physicality more adapted to the awakening of consciousness than in the chakra system.

---

[132]Teilhard de Chardin, *The Phenomenon of Man*, 99–100.

[133]As quoted by Michael Dowd in *Thank God for Evolution* (San Francisco/Tulsa: Council Oak Books, 2007), 32.

The Chakras

Cayce's readings are in agreement with most esoteric literature in saying that, " . . . there are centers, areas, conditions in which there evidently must be that contact between the physical, the mental and spiritual. The spiritual contact is through the glandular forces of creative energies . . . "[134] But before we can explore Cayce's information on the chakras from an evolutionary perspective, a couple of clarifications are necessary. The first regards Cayce's frequent reference to the "glandular forces" or "glandular system." By this he means far more than just the organic glandular bodies. Rather, he is referring to the entirety of the chakra system—a complex, multi-leveled interface between flesh and spirit. Each center is a complex meeting place of glandular body, neurological function, and subtle energy vortex (the latter actually operating on successively finer levels of the unseen world). We get the Hindu term *chakras*—literally meaning wheels—because they are swirling vortices of energy.* From these main centers, the subtle energy is distributed throughout the body in channels called *nadis* (literally "rivers" or "flow"). In Chinese medicine, the larger collection areas are called *dan tiens* (literally "elixir fields") with meridians being the channels that circulate the subtle energy throughout the body.

While Cayce never directly used the terminology of either the yogic or Chinese traditions, the readings offer a rich and detailed view of the body's subtle energy system that is consistent with the general principles of both. Perhaps because the chakra system was better known to Cayce's questioners than was the Chinese system of dan tiens and meridians, we find more data in his readings that is tied to the chakra tradition and so that will be our principal focus here. In consistency with ancient traditions, Cayce emphasizes the importance of the physiological correlates to the energetic aspect of the chakras and so we most often find the readings using "glands" or "glandular system" as

---

[134]263-13

*Interestingly, we find what may well be reference to the chakras in the Hebrew scriptures, where in Ezekiel 1:20 we read, "For the spirit of the living creature was in the wheels" and in Daniel 7:9 we read, "The Ancient of Days has wheels of burning fire."

shorthand for "chakras;" for example, "The soul body manifesting in the physical, as we have heretofore indicated, finds expression in what we call today the *glandular* systems of the body."[135] He also uses the term "centers" to describe the chakras, as is seen in the quote that began this section.

When we include Cayce's contribution to our understanding of chakras, it is also important to keep in mind that the correlation of chakras with glandular bodies is far from straightforward. We find significant differences among various teachings on the chakras when it comes to linking a particular chakra with a particular gland or other physical organ, and Cayce's identification of these linkages adds yet another set of possibilities to the mix. Fortunately, the assignment of a chakra to a specific organ or glandular body is not nearly as important as recognizing the way that *all* of our internal biology is affected by the flow of these subtle energies. In response to his questioners' eagerness to pin down the how we might link the chakras to their symbolic meanings and the glands to which they correlate, Cayce described these as "relative" and warned against "rote" approaches that can supplant the greater importance of applied experience in living the principles expressed by the chakras. What matters most, from an evolutionary perspective, is that the chakras are bioactive through the glandular and nervous systems and that there is broad agreement across various schools of thought concerning the distinct patterns of energy that characterize each chakra. This will be our emphasis as we look at the individual chakras for their thematic significance.

The Chakra Themes and Human Development

In mediating spiritual energies into biological expression, the chakra system is like the software that comes pre-loaded into a human being. It is geared toward universal stages of evolutionary advance, in that there are basic themes related to each of the seven centers. These themes—which characterize the energy patterning for the respective chakras—tell the story of our evolutionary trajectory from past to present to future. Each theme broadly describes the quality or tone of

[135]2402-1

energy a particular chakra mediates within the body–mind–spirit complex that we call a human being. Together they comprise the pattern of spirit's involution and evolution—learning to express through, master, and ultimately create with matter. The chakras are also repositories of memory, in that they hold the impressions left by our experience with their energies. For example, one woman was told in her Cayce reading that she could catch glimpses of past lives when energy moved through the chakra system[136] and several others were told that the chakra centers express urges that are reflective of past experience.[137] As we will be seeing here and later on in Part Three of this book, these chakra energy themes are recapitulated in the childhood development of each incarnation and can be traced in our collective human history as well. Our personal evolutionary edge will always involve work with chakra themes, especially possible blockages and distortions of chakra energies for, as the Cayce readings remind us, "The glandular forces then are ever akin to the sources from which, through which, the soul dwells within the body."[138]

Our co-creative contribution to collective evolution will also involve expression of all of the chakra energies. Like notes of an octave or colors of the spectrum, each chakra provides a necessary note for the musical scale or color for the palette in its distinctive energy theme. In the hands of the composer or painter, they make great art possible. If a particular chakra energy is blocked or if some tones overbalance others, the creative impulse is impaired. If a chakra's energy is distorted, it can become its own evil twin. Then the tone it gives to the composition is murky. Therefore each chakra's energy has both a constructive, or evolutionary, manifestation and a form of expression that indicates glitches in that evolutionary process.

First Chakra: This "root chakra" at the base of the spine has to do with basic physical survival and our being securely grounded in this world. Remember that involution precedes evolution. Spirit must first vest itself in matter for the process to begin. Related themes revolve around various aspects of feeling safe in this world with our basic

[136]5399-2

[137]263-13; 949-12; 1221-1; 2594-1, for example

[138]281-38

needs cared for. Perhaps not surprisingly, then, the first chakra's basic safety and security needs are a dominant issue in our lives from birth to approximately one and a half years of age.* The Darwinian concept of "survival of the fittest" is very much at play on this level. The coccygeal nerve plexus that relates to this chakra serves the external reproductive organs, eliminations, and the lower limbs.

As we might expect, because this center's energy has to do with having our basic needs met and our feeling safe, secure, and well-grounded in the earth, issues of pervasive insecurity about having our physical needs met can be traced to this chakra level. Poverty consciousness, obesity arising from feelings of scarcity about food, hoarding, excessive concern about keeping a roof over one's head, and fears concerning physical safety are some of the ways this chakra's energy might manifest in an unhealthy way. (Please note that with respect to food, shelter, and safety, we are talking here about situations where actual circumstances do not warrant the level of insecurity one might feel. In the midst of true poverty or when one's home is being foreclosed or in the middle of a war-torn city, such feelings become totally natural.) Deep-seated issues with trust in other people or trust in life itself can be traced to this chakra, especially when the security needs of earliest infancy were not met. Basically, the way we answer the question of whether we see the world and the universe at large as safe/friendly or whether we see it as unsafe/hostile depends on how secure we feel at the level of the first chakra. Lesions of this energy at their worst can manifest as psychosis. Lack of grounding would be a less severe manifestation of inadequate root chakra energy flow. In this, as in all of the other chakras, problems with parts of the physical body served by this chakra's nerve plexus may indicate problems with this chakra's energies.

Second Chakra: This "sacral chakra," located in the lower belly area, is concerned with sexual energies. It is also concerned with imagination, emotion, desire, and creativity. The second chakra's emotional, sexual, and imaginative theme comes into play during toddlerhood,

---

*Different theorists may assign slightly different ages and developmental milestones to the specific chakras, but the general pattern whereby childhood development takes us sequentially through the themes of the first five chakras holds.

as we move into the stage of earliest gender identification and sexual feelings, and a world view that is both magical and imaginative. In the Cayce system, it is identified as the "seat of the soul in the earth," describing it as a door that may be either open or sealed to higher spiritual consciousness. The pelvic nerve plexus related to this chakra serves the bladder, large intestine, internal reproductive organs, and the lumbar region of the back.

Because of its rich energies from the sexual, emotional, and imaginative spheres, this chakra's energies can present us with many complexities in how we channel these aspects of our lives. Early childhood conditioning that involves shaming or repression of emotional or sexual impulses can lead to either continued repression or uncontrolled expression of these energies later in life. Blocked creativity can result when this chakra's energies are blocked. The imaginative power of this center, in its immature form, can also predispose one to magical thinking—the tendency to illogically impute causation to events that are merely correlated in one's experience. For example, "I was angry at Tom and then he had a horrible accident, therefore my angry thoughts caused his accident." Many theorists believe that obsessive–compulsive disorder stems from this level. Beliefs based purely on wish fulfillment would be a less severe manifestation of magical thinking due to immature second chakra energies. Because of its relation to our sexual energies, the inner image we hold of the opposite sex and the balancing of sexual polarities within our own being (anima/animus) is centered at this chakra. Thus, distortions of that image of the opposite sex and/or being "possessed" by one's anima or animus are tied to problems with this chakra's energies.

Third Chakra: Sometimes called the "navel chakra," this is the center concerned with personal power and the two–sided coin of courage and aggression. It is located between the navel and the bottom of the rib cage. Here safety becomes figurative where it was literal with the first chakra, and so issues of ego, status, and self-esteem come into play. The third chakra's personal power and ego development themes begin to kick in around age three as we develop the beginnings of a self that has awareness of being distinct from the body. As we move on toward middle childhood years, a personal ego develops, and we navigate through the rules and roles that are given to us in our family and school environment and find our place in the social orders we are involved in. At its most functional, this is the "healthy ego" described in Chapter 8. In its more limiting manifestations, this same ego learns to craft the many protective masks discussed in that same chapter. The solar plexus falls at this chakra level and serves the esophagus, stomach, small intestines, most of the large intestines, liver, pancreas, spleen, adrenal glands, and kidneys. The nerves that serve the sympathetic and parasympathetic nervous systems also branch from within the solar plexus, thus its involvement in the "fight or flight" response.

As the center for personal power, this chakra is subject to disorders related to ego. In its overbearing state, the energy of this center may manifest as an unbridled power drive, aggression, a need for recognition or social status, and many of the traits that we typically associate with being "egotistical," including the inability to take another's point of view. When the energy of this chakra is not sufficient to give healthy ego strength, lack of confidence, a poorly formed self-identity, inability to assert one's own needs, and timidity may be the result. This is the level of most garden variety neuroses.

Fourth Chakra: Commonly called the "heart center," this is the chakra concerned with earthly love. Compassion and kindness, as well as our sense of affiliation and belonging and need for approval come into play at this level. The fourth chakra's love theme, particularly in terms of affiliations with others, comes into play around age eleven as we develop the reasoning capacities of a mind that can grasp the meaning of relationship and truly take the perspective of another. The cardiac plexus and pulmonary plexus are both proximate to this chakra and are concerned with the heart, lungs, and circulatory system. It is also worth noting that as the middle chakra out of seven, the heart center is the point of both balance and connection between those chakras that channel energies related to the personal concerns of navigating life in the earth (the first through third) and those that bring in transpersonal motivation and higher consciousness (the fifth through seventh).

When this "heart center's" energy is unbalanced or blocked, we find impairments in the ability to give and receive love. Lack of generosity, feelings of hurt, bitterness, jealousy, and overbearing "smother love" are among the manifestations of problems with this chakra's energies.

Patterns of problems with belonging or with having healthy affiliations with others may also manifest. When the heart center's energies
are not clear, there may be an imbalance or even a disconnect between the concerns of the first three and those of the last three chakras.

Fifth Chakra: This center, which falls at the throat level, relates to
the verbal, rational mind, and the expression of our truth. It is also the
level at which we can shift from the limited personal perspective to
consider our place in the wider scheme of things and the higher laws
that give order to that scheme. In Cayce's and some other systems, it is
also related to will. The fifth chakra's theme of rational mind comes
into full expression in adolescence as we develop the capacity for synthetic, creative thinking. Many people stay at this rational level for the
remainder of their lives and never explore the wider context of this
chakra's energy theme; that is, higher reality and one's place within it.
But to do so is to embark on the spiritual path. The throat, shoulders,
arms, and voice are most directly under the control of the pharyngeal
nerve plexus that is related to this chakra.

Problems that may be associated with blocked or unbalanced energy at this level include feelings of not being heard or the inability to
express your ideas or convey who you are. In the light of this center's
strong role in finding one's purpose in the wider context of life and
higher law, identity crises or existential crises may arise from lack of
clarity at this level. Untruth, in the sense of lying to oneself or others,
may also arise from distorted energies at this chakra. Because this is
the will center, problems with excessive willfulness or inability to apply will may also be related to problems with the energy of this center.
The neck, by its very structure, can be a bit of a bottleneck in the free
movement of subtle energies between the torso and the head, so
blocked energy at this level may contribute to energy blockages in the
sixth and seventh chakras.

Sixth Chakra: This "third eye" center at the brow is related to
higher intuition, Christ consciousness, and loving service to humanity.
If the fourth chakra has to do with human love, the sixth has to do
with transhuman love. Its spiritual theme is the manifestation of deity
in humanity and nature. Therefore this is the level of mysticism centered on oneness with nature and/or a personal deity. The energies of
this center open up much more as one pursues spiritual awakening.

The carotid plexus associated with both this chakra and the seventh is concerned with the brain and the sense organs—eyes, ears, nose, tongue, and skin.

Blocked sixth chakra energies may result in symptoms ranging from fuzzy thinking to headaches to sleep disorders, while excessive energies from this center without adequate balance elsewhere in the system can result in psychic disorders and an array of psychosomatic disorders. Sensory problems may also be symptomatic of problems with sixth chakra energies.

Seventh Chakra: This is the "crown chakra" at the top of the head. It is the counterpart to the root chakra in that it is the source of spiritual energy from above, while the root chakra grounds us to the energy of the earth (or the manifest realm) from below. As such, it is the chakra that brings full integration of the spiritual and physical. A full opening of this chakra brings unity consciousness or consciousness that transcends the dualities of the manifest realm. The seventh chakra's theme of transcendent consciousness plays out in experiences of non-dual awareness—timeless, spaceless oneness with all that is. For many spiritual seekers this is the "holy grail" of the spiritual path that may or may not ever be realized in this lifetime. This does not mean, however, that the seventh chakra's flow of spiritual energy from our Source is not present; it has just not yet reached full conscious realization.

Just as the root chakra is our means of staying connected with and fed by the earth, the crown chakra is the master connection to Spirit. It is our link with cosmic energy. If this chakra is not clear, we may feel a pervasive lack of ease or feel constricted or cut off from joy. Extreme worry or anxiety may result as well. Blockage at this level may also manifest in a state of being closed off from or afraid of religion and spirituality. The physical ailments associated with the seventh chakra are much the same as those associated with the sixth—problems with the sensory organs, headaches, and sleep disturbances.

A Big Picture Approach to Chakra Energies

In a comment on this alignment between the chakra themes and human development, Ken Wilber relates the chakra themes to three main stages of moral development which psychologist Carol Gilligan has called ego-centric, ethno-centric and world-centric. At the ego-centric stage what we care about is ourselves; it is "me" centered. At the ethno-centric stage our care extends to "us," meaning ourselves and people like us. At the world-centric stage, as we might expect, our caring extends to all of humanity. Paramahansa Yogananda makes the same point and decries how rarely we make it to the third stage when he says:

> The ordinary human being relates to and identifies with his family first; then his neighbors or persons of his own caste or social position, or members of his own religion; then his race; and finally his nation. There his consciousness stops—his ego imprisoned in concentric barriers, cribbed in an isolated corner of its insular world, cut off from the universality that Jesus and the great ones lived by: "God hath made of one blood all nations."[139]

In relating all of this to the chakras, Wilber says that the chakras are a more detailed version of these three stages and that they represent seven levels of consciousness and energy available to all human beings. "The first 3 chakras—food, sex and power—are roughly stage 1," he says; "chakras 4 and 5—relational heart and communication—are basically stage 2; and chakras 6 and 7—psychic and spiritual—are the epitome of stage 3."[140]

It's important to note that we are not talking about a predictable, linear progression from chakra one to chakra seven as we undergo personal evolutionary growth. We are complex beings with many facets, and this will be reflected in our experience with the energies of the chakras. With the basic chakra energy themes laid down in our makeup over the course of our childhood development, most of us will find ourselves drawing on chakra energies in various sequences in different areas and situations of our lives. For example, one may express very

---

[139]Paramahansa Yogananda, *The Second Coming of the Christ: The Resurrection of the Christ Within You, Vol. 1* (Los Angeles: Self-Realization Fellowship, 2004), 296-97.
[140]Wilber, *Eye of Spirit: An Integral Vision for a World Gone Slightly Mad,*13.

healthy energies of the fourth (heart) chakra while out doing volunteer work but experience jealousy (distorted fourth chakra energy) in a romantic relationship. Also, because each chakra has its evolution-and-life-sustaining function, we can expect to find opportunities to work with the energy of each chakra at successively more expansive levels as we evolve, cycling through deeper and deeper engagement with the energies of each chakra. Thus, someone working with third chakra energies at a level of increased complexity may in fact be farther along the evolutionary trajectory than someone working with fifth chakra energies in a much smaller context (i.e., less complexity).

Still, it would be fair to say that the evolutionary pull is toward more resolution of problems related to the energies/themes of the lower chakras and more opening up of the transpersonal potentials inherent in the energies of the upper chakras. Taking the expansive view of incarnation, our primary evolutionary agenda will be to focus on the healthful, balanced expression of *all* of the chakra energies. Yes, we all have unfinished business related to less-than-optimal expression of some of these chakra energies, and many of us may even have inner wounding at one or more of these chakra levels. We will take all of this into consideration in Chapter 12, when we look at our growth issues in the context of the chakras. For now the most expansive orientation is to approach the chakras as our circuitry of attunement to the energies necessary for our own evolution and as the blueprint for the collective evolution of the human race.

Meditation to Awaken and Balance Chakra Energies

Not surprisingly, the Cayce readings point to meditation as the key to balanced expression of chakra energies:

> ... *meditation* is *emptying* self of all that hinders the creative forces from rising along the natural channels of the physical man to be disseminated through those centers and sources that create the activities of the physical, the mental, the spiritual man; properly done must make one *stronger* mentally, physically.[141]

---

[141]281-47

This excerpt is taken from a series of instructional discourses given for the healing prayer group that formed in 1931 as a central part of the work then being done with the Cayce material.* Many decades ahead of the time when courses in healing modalities have become common, this series of readings was given to provide detailed information on what might almost be called the technology of meditation and healing. Identifiable by the 281 number, these readings recast the biblical book of Revelation from apocalyptic prophecy to detailed symbolic exposition of the inner circuitry that mediates spirit into matter. As such, they are a treasure-trove of helpful and inspirational material concerning meditation, especially as it relates to the spiritual centers in the body.

Unlike many popular approaches today that target specific centers (such as the third eye) for opening, these readings did not recommend such a practice. In one of the 281[142] readings, when the Cayce source had confirmed that his questioners were correct in identifying the seven seals in Revelation with the seven centers, they requested, " . . . advice that will help us in properly opening these centers." He interrupted with a dire warning against such opening until all spiritual deficiencies had been met and one was capable of assimilating *the whole* of the centers' energies. This same word of caution is to be found elsewhere, when he says, " . . . If ye will study to *understand* the opening of the channels or the centers for the deeper meditation, then the spiritual and psychic awakening may be brought forth. But do not allow self to be overcome with this until ye understand how and why centers are opened in meditation . . . [143] There is a place, according to the readings, for disciplined practice that leads to the safe opening of the centers, but for most people it would be premature and dangerous to jump into modalities that target the opening of certain centers before we have established both the understanding and the personal stability to do so. One person was warned quite compellingly against pranayama, or breathing aimed at opening the centers, because she did not have the requisite foundation:

*The healing prayer group has been in continuous operation since its inception.
[142]281–29
[143]1552–1

> If there had been the opportunities and choice as a very young
> individual, for the entity to have studied or to have practised in its
> experience the developing of the emotions through a system called
> Yogi, it would have been well. But in the present, *do not* attempt to
> do such breathing exercises to open the *emotional* centers as
> related to the physical and the spiritual bodies. To do so would be
> harmful in the present stage of activity.[144]

Another was given some helpful advice and information, but also
reminded of the old adage that curiosity killed the cat. [145] Obviously, a
self–centered quest for spiritually scintillating experiences or idle curiosity is not enough. Clarity of intention and purpose is crucial. Numerous people were advised to tend to the health and vitality of the
physical body before attempting to ramp up the chakra energies lest
physical damage be the unintended result of their efforts. Another
person, in a context where she was told that she could effectively channel healing energies to others, was nonetheless warned against targeting certain centers unless she had a far more complete picture of what
she was doing:

> Thus may acute conditions as well as those of a more general
> nature be materially aided . . . by the body raising the vibration of
> itself and transmitting same through radiation by the hands of the
> body. Do not attempt to use centers, segments or the structural
> portions, unless the body considers also that the anatomical
> structure of the body must be entirely understood. For, applying
> such would then become dangerous, unless there is the full
> comprehension, physically, mentally, spiritually of such structure,
> such functioning, such activities of a body.[146]

For the spiritual seeker who is eager for development (and perhaps
even more eager to have experiences of a non–ordinary nature), the
temptation to overlook these warnings can be great at times—espe-

---

[144]2438–1
[145]2475–1
[146]3368–1

cially when someone or some book promises to teach us how to open these centers with marvelous results to our spiritual and personal lives. But we are well advised to take these warnings seriously, for we find in the literature of yoga similar warnings. Sri Aurobindo, for example, describes a "yogic illness" that can occur when the upper centers open before the physical–emotional body is strong enough to handle the energy. In the writings of Gopi Krishna, we read of his harrowing experiences as a result of an opening of the kundalini energies that very nearly killed him. In my own qigong training, the master warned against opening the third eye before the lower centers were properly developed, as he likened it to building a top–heavy house on an insecure foundation. Alice Bailey echoes such warnings about using postures and breathing and centering awareness on the centers, saying that those who do so "are occupying themselves with the form, which is limitation, and not with the spirit which is life." This, she says, can lead to physical, emotional, and nervous disorders and will not accomplish the goal.[147]

Evolutionary force though they are, the chakra energies will best pull us forward if we allow them to open naturally as a consequence of our attunement to Spirit's presence in our lives. Thus, meditation that awakens the chakra system as a whole would be preferable to the targeting of any one center. One person was told in her reading,

> . . . how oft has remaining quiet aided thee in seeing and feeling and experiencing the full cosmic consciousness! Yes! This is found . . . by the opening of those channels within the physical body through which the energies of the Infinite are attuned to the centers through which physical consciousness, mental activity, is attained,—or in deep meditation.[148]

In the same reading where the healing prayer group was advised against specifically targeting the centers to open them, the Cayce source did describe a way that we can safely address the chakra energies in meditation using the Lord's Prayer, the clauses of which ad-

---

[147]Bailey, *The Consciousness of the Atom*, 11.
[148]2109-2

dress the various chakra themes. Prior to this reading the group had made a chart identifying the centers with the glands and prominent symbols in Revelation, including the seven churches, seven seals, four beasts, and four horsemen. The chart also related the planets of the solar system, colors of the spectrum, and segments of the Lord's Prayer to each of the chakras. While affirming that this chart was on the whole correct, the reading—the same one mentioned earlier which advocated application of the underlying meanings implied, rather than any rote understandings—several times indicated that these identifications were not set in stone, saying in one place, "These are very well done. These vary, to be sure, according to the variation of an *experience* . . . of the individual rather than there being set, as it were, a blanket to cover each and every individual."[149]

In the case of the group's correlation of specific clauses of the Lord's Prayer with the particular centers, the reading said that this was "A way, *an* understanding, to the relationships to the Creative Forces"— strongly hinting that we should be careful about seeing it as the only possible approach. With that caveat in mind, we can nonetheless find some great advice about using the Lord's Prayer to safely address the energies of the centers in meditation:

(Q) How should the Lord's Prayer be used in this connection?
(A) As in feeling, as it were, the flow of the meanings of each portion of same throughout the body-physical. For as there is the response to the mental representations of all of these in the *mental* body, it may build into the physical body in the manner as He, thy Lord, thy Brother, so well expressed in, "I have bread ye know not of."[150]

It's interesting to note here that, in contrast to the warning we saw against pranayama if one is not sufficiently prepared emotionally, Cayce is suggesting that we can safely address the chakra energies via the mental body. It comes back to consciousness and the developing ability to use the mind rather than be used by the mind. In this case, we are advised to dwell on the meanings of the words in the Lord's Prayer and allow the consciousness of those meanings to resonate throughout the physical body.

[149]281-29
[150]281-25

THE SEVEN CHAKRA THEMES IN THE LORD'S PRAYER

As it turns out, if one ponders deeply the clauses of the Lord's Prayer, the seven chakra themes will become apparent within it:

Father in heaven: Seventh chakra: It probably needs no explanation that the highest chakra—which mediates the main inflow of transcendent spiritual energies and which has to do with transcendent consciousness and non-dual awareness—is thematically linked with the symbology of the father in heaven.

Hallowed name: Sixth chakra: The linkage here is beautiful as well, for the sixth chakra, in its theme of Christ consciousness and the personalization of deity, gives a name or identity to divine energy in manifestation. When we pray "hallowed be thy name," we are dedicating the spiritual, intuitive energies of the sixth center to highest service to humanity.

Thy will be done: Fifth chakra: The shorthand version of the throat chakra's theme is "will." When we use the rational mind to rise above our purely personal concerns and consider our place and responsibility within the wider context of higher laws, we tap into higher will (in contrast to self-centered will). It is from this place that we can truly voice our truth. We can also note that in praying "Thy will be done on earth as it is in heaven," we are acknowledging our desire to bring divine principles into the realm of manifestation.

Daily bread: First chakra: This is also probably one of the linkages that needs little explanation. The basic needs/security theme of the first chakra stretches "bread" to mean far more than food. It stands as emblematic of everything that fulfills our safety and security needs and grounds us in the earth.

Forgive us our debts as we forgive our debtors: Third chakra: This is the ultimate prayer to address the personal power drives of the small self in its quest for symbolic safety. Lack of forgiveness of self or another can always be traced to something the small ego-self is holding on to as part of the essential self, something that cannot be let go without some loss of who or what we think we are. To forgive and accept forgiveness is the ability of a healthy self-sense and is the natural antidote to the power-and-aggression impulses of distorted third chakra energies.

Lead us not into temptation: **Second chakra**: As the center from which the sexual, emotional, and imaginative energies arise—the possibilities for misuse of its impulses are limited only by the imagination! "Lead us not into temptation" is a call to awaken the most healthful side of the second center's energies.

Deliver us from evil: **Fourth chakra**: The personal love and compassion energies of the heart center, when activated, are indeed our deliverance from all of the evils that distorted human impulses can create. When the heart energies are themselves distorted (as we will be seeing in Chapter 13), the evils of jealousy, the distress of worry, and the despair of disenfranchisement can dominate our experience. When we pray this part of the prayer, we seek to awaken the very best of the heart's gifts in our experience.

For those who pray the concluding "Thine is the kingdom, the power, and the glory," we can see these as addressing the fifth, sixth, and seventh chakras once again, this time in ascending order. Thus the prayer has a nice symmetry.

Remember, it's not that we are to focus on specific chakras as we meditate on these words, but rather we are to let a deepened contemplation of every clause of the prayer resonate throughout the body. The template, "Using the Lord's Prayer in Meditation," below is one example of how this may be done.

Using the Lord's Prayer in Meditation

This meditation is based on the Cayce readings' suggestion that we can use the Lord's Prayer to foster awakened, balanced functioning of all of the chakras. What follows is an example of how we might use the clauses of the Lord's Prayer, along with positive affirmations related to chakra themes, to strengthen the circuitry of the entire chakra system. The affirmations used here are representative of the kind of thought-energy with which we might want to infuse the system, but they are by no means the only expressions that might apply. Feel free to design your own affirmations to reflect the chakras' energies, especially if you are aware of areas of personal challenge, opportunity, or need. In setting your intention for this

meditation practice, keep in mind that the chakra system is the circuitry that mediates Spirit into flesh; as such it is a powerful instrument of evolutionary advance—not only for you as an individual but
through you to the entire human race.

Start by finding a comfortable position and taking a few slow and
conscious breaths ... and realize that the same breath that nour-
ishes your body with life-giving oxygen carries the subtle energy of
Spirit as well. Just picture that inflow in detail ... the breath filling
the lungs ... the oxygen extracted in the air sacs and sent through
the tiny capillaries into the bloodstream ... pumped by the heart
throughout your body ... flooding cells with life-giving oxygen. Picture
it as light flowing throughout your circulatory system ... to
every organ ... every bone ... every muscle ... every tendon and
ligament ... every nerve ... all of them flooded with pure light. And
then picture and imagine the circulatory system for your subtle energies, swirling vortices of light energy ... one at the very base of your
spine ... one below the navel ... one just a little above the
navel ... one at the heart ... one in the throat ... one in the very
center of your skull ... one at the top of your head. Picture and imagine them all, alive with Spirit-flow, spinning clockwise, as it would
appear from outside your body looking at you ... each connected at
its core to a line that runs up the spine into the head ... connected
to the nervous and glandular systems of your body ... and connected
to an inexhaustible source of life energy all around you ...
Hold the image of energy flowing in through all of the centers ... distributed throughout the body with its own circulatory system for
subtle energies ... channels and conduits through which spirit flows
throughout your body ... Think of and imagine your body as a lighted
network of Spirit-flow, fed by the swirling energy of all seven
centers ... And while you hold that image ... let your mind, your intention, your very consciousness be absorbed in the meaning of the
words in the Lord's Prayer. Feel the flow of the meaning for each
statement *throughout* your body (*not* in particular chakras), and then
add your own silent prayer that is aligned with that meaning. Once
you have slowly and deliberately gone through the prayer in this
way, just rest ... again hold that image of the seven flowing

centers ... flooding your being with the currents of light ... and absorb these truths into your entire body ... let them flow throughout your energy circuitry:

Our Father who art in heaven ... I am nourished by a deep connection with my spiritual source.

Hallowed be thy name ... I see the manifestations of God all around me ... in nature, in acts of love, in sparks of wisdom that bubble up through me. I am attuned to spiritual insight, and it comes to me from within and from others who are also attuned.

Thy kingdom come, thy will be done on earth as it is in heaven . . . I know that my life is part of the great unfolding of divine purpose in the earth, and I surrender myself to the currents of truth that stand ready to guide my every choice.

Give us this day our daily bread. I trust in the limitless abundance that is my birthright as a beloved child of God.

And forgive us our debts as we forgive our debtors ... I let go of all need to judge or compare myself with others. I stand clear in the purity of who I am in this moment. I have all the courage I need to face every challenge in life.

And lead us not into temptation ... My powers of imagination and creativity are unleashed in service to evolving expression ... My sexuality is a source of deep connection to life itself.

But deliver us from evil ... My heart is expanding in the warm light of ever deeper love, compassion, and kindness ... My heart is like a beautiful flower opening to the morning sun . . .

Continue to hold that image of the seven swirling, flowing centers ... flooding your being with the currents of light ... And absorb these truths ... into your very body ... feel their meaning flowing through you ...

Our Father who art in heaven ... I am one with the infinite source and eternal cause of all creation ... I have been endowed with the image and likeness of God.

Hallowed be thy name ... Light fills me and awakens the deepest impulses to serve the world in love.

Thy kingdom come, thy will be done on earth as it is in heaven ... I offer my voice and my hands to do the work of God in the world.

Give us this day our daily bread. I am grounded and sure. I take care of my physical body, for it gives me the means to experience the gifts of life in this world.

And forgive us our debts as we forgive our debtors ... I am strong and confident as I release myself and others from old patterns that need no longer limit us. I free myself as I free all others who have wronged me, for they have done so only in ignorance of the truth that sets us free.

And lead us not into temptation ... My emotions serve to connect me to life in deep and meaningful ways. I allow myself to experience them fully and then release them completely when their time has passed.

But deliver us from evil ... My deep bond with humanity finds expression in strong and satisfying affiliations with other people. I easily and naturally join with individuals and groups as my inner self leads me to. I just as naturally let go of associations that no longer serve the greatest good.

Continue to hold that image of the seven swirling, flowing centers ... flooding your being with the currents of light ... filling your very body with these truths ...

Our Father who art in heaven ... I am made of inexhaustible, expansive God-force.

Hallowed be thy name ... My vision of divine manifestation in the cosmos knows no limitations. I delight in its unfolding before me day by day.

Thy kingdom come, thy will be done on earth as it is in heaven ... I find purpose in the smallest tasks and activities of my day, for I see them through the lens of my divine nature and perform them in the consciousness of who I really am.

Give us this day our daily bread ... I am secure, for my source is nothing less than the One who brings entire worlds into being. I will have all the energy I need for the work of today. Everything will be provided for me to do those things that care for the practicalities of life. My basic needs are in alignment with what God has called good; therefore it is in divine order that they be met.

And forgive us our debts as we forgive our debtors ... It is easy to forgive, for I make my own peace of mind. I am internally secure and this frees me from any need to lift myself up at the expense of others. I see the worth in others and this causes me to value myself as well. I admire others' success and this feeds my own success. I acknowledge my accomplishments with gratitude.

And lead us not into temptation ... My senses are alive to the spirituality of the flesh. Every cell of my body is enlivened with Spirit and therefore my pleasure in sexuality is enhanced. My creativity is inspired by the evidence of creation all around me and my emotions respond in deep and satisfying ways.

But deliver us from evil ... My heart is free of any past burdens or constrictions. My heart leads me onward along the currents of love and inward to the depths of authentic connection with all of life. I am alive to love. My life, my relationships, my activities, my very being pulses with the heart of the Universe.

At this point you may make additional rounds through the clauses of the prayer (either by itself or adding relevant affirmations) or move toward the close:

For thine is the kingdom ... My life speaks truth.
And the power ... My joy is in living my vision of God's love in the earth.
And the glory forever ... My destiny is sealed in the radiant, loving light of God that is my source and my true Self.

Complete your meditation by resting in that radiant, loving light for as long as you wish to. And whenever you feel ready, just open your eyes and come back outside, going forth into your life with all your spiritual circuits alive.

This is one more way to infuse the physical matter of our bodies with awakened consciousness. The important point for us, in looking at chakra energies as integral to our makeup, is to notice how our very biology functions from the start to mediate Spirit into flesh. Targeting a specific chakra may be risky, but filling all of the chakras' energies with consciousness aligned around their highest function strengthens them as the instruments of attunement that they are. According to Cayce, " . . . the soul of man, the body of man, the mind of man—is nearer to limitlessness than anything in creation."[151] These bodies of ours are not hunks of flesh that blind us to our evolutionary future as God-realized humans, but rather intricate instruments for the bringing of divine consciousness into materiality. In so doing, we participate in the grand evolutionary drive to bring order of chaos.

[151]281-55

PART THREE:
BRINGING ORDER OUT OF CHAOS

For as the earth is *only* a portion of a mighty array of forces and influences in our *own* little solar system, so man—though but a speck upon the earth and only as a grain in the universe—is a portion of that divinity that urges *on* and *on* and *on* and *on*! that makes for that eternal hope, that spark of light, that thread of soul in infinity itself!   1298-1

In every form, in mineral, in vegetable, in animal, in man, this expansive energy of the Logos is ceaselessly working. That is the evolutionary force, the lifting life within the forms, the rising energy that science glimpses, but knows not whence it comes.

Annie Besant, Esoteric Christianity*

---

*Annie Besant, (1905, p. 73), *Esoteric Christianity: Or The Lesser Mysteries,* e-book.

Chapter 11:
Beyond Darwin:
The Science of Evolution Redefines
Our Models of Spirituality

> ... Life in all of its phases, its expressions, is a manifestation of that force or power we call God, or that is called God. Then Life is continuous. For that force, that power which has brought the earth, the universe and all the influences in same into being, is a continuous thing—is a first premise. 1567-2

> No man can study modern Science without a change coming over his view of truth. Henry Drummond, *Natural Law in the Spiritual World* *

Several years ago, I led a retreat for church women called "The Way of the Heart." Much of the informational backdrop to the retreat's experiential component was drawn from fascinating research on the heart's electromagnetic field. We looked into some findings from the field of psychoneuroimmunology, which explores the roles that our thoughts have on neurological function within the body and how those in turn affect our immune system. We worked with breath-based practices that focus on the heart region of the body. We did it all within a framework based on the various biblical meanings of the word heart, and we applied the combined information to a devotional life centered on Jesus. For the most part the retreat was very well received. But one woman did not like it at all. It was pretty evident in her body language throughout the weekend and confirmed on her retreat evaluation, where she wrote that she had wanted something about her faith and instead it had been like attending a science class. At the time I wrote her reaction off as a product of her known fundamentalist leanings. But then more recently something that occurred in

---

*Drummond, *Natural Law in the Spiritual World*, 15.

a very different setting made me wonder all over again about the disconnect that many people feel between science and spirituality.

A spiritually progressive book discussion group, to which I belong, was reading *The Biology of Belief* by Bruce Lipton. In that book Dr. Lipton provides a short course in cell biology, written very engagingly for the layperson. Only near the end does he fully connect the dots regarding the implications of his biological thesis for the beliefs with which we shape our lives. For more than a few people in the class, the biological detail which comprises the meat of the book did not have spiritual significance until the end when he tied it all together. "I wish I'd read this chapter first" was a sentiment shared by several. At first I was baffled by this reaction. But upon reflection it struck me that we have been conditioned by our education, our culture, and most of all, our religious institutions to keep science and spirituality compartmentalized. For the majority of modern, educated, intelligent, and even spiritually aware people, there is nothing especially "spiritual" in looking at the inner workings of a cell—or of a star, for that matter. It may be interesting, but it does nothing to stir their spiritual sensibilities.

When you think about it, this disconnect, widespread though it is, is rather bizarre. Science and religion are both attempts to look beyond the surface of things in order to discern deeper underlying processes and principles. Both seek to understand the mysteries of existence, and both seek to improve the lot of humanity through a better understanding of how things work. As Albert Einstein said, "All religions, arts, and sciences are branches of the same tree. All these aspirations are directed toward ennobling man's life, lifting it from the sphere of mere physical existence and leading the individual towards freedom."[152] Yet the respective exponents of these disciplines have not always seen it this way.

The story of how science and religion split—for they have not always been held apart—is better told in other places, so I will not belabor it here. Suffice it to say that science had little choice but to carve out a domain sealed off from a religious establishment that responded to pioneers in scientific discovery by stretching them on the rack and

---

[152]As quoted on thinkexist.com

burning them at the stake. Eventually such religion could only preserve itself in the face of mounting scientific evidence that challenged its world view by retreating to its own corner and ruling over a domain kept untouched by science. Today, however, in an age where science probes the depths of unseen worlds both within us and beyond us, the distance between laboratory and cathedral is getting smaller. If one accepts the premise that, as Cayce put it, " . . . all nature, all mankind, all expressions in materiality are manifestations of a higher force or influence called God,"[153] then unbiased spiritual exploration should eventually lead us to the same discoveries that are to be found in objective science and vice versa. And since knowledge is something that grows over time, it would seem logical that advances in scientific knowledge should trump religious dogmas that were formed in historical contexts where knowledge was considerably less.

I'm not suggesting that we should change the articles of our faith with each new scientific finding. After all, the journey from scientific theory to scientific fact is a long one, with many twists and revisions along the way. But over the long haul, as science is able to tell us more about the properties of stars, cells, and virtually everything in between, and as it is able to elucidate the processes and laws that operate in our universe, this can't *not* influence the thoughtful theist's spirituality as well. Henry Drummond describes the epiphany wherein his spiritual model of the world was re-shaped by nineteenth century scientific advancements in this way:

> I discovered myself enunciating Spiritual Law in the exact terms of Biology and Physics. Now this was not simply a scientific coloring given to Religion, the mere freshening of the theological air with natural facts and illustrations. It was an entire re-casting of truth. And when I came seriously to consider what it involved, I saw, or seemed to see, that it meant essentially the introduction of Natural Law into the Spiritual World.[154]

---

[153]1983–1

[154]Drummond, *Natural Law in the Spiritual World,* 6–7.

If this was true more than a hundred years ago, how much truer is it today when average people can take mind–boggling trips through space that stretches and twists, time that bends, and a universe that may actually be a "multiverse" as they watch PBS's *Nova* and programs like it? It becomes increasingly untenable for those who may watch such programs on, say, a Thursday evening to pretend at a religious service the next Sunday to believe the exact same things that people believed 2,000—4,000 years ago. We need a new spirituality for the twenty–first century that adequately reflects twenty–first century science. And where better to find it than in evolutionary spirituality, which posits interlocking development on the cosmological, biological, and spiritual levels? Yet has there ever been a scientific discovery more hotly contended in religious circles than evolution? Perhaps it's because the evolutionary view calls for us to make changes in the way we view not only the world and its origins, but ourselves and our concept of God as well.

Changing Views of the World, God, and Humanity

Back in the Victorian era, Darwinism brought a huge crisis of faith for many people because they had assumed a static model of creation, one which happened all at once in the beginning and had no room for ongoing development. In making this assumption, they were in tune with the dominant model of eighteenth century Enlightenment, where the universe was seen as a thing, a mechanism, the proverbial watch that is gradually winding down. At first that might not sound like a very spiritual basis for one's religious world view, but think about it: This was a model that accommodated the view that God stood apart from the world. God had created a perfect world at the beginning and sinful humans had ruined it. So a world in gradual decay, a world that's running down, is just the kind of world we might expect to see. And, of course, given that this is a doomed world, we would be merely biding our time here, waiting for heaven. We see this thinking even today, in certain religious ideologies where a major con-flagration in the Middle East would be the harbinger of the long-awaited return of Christ. Such a view is not particularly concerned with the evolution of this world, but rather with those things that will put an ailing world out of its misery.

Nor is the assumption of a static creation the only thing blocking religionists, both past and present, from embracing evolution. They are also often particularly offended by the idea that human beings could have had biological antecedents that were less than human. For most anti-evolutionists, placing humans as a branch of a great phylogenetic tree robs us of our spiritual significance. Just as many of the faithful in Galileo's day would rather ignore scientific evidence than adjust the underlying assumptions of their faith, the same human tendency arose when Darwin's theory was brought forth. In a famous debate between the Anglican Bishop Samuel Wilberforce and Thomas Henry Huxley, biologist and early advocate of evolution, Wilberforce is reported to have asked Huxley whether he was descended from an ape on his grandfather's side or on his grandmother's. Undaunted, Huxley replied, "I would rather be the offspring of two apes than be a man and afraid to face the truth."*

If the religious establishment of Darwin's day was offended by evolution's implications for the nature of the world and humanity's origins, how much more so would they be when the prevailing concept of God was threatened as well? Many assumed that acceptance of evolution was, *ipso facto,* a leap to atheism. As a case in point, British novelist and poet Thomas Hardy was widely condemned as an atheist because some of the themes in his work challenged Victorian-era religious dogmas in favor of a more naturalistic, evolutionary world view. Yet Hardy himself rejected the charge of atheism, saying "I have never understood how anybody can be one except in the sense of disbelieving in a tribal god, man-shaped, fiery-faced and tyrannous, who flies into a rage on the slightest provocation." He goes on to say that "Fifty meanings attach to the word 'God' nowadays, the only reasonable meaning being the *Cause of Things,* whatever that cause may be."[155] Like Hardy, some religious thinkers of Darwin's day were flexible enough

---

*Accounts of this exchange vary, and there was no direct transcript taken at the time of the actual debate. Different accounts of it appear in the writings of witnesses and the letters of Huxley himself. But the essence of all these accounts concurs with the version given here.

[155]Thomas Hardy, *The Life and Work of Thomas Hardy,* ed. Michael Millgate (Athens: The University of Georgia Press, 1985), 406.

to accommodate new scientific understandings into their personal theology. In addition to Henry Drummond, whom we've already met, early synthesizers of evolution with theism included Alfred Russel Wallace, who co-authored a paper on natural selection with Darwin and also embraced the concept of an underlying spiritual dimension to life and consciousness; Presbyterian American botanist Asa Gray, novelist and Church of England priest Charles Kingsley; and computing pioneer Charles Babbage. But they were the exception rather than the rule. Most of the faithful held tenaciously to a world view that excluded evolution from the canon of acceptable theistic ideas.

We see some of these same fears and assumptions fueling the creationism vs. evolution debates of our day, where those who reject evolution on religious grounds make the huge assumption that it deprives us of our spiritual nature and/or removes God from our world view entirely. Such fears are largely unfounded, for while the scientific viewpoint may not *require* a divine presence in the cosmos or a soul for humankind, neither does it automatically deny either one. Rather, it calls those who are theistic to expand and perhaps even revise their understanding of God—a mental-emotional operation that does not always come easily to a human nature that likes to have the big questions of life settled once and for all! As a result, people may unknowingly substitute faith in the rightness of their beliefs for faith in a *living* God. A "living God"—in contrast to a God who is ossified in past epochs—is one who is so much larger than our most expansive imaginings that *all* human understandings are doomed to obsolescence sooner or later. This is a God who evolves as we evolve, a God who grows as our factual knowledge of the universe grows, for as Michael Dowd, author of the acclaimed *Thank God for Evolution*, so aptly puts it, "Facts are God's native tongue."[156]

"The world must have a God," said Teilhard de Chardin, "but our concept of God must be extended as the dimensions of our world are extended."[157] As in the day of Darwin and later that of Teilhard, this is the challenge today that evolution brings to religion. It is not enough

[156]Dowd, *Thank God for Evolution*, 68.
[157]As quoted by Carter Phipps in "A Theologian of Renewal," *EnlightenNext Magazine* (December 2009–February 2009), retrieved from enlightennext.org.

to simply substitute the word "spirituality" for "religion" and think that we have done away with limitation. The common "religion vs. spirituality" distinction may be a useful way of distinguishing dogmatic systems from approaches that are more open, but religion is ultimately nothing more or less than one's linkage to a Something Greater. The transformation we are living through is not the death of religion, but religion's painful coming of age in the twenty-first century. With the huge changes that evolution brings to our collective world view, both the stakes and the opportunities are high. The old argument of the nineteenth and twentieth centuries continues into the twenty-first century with some religious people defending the same tribal God against the encroachment of science, thereby providing fodder for the cannons of the most outspoken atheists of our day. For, make no mistake about it, when you examine the forceful atheistic objections of a Richard Dawkins, for example, all but the defenders of this tribal God will find themselves in full agreement that the God Dawkins refutes can't possibly exist. The jury is still out on how some branches of religious faith will deal with this challenge and what will be the long-term result of the stand they take, but the potential is there for the dogmas of religion's earlier days to give way to glorious engagement with a much bigger, more astounding Reality than early formulators of the various faiths could have dreamed of. One thing seems certain: In the words of philosopher, physicist, and mathematician Alfred North Whitehead, "Religion will not retain its old power until it faces change in the same spirit as science."[158]

But then again, we might temper Whitehead's enthusiasm for science's ability to roll with the punches by pointing out that science, too, can get locked in to prevailing theories and resist inconsistent new information until it accumulates to a point where it becomes impossible to ignore. As American physicist, historian, and philosopher of science Thomas Kuhn pointed out in his landmark work *The Structure of Scientific Revolutions*, it takes more than new data to change the prevailing scientific view. The new data must be amassed and interpreted with a growing consensus before it reaches the critical mass

[158]Alfred North Whitehead, "Religion and Science," *The Atlantic Magazine* (August, 1925), retrieved from theatlantic.com/magazine.

that changes the accepted paradigm. If the accepted religious paradigm of Darwin's time met a major challenge in evolution, the secular, scientific paradigm of a mechanistic world—one that is running down—was challenged as well. Prior to the introduction of evolutionary thinking, whether you believed that a sinful humanity had spoiled the perfect creation or took the scientific position that the universe is a mechanism that is running out of steam, you were still left with a universe that was not going anywhere. Evolution changed all of that, calling on the scientifically minded as well as the religious to take a new look at the directionality of the cosmos, and in many ways the scientific world was almost as slow as the religious one to catch the full implications of evolutionary advance. For example, many readers will recall an education in the second half of the twentieth century in which they were taught biological evolution simultaneously with cosmological *devolution*—the old model that suggested the universe was like a watch that had been wound up at the beginning and has been winding down ever since. Yet over time, examples of evolution on both the biological and cosmological levels yielded a growing body of evidence that not everything is winding down; some things are winding *up*, so to speak. No wonder this data challenged the established scientific paradigm; it is nothing short of astounding when the second law of thermodynamics is taken into consideration.

Entropy vs. Creative Advance

The second law of thermodynamics, also known as the law of entropy, does indeed support the running-down-watch model. By it we see how things do tend to revert toward a mean, to disorganize and disintegrate over time rather than leap forward to something new. For example, the same principle that causes the coldness of ice to chill the lukewarm drink in your glass causes the heat in one room to flow out into a less warm adjoining space. The higher pressure air in your bicycle tire will flow out a pinhole into the less dense air around it. A rock erodes to sand over time and a piece of iron will slowly rust into its oxidized elements. Everything breaks down over time. We all know this to be true; ask any homeowner! This is the process called entropy, and it is often associated with decline and decay.

But entropy turns out to be only half the story. The old Newtonian model which gave rise to that analogy of a clock that was running down did not reckon on another force in the universe, a force that Albert North Whitehead called "creative advance into novelty." Entropy notwithstanding, there is a directionality toward increased differentiation, organization, and complexity over time. Right alongside the "running down" character of entropy, we find an equally ubiquitous organizing force in this universe. We have the well-known phenomenon by which the pendulums of multiple clocks in the same room, which may start out swinging in a variety of rhythms, will come into synchronization with one another over time. The water that leaves your bathtub when you open the drain will organize itself into a whirlpool. New stars are being born in the universe, despite the fact that we are getting further away in time from the Big Bang's energetic burst. Unlike the regression toward a mean that occurs when ice melts in a drink or a breakdown of structure such as occurs when rocks erode into sand, the evolutionary direction builds *up* over time. When we look at the life forms of this planet, we see that over time they get more complex and highly advanced rather than regressing toward less organized, more primitive states.

Out of a chaotic set of conditions and possibilities beginning as far back as the Big Bang, the directionality of creation brings order out of chaos. As the Big History Project founded by Bill Gates and David Christian points out, there have been key times in the history of the universe when so-called "Goldilocks conditions" came together in such a way as to bring forth something new, seemingly out of nowhere.* For example, 200 million years after the Big Bang, when gravity within more dense areas of the clouds of helium and hydrogen brought about compaction, which in turn increased the temperature to a threshold of ten million degrees, the protons in the hydrogen and helium fused, bringing forth the explosive birth of stars. Much later, the "Goldilocks conditions" on earth—a variety of elements as the building blocks of life, water warmed by vents in the ocean that channeled the earth's interior heat, a planet just close enough but not too close to the sun, to

---

*See bighistoryproject.com for more information.

name just a few—were such that life sprang forth. The important thing about evolutionary thresholds is that what the new combination turns out to be is greater than the sum of its parts. Two hydrogen atoms and one oxygen atom may come together to make water, but once that happens, water has characteristics that neither of its components had by itself. An essentially new property has emerged. Now some would credit such emergence to an underlying force and some would see it as happenstance, but no one can deny that there is directionality to this process. Again and again over the course of long-term history, we see evolutionary leaps forward that changed everything, and it's hard not to see in these leaps an inherently creative principle embedded in the universe, a trajectory of growth and development. Some would call that principle God. Some would call it Creative Force. Edgar Cayce called it both.

As we have read in the Cayce readings, "In the beginning when chaos existed in the creating of the earth, the Spirit of God moved over the face of same and out of chaos came the world—with its beauty in natural form, or in nature."[159] It is here within a universe that has a trajectory of growth and development that we find a God who is up to something in this world and the call to us of co-creatorship. Once we heed this call, the interplay of entropy and creative advance take on deep personal significance—a significance that shapes the very essence of what it means to be on the spiritual path. Entropy is undeniably happening, yet in its midst so is there also ongoing creation. What we don't find anywhere is stagnation. Things—and we—either progress and grow or we decline into decay. But with us or without us, time's arrow is pointing forward.

In a world where one force is undeniably breaking things down while another is undeniably breaking forth into newness, we are called to accept the inevitability of change and death while simultaneously giving our energy to the onward-moving direction of Life. Not in a stance of war against entropy, for one of the hardest lessons of the spiritual path is that we must accept the inevitable passing away of all forms; but rather to follow the currents of life in the midst of death,

[159]3976-8

creation in the midst of dissolution, and order in the midst of chaos. Over the next four chapters we will be taking a somewhat detailed approach to that process, returning in Chapter 13 particularly to un-bundle the interplay between entropy and evolution's trajectory. But first, to keep it real and personal (rather than merely theoretical), let's go to the places in each of our lives where evolution's call can always be found—those places where we feel stuck or stagnating.

Stuck States

In considering the evolutionary premise that there is no stagnation, we've probably all experienced the growth spurts that come from an inner drive to move onward and upward—in fact, as we have already seen, it has been the force that drove our development from infancy onward. But we are also faced with the unavoidable fact that most (if not all) of us do indeed feel stuck at times with respect to certain situations in our lives. As a practicing hypnotherapist and life coach, I have observed over the course of many years that for most people there is no condition more disturbing than the sense that they aren't *going* anywhere. In fact, such "stuck states" are the number one reason people come to see me. The anxiety that usually accompanies stuck states testifies to a knowing deep within us that stagnation cannot go on indefinitely but must eventually result in either a leap forward or dissolution.

The good news is that when we recognize that we are stuck, we are actually experiencing the stirring of the evolutionary drive within us. People who are completely out of touch with the evolutionary drive may *be* stuck, but they don't know it. This is not to say that only those who recognize the evolutionary drive by name are engaged by it. Many people who are living the evolutionary principle do not label it as such, just as many people who resist the evolutionary drive have no idea that that's what they are doing. I simply want to point out that when we do recognize we are stuck and feel deep discomfort about it, this is the sound of evolution knocking at our door. It behooves all of us, then, to be aware of those places in our lives where something wants to move forward and something else seems to be holding us back; because these are our evolutionary thresholds. We will be looking at strategies for traversing those thresholds in subsequent chapters, but first it's important to know where in our lives such thresholds exist. To get a sense of where your own thresholds might be, consider the questions below under the title, "Where Are You Feeling Stuck?

Where Are You Feeling Stuck?

Where are you experiencing chaos in your life right now? Where is the system of your life on overload? When and where do you find yourself playing out the same old dysfunctional patterns of response to a difficult life situation? Consider this a snapshot of where you find yourself now. Make a few brief notes to yourself about any issues you are aware of in the following areas:

- Undesirable habits and behaviors that you have been unsuccessful in changing thus far

- Unwanted and limiting attitudes and emotions that interfere with your living the best version of life that you can imagine

- Health challenges

- Interpersonal challenges such as unresolved relationship issues, problematic ongoing responsibilities involving another person, patterns of worry, fear, jealousy, etc. concerning another person.

- Life circumstances, struggles, or situational problems with job, finances, lack of opportunity, etc.

- Anything else that may occur to you

Now go back and consider some of the practices and reflective exercises you have encountered in earlier chapters. There may have been times when you felt moved to follow through on some aspect of the evolutionary perspective, but then the intention was lost as other demands or interests took over your priorities. This is yet another

way that stuckness manifests: quick bursts of inspiration and intention that fizzle out before they are translated into action. Below is a
list of some of the places in earlier pages of this book where you
may have felt the impetus toward a specific evolutionary action:

- At the end of the exercise "Examining Your Response to the Evolutionary Call" (p. 55) you were asked to notice things you do or
  fail to do which act as a drag on the evolutionary advance and
  then select just one of these as a focus of attention and more
  consistent effort.

- All of Chapter 6 emphasized the key role of meditative practices
  centered on the "I am" awareness in cultivating evolutionary
  consciousness. Several variations were described and you were
  encouraged to make such meditation a part of daily life.

- The exercise in Chapter 7 ("Changing the Filters on Your Lens,"
  p. 88) culminated in the suggestion that whenever you find your
  thoughts gravitating toward the remedial perspective, you consciously and deliberately consider an alternative, expansive view
  of the situation.

- The challenge presented in Chapter 8 calls for a vigilant but
  somewhat playful awareness of ego's many disguises. The exercise "Stalking the Wild Ego" (p. 111) gives some ideas for how
  to do this.

- The evolutionary awareness that we are corpuscles in the body
  of God (Chapter 9) can be enhanced through meditative awareness (an example appears on p. 122) and acted on when we
  remember that our consciousness is God's nervous system and
  our acts of love are God's bloodstream. The aim is to be corpuscles that bring life, growth, and vitality to God's "body" and
  catch ourselves when we are instead being cells that bring death,
  destruction, and disease.

- Biology that supports our spiritual growth is a great evolutionary attainment (Chapter 10). Working with the chakra energies is a very practical way that we can give form to further evolution. When we cultivate attitudes and actions that are supportive of each chakra's constructive energy, we cooperate with the evolutionary force. A practice like using the Lord's Prayer for meditation (p. 146) is one way to do this.

What has been your response to each of these potential evolutionary actions or practices? As you go over the list above notice:

- The ones that you are, in fact, working with. These are not likely to be related to stuck states for you.

- Which ones never mobilized your intention to act. These are not likely to be indicative of stuckness either. Not everyone will feel called to respond to the same actions. The exercises in this book are suggestions, not dictates!

- The items that sparked an initial impulse to act, but which you have since forgotten or continued to put off doing. It is this last group that we are most interested in here, for these are the places where old patterns of stuckness may have arrested an incipient move forward.

The Convergence and the Potential

And so we return to where we began in this chapter: a spirituality that is informed by the observations and discoveries of science, a path that places us firmly within the cosmos in which we find ourselves, a vision that shapes our meaning and purpose within the framework of the great, unfolding story of an evolving universe. Here there are no divisions between the secular and the spiritual, for we are getting closer and closer to the realization that we cannot sequester the spiritual side of life into a separate little box where it doesn't flow over into the other areas of our lives. Our future as a human race depends to a large degree on how well we are able to keep our collective eye on the big picture. An infusion of spiritual influence may help us do this, so long as it is not a prescriptive or coercive movement that presumes to dictate the terms of spirituality for all people and so long as it is a spirituality that has a living, breathing relationship with science. Alice Bailey expressed the hope that science and spirituality would one day come together, but recognized that it would require a unifying philosophy for it to do so:

> I hope we shall come to the realisation that the man who is only interested in the scientific aspect, and who confines himself to the study of those manifestations which are purely material, is just as much occupied with the study of the divine as is his frankly religious brother who only concerns himself with the spiritual side; and that the philosopher is, after all, occupied in emphasising for us the very necessary aspect of the intelligence which links the matter aspect and the spiritual, and blends them into one coherent whole. Perhaps by the union of these three lines of science, religion, and philosophy, we may get a working knowledge of the truth as it is, remembering at the same time that "truth lies within ourselves."[160]

With evolution of knowledge and understanding in all of these fields, we see the very distinct possibility of that hope being realized, for as Teilhard de Chardin pointed out, "Like the meridians as they approach the poles, science, philosophy and religion are bound to converge as they draw nearer to the whole."[161] It remains to be seen what we, with our present opportunity to manifest in the earth, will do with this convergence. As Richard Bucke poetically put it:

> As life arose in a world without life, where Simple Consciousness came into existence where before was mere vitality without perception; as Self Consciousness leaping widewinged from Simple Consciousness soared forth over land and sea, so shall the race of man which has been thus established, continuing its beginningless and endless ascent, make other steps (the next of which it is now

---

[160]Bailey, *The Consciousness of the Atom*, 11.
[161]Teilhard de Chardin, *The Phenomenon of Man*, 30.

in the act of climbing) and attain to yet higher life than any heretofore experienced or even conceived.[162]

Whether we do, in fact, attain that higher life and what it will look like once we get there may depend largely on how we negotiate our ongoing travels up the great spiral of life.

---

[162]Bucke, *Cosmic Consciousness*, 22.

Chapter 12:
Our Path up the Spiral of Life

(Q) Explain how the example of Man's developing and improving his mode of living scientifically on earth, for example in medical work and all other sciences, proves his development and evolution on earth and other planes.

(A) Man's development, as given, is of man's understanding and applying the laws of the Universe, and as man applies those, man develops, man brings up the whole generation of man . . .   900-70

We are evolving, in ways that Science cannot measure, to ends that Theology dares not contemplate.   E.M. Forster, *Howard's End**

*T*he evolutionary force driving the world of manifest form is apparent all around us, from nature as we experience it on this earth to the far reaches of deep space. And as we have been seeing, the discovery of evolution holds the potential to place a new frame of meaning around our existence. It brings not just an addition to our knowledge, but a new organizing principle that shapes our views of spirituality, history, and life itself. In the words of Julian Huxley, evolutionary biologist and grandson of Thomas Henry Huxley:

> With the adoption of the evolutionary approach in non-biological fields, from cosmology to human affairs, we are beginning to realize that biological evolution is only one aspect of evolution in general. Evolution in the extended sense can be defined as a directional and essentially irreversible process occurring in time, which in its course gives rise to an increase of variety and an increasingly high level of organization, in its products. Our present knowledge indeed forces us to the view that the whole of reality is evolution—a single process of self-transformation.[163]

---

*E.M. Forster, *Howard's End* (New York: Vintage Books, 1954), 241.

[163]Julian Huxley, "Evolution and Genetics," in *What Is Science?*, ed. James R. Newman (New York: Simon and Shuster, 1955) 278.

Key to our understanding of both personal and collective evolution is this realization spoken of by Huxley—that we are, indeed, involved in a "single process of self-transformation." There is one evolution taking place. It involves a cosmos. It involves all life within that cosmos. It involves our individual development, and it involves civilization as a whole. Just as we can see evidence of or kinship with all biological life in the stages of fetal development, the linkage between our personal and collective evolution becomes apparent when we view history through the lens of the same developmental themes that characterize our childhood development.

Using the chakra themes, we can see in the early hunter–gatherer tribes, for example, a fledgling humanity devoted almost entirely to the basic survival needs of the first chakra. We can think of this as representing the infancy period of human civilization, which is then recapitulated in the infancy of each individual human being. As tribal cultures developed, we can trace second chakra themes. What appears in childhood as budding imagination, magical thinking, a developing emotional life, and first stirrings of sexuality made its appearance in human history with the emergence of fertility cults, expanding artistic expression, and the magical world views that characterized those early cultures. The power drives of the third chakra theme gave rise to cultures where power rested not so much with the tribe as with those who rose to strong leadership. The age of city–states and later monarchies began. In the gradual spread of more democratic cultural values we can detect fourth chakra themes of belonging, membership, and affiliation around a common mythos and strong national identities— often linked with that nation's dominant religion. The age of scientific advance bears much of the fifth chakra's theme of rational mind that looks for over–arching patterns that make sense of things.

The human race today is perched atop its current collective evolutionary attainment of rational mind. In that respect, it is analogous to a young adult. Remember that in the context of "deep time" or "big history" we are still a young species. Much of childhood is still with us and much of true maturity is still in our future. And just as the majority of human beings "naturally" develop to the rational stage and then will either stay there for the rest of their lives or continue in a more conscious, chosen way to develop beyond that attainment, the human race is at a point where further evolutionary development is likely to happen only as the result of chosen development, because the very nature of movement beyond this point is one of "waking up" to the higher potentials within us. As the spiritual awareness of more and more people moves beyond the constraints of mythic religions that stress membership in the group through adherence to its rules and beliefs and as the sensibilities of more and more people extend beyond rigid ethnic and national identities, we can see an evolutionary pull toward the themes of higher fifth chakra energies and onward to the sixth chakra.

It's important to keep in mind that these are general cultural, historical trends that trace the basic developmental lines of human civilization. They are not meant to be absolute or universal. They are a depiction of the aggregate and do not address the exceptions. This makes it especially important not to equate "lower" chakra energies with "worse," "less valuable," or "less advanced." Just as a balanced, healthy person draws on the life-enhancing energies of *all* the chakras, a balanced, healthy humanity needs all of these energies as well. The most advanced human culture would still need to have security at the first chakra level and will face its primal survival instincts if that security is threatened. The most enlightened of cultures will still need to continuously monitor itself for proper use of personal power at the third chakra level. Nor does a collective cultural growth to, let's say, fourth chakra values mean that the destructive versions of the second and third chakra energies will be totally absent. And just because there is wider engagement with sixth chakra energies today than there was, perhaps, a thousand years ago, it does not mean that these characteristics were completely absent at that earlier time. Rather, we are looking at very broad trends that take their greatest significance against the backdrop of big history. The general trend of human cultural evolution, just like our individual evolution, is pulling us toward ever-deeper engagement with the energies of the higher chakras even as it is manifesting greater health or stability in the expression of the lower chakra energies.

The details and nuances of how these personal and cultural advances operate and cross-pollinate one another, while germane to what we are considering here in this book, would nonetheless involve us in a large quantity of information that has already been dealt with elsewhere with far more expertise than I can bring to the subject matter. For that reason, I would recommend several resources for the reader who wants to go deeper. Two of Ken Wilber's early works, *The Atman Project* and *Up from Eden*, deal with personal and cultural evolution respectively in considerable depth, while his *A Brief History of Everything* and *A Theory of Everything* represent his later thinking in more condensed form. And no approach to cultural evolutionary advancement would be truly complete without reference to the groundbreaking model called "Spiral Dynamics," which is expounded in the book *Spiral Dynamics: Mastering Values, Leadership and Change* by Don Beck and Christopher Cowan. Spiral Dynamics, a theory of human development based on the work of psychologist Clare Graves, describes both the adaptive strengths and destructive characteristics of common human value systems. Each value system is assigned a color label as a means of getting beyond notions of race, nationality, or ethnicity (sort of the way Sesame Street did this by using colors other than human skin tones for its diverse cast of characters). Dr. Beck, who along with co-author Cowan developed Graves' thinking into the Spiral Dynamics model, is a leading global authority on value systems and societal change. In his professional consulting, he has applied the principles of Spiral Dynamics for over thirty years in such "real world" contexts as the peaceful end of apartheid in South Africa and The Center for Human Emergence–Middle East (where he served as senior advisor).

The salient point for us right now is that we see a fascinating pattern whereby the developmental experience of the individual is an up–close–and–personal version of the development of the human race—one evolution manifesting at multiple levels where there are patterns within patterns within patterns. It would seem that there must be some organizing principle to it.

In the Beginning Was the Word

Observation of life and the world will show us that the "single process of self-transformation" in which we are engaged involves interlocking levels of one great pattern. If we are to anchor this pattern in the Cayce cosmology, we would have to say that it all begins with the Word. In response to a question about how souls may be entangled in other systems similar to those we experience in matter, the Cayce source begins the response with, "it is well that the premise be given from which such answers would be made." What is that premise upon which all of our ponderings about worlds seen and unseen should be based? Paraphrasing the opening to the Gospel of John, the reading says,

> These you may find in the indication that in the beginning was the Word, and the Word was with God—the same. Without Him there was not anything made that was made. Thus in the answers we may find that, though there may be worlds, many universes, even much as to solar systems, greater than our own that we enjoy in the present, this earthly experience on this earth is a mere speck when considered even with our own solar system. Yet the soul of man, thy soul, encompasses ALL in this solar system or in others.[164]

If we are to unbundle the magnificence of the thought in this reading, we must look at the meaning of *Word*. This term, *logos* in Greek, means far more than the simple unit that is a building block of language. *Logos* was used among the Greeks to represent variously thought, speech, meaning, reason, and proportion. According to the Greek philosopher Heraclitis (who was born more than 500 years before the Gospel of John used the term), *logos* is the fundamental order of the cosmos. The Stoics equated the term with the divine principle of active reason that animates the universe. There can be little doubt that John's choice of the term *logos* to tell his version of the creation story reflected these philosophical nuances of meaning, for all of this texture of meaning was established hundreds of years before the Hellenistically influenced Gospel of John was composed.

In building everything on the premise that the Word was present in the beginning and that it is the same as God, Cayce is pointing to the divine order, template, or pattern that underlies everything. This is why, in the reading excerpted above, he could first diminish our

---

[164]5755-2

earthly experience to a "mere speck" and then in the next breath say
that we encompass everything in our own solar system and others as
well within our souls. We have already seen this same principle addressed in the assertion that we are corpuscles in the body of God and
that within us are universes in the making. In the hermetic teachings,
we find this same principle expressed in the simple phrase, "as above,
so below; as without, so within."

Here we revisit a concept touched upon in Chapter 8: things that
are simultaneously whole in themselves and a part of something larger
than themselves. An atom is part of a molecule and a molecule is part
of a cell which is part of an organ which is part of a living thing.
Letters form words that form sentences which form paragraphs and so
on. A person is part of a family which is part of a community which is
part of a nation which is part of the world. Everything is both whole
unto itself and a part of something beyond itself. Arthur Koestler
coined the term "holon" to denote this quality of being a whole and a
part at the same time.

Although he may not have used the term (which hadn't yet been
coined), Edgar Cayce described our ultimate nature as being that of a
holon when he said that we can know ourselves to be ourselves and
yet be one with God. We are whole unto ourselves, and yet we are also
part of that greater Allness that we call God. We are corpuscles in the
body of God and within the corpuscles of our own bodies we contain
universes. Thus we see holons comprising holons comprising holons
and the adage "As above, so below; as without so within." This is the
pattern, and the dynamics by which holons come together or dissolve
into their component parts is a picture of both entropy and creative
advance into novelty.

When holons come together to form larger patterns of wholeness,
we find greater complexity, for now the combined complexities of the
constituent parts have woven together to create something new.
Teilhard de Chardin described it this way:

> . . . modern thought is . . . beginning to see that there is definitely
> *more* in the molecule than in the atom, *more* in the cell than in the
> molecule, *more* in society than in the individual, *more* in the

mathematical construction than in the calculations and theorems. We are now inclined to admit that at each further degree of combination *something* which is irreducible to isolated elements *emerges* in a new order.[165]

We might see this as a movement to wider and wider contexts within which the holon exists. For example, the tree growing in your yard has more complexity than algae. Yet the same chloroplasts within the cells of that tree's leaves are to be found in algae. To get from algae to tree, cells that perform photosynthesis had to join along the way with cells that make up roots, stems, leaves, and vascular tissue—none of which are to be found in algae, but all of which are necessary to the life of a tree. So we could see the tree's relatively greater complexity as a much wider context in which its chloroplasts exist—while each chloroplast nonetheless remains whole unto itself. This pattern applies to all things. The same pattern that takes us from algae to a tree can be seen from atom to molecule to grain of earth to rock to planet. At the level of planet, a grain that is part of the composition of the Earth exists in a far more diverse and complex context than it does all by itself as a single grain made up of molecules.

Now what does all this about trees and algae and grains of earth have to do with us? We, too, are drawn by the evolutionary impulse to ever wider and more complex contexts for our being. Not to lose ourselves in sameness (for the distinctness of the cell and the grain of earth is necessary for it to fill its place in the whole), but to expand our field of participation in the whole, we move onward along the evolutionary trajectory.

The Leading Edge of the Evolutionary Trajectory

Back in Chapter 4 we looked at a Cayce reading (900-340) which tells us that the various kingdoms of nature give us a way of conceiving the evolutionary scheme of things. The epigraph for Chapter 1 was also taken from this reading, which is especially rich in its evolutionary perspective. We return to it now for further illumination concern-

---

[165]Teilhard de Chardin, *The Phenomenon of Man*, 267-68.

ing the evolutionary trajectory, for in it we find ourselves placed in a context where our world is one of many. Anticipating what modern astronomy tells us about the vast amounts of time it takes images from the stars to reach us from outer space, this reading points out that as we look up to space, we see beginnings just like that of the Earth. We're told that the pattern of creation is the same across time and space, and the same creative energy that birthed our sphere is still its organizing principle. Here we see the ongoing creative advance—the presence of a pattern of creation that runs through the universe.

But that's not all. As this reading goes on to comment on the coming of humankind, it says that the advent of humanity involved a "combining all of the forms of creation so far created." By coming up through what the reading calls "dividing points" between the mineral, plant, animal, and human stages of creation (these seem to be equivalent to the "thresholds" discussed in the last chapter), the very evolutionary force itself was imbued with "understanding." In this statement, the reading is amazingly prescient of contemporary evolutionary thinking. Compare this comment from Tom Atlee, evolutionary thinker and founder of the Co-Intelligence Institute:

> To the extent we *are* evolution, *humans becoming aware of the reality and dynamics of evolution is evolution becoming aware of itself.* And as we learn to apply our knowledge of evolution to our evolutionary role, and reach out into the world with conscious evolutionary intent and impact, *we are not just humans doing our own evolution consciously. We are evolution, itself, becoming conscious.*[166]

Echoes of Cayce's assertion that the evolutionary force gains understanding through its journey up from mineral to plant to animal to human are unmistakable in such comments from Atlee, as they are in numerous similar ones from his evolutionary colleagues. To return, then, to the very remarkable ideas in reading 900-340, the culminating

---

[166]"Tom Atlee's Take on Conscious Evolution" retrieved from wikia.com, emphasis original.

point of this entire process is nothing less than that the soul, through the will, "might make itself One with that Creation." The reading concludes:

> . . . There you have reincarnation, there you have evolution, there you have the mineral kingdom, the plant kingdom, the animal kingdom, each developing towards its own source, yet all belonging and becoming one in that force as it develops itself to become one with the Creative Energy, and one with the God. The one then surviving in the earth, through mineral, through plant kingdom, through the vegetable kingdom, through the animal kingdom, each as the geological survey shows, held its sway in the earth, pass from one into the other; yet man given that to be lord over all, and the *only* survivor of that creation.

From this we see that the readings would certainly agree that we stand at the leading edge of what has been a long evolutionary journey up what many evolutionary thinkers have depicted as the spiral of life.

The Spiral of Life

The spiral is an apt image of the evolutionary advance—far more fitting than a depiction of straight linear ascent—because it conveys the way we continue to encounter the same pattern at ever-higher levels of manifestation and wider contexts of meaning. This is true of not only externally observable evolution, but also our personal growth experience.

We often find ourselves confronting the same issues and patterns repeatedly in our lives and erroneously concluding that the repetition means we have not made progress. Yet, if we will look more carefully, we will usually see that we are meeting the pattern at a higher level or in a broader context than before. Take, for example, an emotional challenge like fear of speaking one's truth. For the one dealing with such an issue, the way you met that fear as a child may have been quite different from the way you met it as a young adult, and the way you meet it as a mature adult may be different still. You may well be facing the same root pattern of fear of speaking your truth, but notice how you have to meet it at both higher levels of challenge and within the broader context that your ongoing experience provides. The child may fear and not even know why. The young adult may experience the same fear and understand more about where the perceived threat lies. With maturation, there may be growing insight about the responses one makes to the fear and the motives of others who may be involved in the fear-inducing situation. There may even be the introduction of spiritual understanding along the way. We may not be skyrocketing beyond fear forever and always, but rather meeting it each time the spiral curves back around to that pattern. And so we spiral upward. In this way, we grow.

The nautilus, with its spiral shape, has long been a favorite metaphor of this spiraling spiritual growth. It is such a perfect metaphor because it shows both our spiraling, expansive growth and how encased and calcified we can nonetheless become at each stage that we attain. Oliver Wendell Holmes' poem, "The Chambered Nautilus," describes the way the nautilus builds successive chambers of pearly shell to live in, each one more commodious than the one before:

> Still, as the spiral grew,
> He left the past year's dwelling for the new,
> Stole with soft step its shining archway through,
> Built up its idle door,
> Stretched in his last-found home, and knew the old no more.

There is metaphoric value in noting that although the shell of the nautilus is the outer, visible record of its growth, it is the growth of the living animal inside of it that necessitates successively larger chambers. As Holmes expressed it in prose, "Once the mind has been stretched to a new idea, it will never again return to its original size." We hear this same idea from theosophist C.W. Leadbeater:

> The whole process is one of steady evolution from lower forms to higher, from the simpler to the more complex. But what is evolving is not primarily the form, but the life within it. The forms also evolve and grow better as time passes; but this is in order that they may

be appropriate vehicles for more and more advanced waves of life.[167]

Like the nautilus, you and I must expand the contexts and bound-aries of our lives in order to manifest more developed expressions of Spirit, the life force within us. To do that, we find ourselves running up against the very walls of our previous contexts and boundaries. These include our ideas about who we are; the interpretations we put on our circumstances; our beliefs about what is and is not possible; the emo-tions that have taken on a life of their own within our internal reali-ties; patterns of behavior that we repeatedly exhibit—either because we feel powerless to change the behavior or because we remain un-conscious of it; and our notions of what we are and are not willing to do for the sake of evolution. We have previously approached these contexts and boundaries as we considered unmasking the ego, replac-ing a remedial view of incarnation with an expansive one and explor-ing our willingness to respond to the evolutionary call. Now these things come together as the framework and plaster of our chamber walls. If we are to "steal with soft step" through the "shining archway" of our next-larger chamber (to borrow the language of Holmes' beau-tiful poem), we must come face to face with our current chamber walls and be ready to dismantle them. To help with this process, "Examining the Walls of Your Current Chamber" below provides some points for pondering.

What Are Your Current Walls Made Of?

In the context of our spiraling nautilus metaphor, look again at the places where you feel stuck, blocked, or constrained in a state (chamber) that the truer, deeper you has outgrown. There may be one main "stuck state" that you experience in your life right now or there may be several situations that feed into a place where you feel stuck. In either case, take a moment to really feel your "stuckness."

---

[167]Leadbeater, *A Textbook of Theosophy*, 20.

From that perspective, reflect and/or journal on the following questions:

- When you are in the midst of feeling stuck, what do you tend to identify as the cause of your stuckness?

- Who are you when you experience this? Feel into the self that you experience yourself to be. Get in touch with the self-sense or self-identity that predominates in your inner world when you are experiencing this stuckness. What do you believe about yourself? What do you believe about life or other people?

- If your stuckness were the result of a force outside of you that causes you to remain stuck, what motive would you assign to that force?

- If your stuckness were to be the result of a part of you deliberately not making progress (the old inner saboteur theory), what motive would you ascribe to that part?

- What emotions arise when you experience this stuckness?

- What feels impossible when you are stuck?

- What effort are you willing to make when you feel stuck? What effort do you find yourself unwilling to make?

- How important is your own evolution when you are stuck? How important is overall evolution when you are stuck?

You may not have answers to each and every one of these questions, and that's okay. Just be sure that you do not prematurely dismiss any question, as it may be the one you most need to ask yourself. We are not looking for answers or solutions to your stuckness in this reflective exercise—just increased awareness concerning the architecture of your chamber walls.

From all of the foregoing, we can see that for one committed to the evolutionary path the questions will always be things like: Where am I feeling pinched, stuck, or challenged? What are the structures of belief, lifestyle, or habit that are boxing in the part of me that wants to expand? Where are the strictures so tight as to stunt further growth? When we can answer these questions, we have found our evolutionary edge.

Engaging Your Evolutionary Edge

In our most persistent manifestations of limitation we will usually recognize the distortion or blockage of a particular chakra's energy. (A chart summarizing the chakra energy themes discussed in Chapter 10 appears on page 184. It may be helpful to review this information in the light of what you noticed when examining your "chamber walls.") We may also recognize challenged chakra energies when they manifest as circumstances that we draw to ourselves. Because each chakra is integrally linked with the body via the nervous and glandular systems, distortions or blockages of chakra energy can even appear as physical symptoms. This comment from the Cayce readings pretty much sums up the breadth of impact we experience from chakra energies:

> Thus we find the connection, the association of the spiritual being with the mental self, at those centers from which the reflexes react to all of the organs, all of the emotions, all of the activities of a physical body.[168]

One important caveat is that in surveying these possible manifestations of less-than-optimal function of the chakras' energies, it's important to look for recurring patterns or longstanding situations in our lives rather than jump to conclusions based on short-term problems in one area of life or another. We are looking for those things that may be clues to our evolutionary growing edges rather than attempt-

---

[168]263-13

Chart 1: A Review of Chakra Energies
(Please see Chapter 10 for a more complete discussion of this material)

Chakra	Positive Energy	Blocked or Distorted Energy
1	being securely grounded in this world; feeling safe in this world with trust that basic needs will be cared for; basic life energies	insecurity re: having physical needs met; poverty consciousness; obesity arising from feelings of scarcity; hoarding; excessive concern over keeping a roof over one's head; fears concerning physical safety; deep-seated issues with trust; lack of grounding; problems with eliminations, lower limbs, male reproductive organs
2	sexual energies; imagination, desire and creativity; emotional connection	blockage or excess of sexual energies; unhealthy relationship with one's anima/animus; blocked creativity; excessive emotionality; magical thinking; problems with bladder, large intestine, internal reproductive organs or lumbar region of the back
3	personal power; establishing a healthy ego-identify; self-esteem; courage	power drives; social status-seeking; egotism; self-importance; aggression; anger; control issues or their opposites—lack of confidence, a poorly-formed self-identity, inability to assert one's own needs; timidity; problems with esophagus, stomach, small intestines, most of the large intestines, liver, pancreas, spleen, adrenal glands, and kidneys
4	love, compassion and kindness, affiliation and belonging	impairments in the ability to give and receive love; lack of generosity, feelings of hurt, bitterness, jealousy and overbearing "smother love," need for approval; problems with belonging, or having healthy affiliations with others; problems with the heart, lungs, and circulatory system
5	expression of your truth; shift from limited personal perspective to place in the wider scheme of things and higher laws; use of will	feelings of not being heard, or the inability to express your ideas or convey who you are; identity crises or existential crises stemming from not knowing your place in the larger order of things; untruth, in the sense of lying to oneself or others; excessive willfulness or inability to apply will; problems with throat, shoulders, arms, and voice
6	higher intuition, Christ consciousness and loving service to humanity; vision; understanding	fuzzy thinking; psychic disorders; psychosomatic disorders; headaches; problems with brain and the sense organs
7	source of spiritual energy from above; expansiveness; unity consciousness	pervasive lack of ease; feeling constricted or cut off from joy; extreme worry or anxiety; being closed off from or afraid of religion and spirituality; problems with the sensory organs, headaches, and sleep disturbances

ing to come up with a laundry list of what may be wrong with us!

The great value in tying our evolutionary edge to the chakra energy themes is twofold. First, it places our personal struggles and strivings against the backdrop of archetypal themes that are the work of a soul in the earth. When we come against our personal challenges, we are not flawed or broken or failures but instead members of the human race, representatives of the entire influx of souls who are here with a task to accomplish. Second, when we realize that our struggles, personal though they may be, involve energies that are universally available, we find a rich resource in the functional, life-enhancing potential within the very chakra that is the locus of the problem. This is in keeping with the Cayce readings' definition of evil as being "just a little under good" or as "good misapplied." When we recognize chakra themes in our areas of struggle or limitation, we can more easily identify the more life-enhancing version of that same chakra's energies and seek to apply those in our lives, thus engaging our evolutionary edges rather than denying them or running from them in fear.

This is much easier said than done, of course, for we can be such walking contradictions. As much as we aspire to the heights of spiritual growth, when faced with real challenges to our entrenched ways of being, self-protective fear is the all-too-common response. Anyone who has ever been serious about spiritual growth will know that the tendency to back off and retrench in our stuckness is a force to be reckoned with. Sooner or later, we all face those times when all of the spiritual inspiration and knowledge we have accumulated through reading or attending workshops or participating in online discussions is not quite enough to push us through that threshold of change. Sooner or later, we come up against the chaos that generally precedes times of evolutionary advance. We may look back later and see that some of these times of life struggle and unsettling chaos have brought us the greatest advances in awakening to our souls and the ability to live from the soul's perspective. How true it is, as French playwright and actor Moliere said, that "the greater the obstacle, the more glory in overcoming it." But that may not always be apparent while we are in the midst of the situation. It's hard to realize while you're going through it that evolution brings order out of chaos.

Chapter 13:
Out of Chaos, Something New Arises

We find in certain periods in the life there have been those influences that would appear that all was lost to the entity, in the physical, material, and in the filial conditions, yet, as is seen, better judgment or better application of self has often brought out of chaos those conditions that have become satisfactory, or the entity has builded upon the ashes of blasted hopes.   4185-1

> . . . she sat there in her big fur cloak . . . with eyes that looked outwards, yet brooded inwardly, April-eyes, that were turned towards the summer that was coming. And all the past was poured into that, even as the squalls and tempests of winter are transmuted into and feed the luxuriance of June-time. The sorrow and the pain that were past had become herself; they were over, but their passage had left her more patient, more tolerant, more loving . . . . Her expectancy was not that of ignorance; she knew, and still looked forward.
>
> E.F. Benson, *Daisy's Aunt**

*I*n the years that followed my original dream about Kings Dominion, I developed a great love of theme parks. This is quite paradoxical because most people think of theme parks as places where you go on rides—and I was one of the world's biggest chickens when it comes to rides. From the earliest days when our family made its annual visit to the legendary Palisades Amusement Park, high on the edge of the New Jersey Palisades overlooking the Hudson River and Manhattan, my speed was carousel, not roller coaster. I was terrified of being hurled into nothingness as a roller coaster car took perilous turns or made sudden drops. I preferred to go safely round and round on a pretty hobby horse. I loved to soak up the exciting atmosphere and feel the sense of mystery that the park stirred in me, but I didn't really want to *do* anything that pushed me past my comfort zone.

---

*E.F. (Edward Frederic) Benson, (1910) *Daisy's Aunt*, e-book.

Many years later, when I became a parent and began taking my young son to theme parks, I noticed a similar reluctance in him. Not wanting him to inherit my timidity, I made the decision to stretch a bit and do one ride each year that was one notch more intimidating than the rides we had done the year before. And although I was doing this under the aegis of motherly duty, I also realized that it was really important for me to stretch a bit. It will become apparent that I had a long way to go as I confess that when I finally got to Kings Dominion the summer my son was six, it took all of the courage I had to ride the Scooby–Doo Roller Coaster in Hanna–Barbera Land, the kiddie section of the park. But ride it I did, and every year thereafter I would stretch a little bit more, next braving the log flume and then the bobsled—right up to the trip to Disney World when I decided I would face the Twilight Zone Tower of Terror.

For those who may not know what the Tower of Terror is, it is a ride that involves going up in an elevator in a haunted hotel and then being dropped thirteen floors—straight down. Not a pleasant thought, but I was going to do it. That's all there was to it. And when I finally decided it was time, I remember having a surreal feeling as I got in the line. (Those who know no such terror in response to rides may find this incredible; those who fear will understand what I am saying.) I remember feeling like something was just moving my legs for me as I shuffled along in the line. As I got closer to the point of no return, my self-talk increasingly turned to something along the lines of "What are you doing? You were crazy to think you wanted to do this." And to make matters worse, there were a couple of people who were right next to me in line (and were therefore going to be in the same little car with me) who were just as terrified as I was. During our entire shuffle toward our fate, all they did was talk about how terrifying the ride was and all of the horrible things that could go wrong when we took the plunge.

Have you ever felt that way about a ride you've been on? It may have been one of those times when, even though your soul might have really wanted to be there, once you were in line and were getting closer to the big drop, you were asking yourself, "*What* was I thinking? Is there any way to get out of this?" I know that I looked very seriously at that one last escape route they give you just before you are irrevocably strapped into the ride on the day I took on the Tower of Terror, but I'd promised myself I wouldn't take the escape route. I just kept telling myself that it would be alright; it *felt* like I was going to die, but I really wouldn't die. I made myself get into that elevator car, heart pounding. Because sometimes we just have to get in and take the ride, no matter what's going on in our thoughts and emotions. No matter how much we want to resist, our path up the spiral really leaves us no choice.

Meeting Our Walls of Resistance

No one ever said that evolutionary advance was smooth or easy. Unlike spiritual teachings that suggest everything flows effortlessly when we are on the right track, the evolutionary approach frames the challenges, setbacks, and pure chaos that life so often entails as the inevitable fallout of a process that is continually rearranging the "stuff" of creation into new forms. According to the Cayce source, that process wherein the Spirit moved over the roiling elements of a birthing cosmos to bring order out of chaos at the dawn of time continues to be the dynamic of evolution to this day. And we are an integral part of that process, for we're told that only as this spirit is "magnified" in the hearts and minds and souls of people will we find " . . . the answer to the world conditions as they exist today."[169] The call to personal responsibility for bringing order out of chaos is unmistakable in numerous readings, including this one: " . . . the entity should seek, through those forces from within self, that there may come the understanding as to that way in which the entity may act in the physical, that will bring light, peace, out of chaos and trouble . . . "[170] In us and through us, the force of evolution finds expression as we become agents who bring order out of chaos. Depending on how you look at it, this is our greatest blessing and our greatest source of pain and struggle.

The idea that we can be conscious agents of evolutionary transformation sounds great on paper. There's something glorious in being "starstuff pondering the stars." There is deep satisfaction to be found in

---

[169]3976-8
[170]900-216

visions of fully awakened consciousness that will eradicate our fears, even as it imbues our lives with purpose and meaning. There is excitement in the possibility that we may live to see the dawning of a truly new age. Who wouldn't want to go there? Well, the truth is *we* don't want to go there—a good deal of the time, anyway. As evolutionary spiritual teacher Andrew Cohen is fond of saying, "Everybody wants to get enlightened, but nobody wants to change." And it's true. Evolution, by its very definition, is change; and change is uncomfortable for most of us. Even those who tolerate or even seek change in things like jobs or residences or relationships are usually not any more flexible than the rest of us when it comes to interior change. To accept the commitment of an evolutionary spiritual path is to accept the need for conscious choice in the midst of the chaos that often ensues when the forces of evolution clash with our confining but comfortably familiar limitations. The old saw about "the devil you know is better than the devil you don't know" describes well the common tendency for us to cling to even painful or disagreeable conditions rather than embark on what we perceive as the greater discomfort of making change.

To complicate things further, our limitations are not always an obvious problem in our lives. While they may become obvious when we face a crisis situation, up until that point we may experience our limitations as the more subtle drive to maintain a status quo that is relatively comfortable. But because every stage of consciousness is limited in comparison to the stage beyond it—even as it's also expansive in comparison to earlier stages—we are all limited in some ways. While the evolutionary path calls us to continually press beyond whatever our current limitations may be, we nonetheless meet significant interior inertia whenever we face the hump in the road that every threshold of deep change presents. The source of that inertia is the current ego-self, who believes that who and where we are right now is something to be defended at all costs. If you have ever consistently attempted anything like the work of unmasking ego that is described in Chapter 8, you will have seen ample evidence of this!

Ego's resistance notwithstanding, if we are committed to evolution—or even interested in truly freeing ourselves from the misery of our stuck states—we must find a way to allow something new to arise within us. To that end, there are three principles that form the basis of this chapter. First, the structure of stuckness is in trying to solve a problem at the level where it exists. Second, the ego will always be invested in keeping us at exactly the level where we currently find ourselves. Third, even though transcending our places of stuckness feels like a little death, once we have made the transition we find that everything of value has been preserved to manifest at a higher level. We will start with the last principle and work our way back to the first.

For Something New to Happen, Something Old Must Die

A little more than ten years ago, our neighborhood was hit hard by Hurricane Isabel. While we were personally spared damage, the area was strewn with downed loblolly pines—which typically tower 60-100 feet above the ground. After the initial clean-up, the logs lining the streets were so high that they formed 10-foot walls on either side, making virtual tunnels that we had to drive through. The air smelled like a lumber camp for many weeks. One neighbor's yard was particularly hard hit, with about seven or eight trees down in the front alone. All in all, it felt like the neighborhood's natural beauty had been ravaged, with something forever lost.

Then, one day a little more than a year later, I went out for a walk on a mild winter morning. As the bare front yard of the neighbor who had lost so many trees came into view, suddenly I noticed something. Where those downed trees had once stood, a profusion of loblolly saplings had sprung up—ten, twenty, thirty of them, already between three and four feet high. A regular nursery of new pines was ready to start the life cycle all over again. In one of those rushes of spiritual comfort that have a way of gracing us when we least expect it, I experienced deep inner knowing that life is the expression, the irrepressible expression, of God. I found myself moved to tears.

When I see the loblolly saplings growing up where once there were only fallen trees, I have new appreciation for Goethe's comment that "Nature invented death in order to have much life." The truth is that when we can take the larger view that the evolutionary process calls us to, we can see the seeds of transformation in countless occurrences that would otherwise look like death. In fact, life is born out of death, for without the death of stars, there would be no planets or elements like carbon and iron and calcium with which to build our bodies. A group of scientists at Cal Tech recently published a paper that discussed how a magnetic pole shift 500 million years ago directly preceded a proliferation of life forms at twenty times the normal rate.[171] Nothing has come close to it since. Out of what would have been utter devastation at the time, new life arose in abundance. Programmed cell death is necessary to human development and the preservation of life. For example, during the embryonic stages of human development, cells in the early paddle-like hand die so that they can be re-absorbed to form the structure of fingers. Different forms of this programmed cell death take place throughout life to maintain bodily function and allow old cells to be replaced with new ones. Without rock eroding, there would be no soil in which to grow plants. When faced with the evolutionary forces in our own lives, it may seem at times like we are being eroded into soil, but perhaps it's more like the old country song that says, "I'm just an old chunk of coal, but I'm gonna be a diamond someday."

Everywhere we look, the change of form called death promotes new and continued forms of life. Evolution tells us that even the conclusion of a particular incarnation has a higher purpose that serves both our personal and the collective advance. As Edgar Cayce put it in one reading, use of the deeper perceptions would show us that " . . . death is . . . but the beginning of another form of phenomenized force in the earth's plane . . . "[172] The use of the word *phenomenized* is especially interesting here because the readings use that word repeatedly and consistently to mean "showing up in material form." So we can take this comment to mean that a death is literally a preparation for a new life *in the earth.* It is a chance to rearrange the components of our soul history for a fresh take on what it means to incarnate spirit in human form. As L.W. Rogers points out:

Every process in nature has a part to play in evolution and therefore

---

[171]Science Mysteries: Pole Shift: "Earth Loses its Balance a Half Billion Years Ago," retrieved from World-Mysteries.com.
[172]136-18

> death is as necessary as life and as beneficial as birth. Death is the destroyer of the useless . . . [Death is] when the physical body has fulfilled its mission and completely accomplished the purpose for which it exists. To continue life in a physical body beyond that point is to waste energy and lose time in the evolutionary journey . . . The soul is in the position of an artisan obliged to work with broken and rusted tools.[173]

That's not to say that once we embrace evolution, we joyously skip our way through the losses and bereavements of life. But we do at least have a framework of meaning within which to place our emotions of personal sorrow. This principle is no less true when we experience the emotions of sadness that so often accompany the mini-deaths that each life transition takes us through. French writer Anatole France describes something that probably all of us have felt at one time or another as we underwent a major life change: "All changes, even the most longed for, have their melancholy; for what we leave behind us is a part of ourselves; we must die to one life before we can enter another." No wonder it often takes a significant push to budge us onward in our growth. Yet if we can look back on our lives with some measure of objectivity, most of us will recognize that it is in the stress, pressure points, and pure chaos of life that our leaps forward have often taken place. As Michael Dowd points out in *Thank God for Evolution,* "As it turns out, every evolutionary advance and every creative breakthrough in the history of the Universe, as best we can tell, was preceded by some difficulty, often of great severity."[174] This is true on the macro level of planets and stars, and it is true within the microcosm of our own beings. Extending its reach beyond potential character-building benefits in humans, difficulty actually seems to be part of the engine of biological evolution. "Evolution happens when DNA reorganizes in response to stress. Every crisis is thus an opportunity for new evolution," says futurist and evolutionary biologist Elisabet Sahtouris.[175]

---

[173]Rogers, *Elementary Theosophy,* 61.

[174]Dowd, *Thank God for Evolution,* 45.

[175]Elisabet Sahtouris, "Planetary and Personal Health: Global Health and Agriculture," retrieved from sahtouris.com.

We find a fascinating model for this view of change in the work of Russian physical chemist Ilya Prigogine and his theory of "dissipative structures" and "self-organizing systems." In essence, Prigogine posited that when any system is thrown into overload, the resulting chaos will disrupt the equilibrium in that system to such a point that only two outcomes can ensue: it will either leap forward to a higher level of organization that will be able to handle the conditions that had been causing the chaos, or the chaotic system will fall apart (dissipate into its components). The former is what we have been calling creative advance, with the latter being a manifestation of entropy.

Now the important thing about the self-organizing occurrence is precisely that it is *self*-organizing—that is, there is no external planner or organizer imposing the new, adaptive organization. As applied to our view of evolution, self-organization, probably more than any other factor, is what distinguishes the purposeful evolution we have been considering from so-called "intelligent design." In the latter, God is an external architect directing the path of evolution, where in the former, evolutionary advance bubbles up from the forward-reaching life inherent within all elements of the cosmos. In self-organizing systems, members or components of the system form coherent, functional patterns that maintain equilibrium within the system. We see this, for example, in flocking, herding, and schooling behavior of animals.* When single-celled life-forms first came together to form multi-celled life forms, that was another example of a self-organizing system. The Internet has been largely a self-organizing system—networks springing up from people coming together in cyberspace. Our subjective internal worlds, where we have juggled all of the input from our life experiences, our conditioning, and whatever is native to our biological state and inborn temperament into an overall sense of self, is a self-organizing system. For the purpose of this discussion, we will call it a "self-system."

Up to a point, self-organizing systems can adapt to changing conditions. But as the system continues to grow in complexity with the

---

*There are many amazing videos online that show the flocking behavior in starlings called murmuration, which very graphically illustrate this kind of spontaneous organization that seems to arise out of nowhere.

addition of more and more new components (think members in an organization, ideas in a mind, items on a growing to-do list, cars on a crowded highway system, emotions in a psyche), the ability to maintain structure begins to erode. In short, chaos threatens to destroy the structure. It is at this point that either the law of entropy will break the system down to a level where its component parts can once again exist in equilibrium or a new self-organizing system will emerge, one that can handle the increased input of more members, ideas, to-do list items, cars, or emotions, as the case may be.

This is the growing edge of evolution. The old system must "die" if a new, more adaptive one is to take its place. Prior to this point of crisis, the system can maintain itself by releasing some of the input that brought things to the chaotic boiling point. This leads us to a key characteristic of a dissipative system: it is open to a flow of exchange of energy and matter to and from its environment. When flow into the system (what I'm calling input) builds to the chaotic point, the system can release the pressure by letting some of the build-up flow back out to the environment. For example, an organization can allow members to leave, we can reject pressure-building ideas, cross off items on the to-do list, try to limit traffic flow onto a crowded highway during rush hour or blow off our emotions through temper or tears. In that way, a stability of sorts is maintained.

Yet sometimes input increases at such a rate that the system just can't dissipate enough input to maintain its stability. The pressure on an organization to change becomes greater than its ability to dismiss advocates of change. New ideas will find their way into our awareness and we can't "unknow" what we know. (This is often what happens when childhood religious faith is finally overcome by adult rational scientific knowledge and a crisis of faith occurs.) Nonnegotiable demands on our time grow more quickly than our ability to create time for them. Traffic still flows onto the highways at levels that exceed the system's ability to handle it. Emotions build despite our letting off steam.

It's at this point when we really have only two choices: go with the leap to a new level of organization that can handle the current overload or disintegrate to an earlier structure. Therefore the organization either shrinks back to some archival version of its once glorious self or it remakes itself for a new time and a new set of circumstances. We find new contexts and world views to accommodate the ideas that had been overloading the old world view or we hunker down and cling to what we believed before the disturbing new information came in. We discover new ways to structure our time or new value systems about what's worth doing in order to respond to the growing to–do list or we fall into the paralysis of overwhelm. We add lanes to the highway system or transportation comes to a screeching halt. We leap to an entirely different level of relationship with our emotions that is more adaptive than either blowing off steam or repressing them, or we spiral down into deeper dysfunction. When the first possibility in each of these scenarios occurs, an evolutionary advance has taken place, an advance that would never have been, had it not been that pressure on the system forced the issue.

Teilhard de Chardin theorized that the fact that the earth is a globe, where the spread of humankind looped back on itself rather than endlessly extending away from its ancestral sources, created a certain pressure that forced the evolutionary drive to turn to consciousness rather than the development of additional biological forms. Just as an unpruned plant may become spread out and "leggy" while a pruned one turns its resources inward to produce more blossoms and fruit, a humanity that could have spread endlessly across physical space may not have turned its evolutionary drive inward to the domain of mind and consciousness. But as the case turned out, human beings in growing proximity to each other gave rise to culture which in turn fostered growth in consciousness via what we might almost think of as increasingly concentrated cross–pollination at the level of mind. Teilhard de Chardin called it "psychic permeability." He spoke of railroads and automobiles and flight as extending the influence of a single human being by increasing the radius of each person's contact with his or her fellow humans, and he pointed to radio as an even more dramatic extension of this consciousness–stimulating proximity among members of the human race. What would he have thought, had he lived to see the way the Internet has linked us even further?

As we face the growing crises of our day, we can see the building of pressure on various systems. Ecologically, economically, politically, sociologically, religiously, and most of all spatially, the world is be–

coming smaller and more interconnected. Our collective crises are rapidly approaching that point where the system just can't dissipate enough overload to maintain stability. Either collapse or creative advance into novelty are simply the only two possibilities before us in the looming future. The choice before us is rather stark, according to Cayce. We can learn how to use divine law to bring order out of chaos, or we can disregard the laws of divine influence and bring chaos and destructive influences.[176] This is the choice between evolution and regression, and it is the only choice of real significance in any crisis we may face collectively or in our personal lives. As Charles Darwin himself said, "It is not the strongest species that survive, nor the most intelligent, but the ones most responsive to change." The Cayce source would concur, repeatedly identifying the ability to adapt as a soul strength that is developed by experience and then carried from lifetime to lifetime.[177] When one of Cayce's close associates presented the trait of adaptability as key to evolution, paraphrasing evolutionary writer Henri Bergson as he did so, the reading affirmed that this was correct.[178] So what is the holdup? Why does it seem to take us so long to wake up and get on with what must be done?

We Can Count On the Ego to Resist Evolution

Adaptive change—that is the pattern of evolution. All of manifestation is a self-organizing system that is open to new input that morphs what has been into what it will become. This applies to the systems of the cosmos, those of collective human structures, and to a viable self-system as well. For just as an ecosystem or a human organization has a certain arrangement of its component parts into a working whole, so too does a human personality have its own self-system that keeps us feeling intact and feeling like "ourselves." Our beliefs, our activities, our habits, our modes of interaction, our memories, our relationship with our bodies—these and many other components all go into making up the self-system that we each think of as being our self. No

---

[176]416-7

[177]333-2, 3873-2, 406-1, 830-1, for example

[178]900-251

wonder we find it daunting to change. No wonder an overload of input that threatens to change any of our component parts can be so destabilizing. Yet there is no standing still. A system must continue to grow and develop with new input or it will dissolve into its component parts. The problem for the human self-system is that the ego has so identified with the current sense of self that it is unable to see a deeper, truer identity that will emerge with the next level of development. We can count on the ego, then, to do everything it can to maintain the status quo—even when to do so is to risk dissolution and entropy rather than creative advance.

Yet the beautiful thing is that, when we stand up to ego's resistance and make that leap toward creative advance, we find that we have not truly lost the valuable components of the old self-system. Rather, we have given them a wider, more functional context in which to breathe. We can find reassurance to face these "mini–death" leaps forward when we stop to realize that anyone who has reached even a minimally adaptive adult identity has already been through this sequence of events many times. Think about it: the "you" that you have grown to be over the course of your life is still the same "you" that you were back before you knew a lot of the things you know now and before you'd had a lot of the growth experiences that you've now had. What's different is the context in which that internal "you" lives. With these thoughts in mind, consider this excerpt from the Cayce readings that so eloquently describes the evolutionary process:

> For truth indeed sets one free, in that truth is *freeing self of that which is the thought of self* and letting every move, every activity be not for the creating of *ease* alone but unto the glory of Him; unto the glory of that influence and force that brought, and *brings* everything into manifestation, into being, from out of the nowhere—the manifestation into which it goes as it cycles in its growth into materiality, and its dissolution into that from which it came.[179]

Notice in the excerpt above that when we free ourselves from something that is only "the thought of self," we are able to glorify the "influ-

---

[179]1580-1, emphasis added

ence and force" that brings manifestation from out of nowhere. We
become part of the very drive of creation, allowing growth to manifest
through us and allowing each form to dissipate in order to make room
for the next cycle of growth. This is the truth that sets us free. It is "the
thought of self" that binds us and the fear of dissolution that keeps the
knots tight. This is why, as we have already seen, the signals that we
may be on the cusp of new levels of freedom are precisely the things
that we tend to find most unpleasant. The places where we are stuck,
the places where we experience system overload of ideas, taxing demands on us, strong unpleasant emotions, or things that trigger our
fears and anxieties—in short, areas of recurrent or acute chaos in our
lives—these are prime opportunities to make an evolutionary leap to a
new level of organization within ourselves. At the crisis of change, it
feels like the death of who we are because we are being called to free
ourselves from our current *thought* of our self. But on the other side of
the transition, we find that what has changed is our *perspective* rather
than our *being*.

We can see this pattern outlined with striking succinctness in this
description by British poet, novelist, and theologian Charles Williams:
"There are always three degrees of consciousness, all infinitely divis-
ible: (i) The old self on the old way; (ii) the old self on the new way; (iii)
the new self on the new way."[180] When we feel stuck, we often experience ourselves as the old self on the new way. We have awakened just
enough to experience a very uncomfortable buildup of pressure in
our self-system, but we haven't yet found the way to become truly the
new self. The ego still has its iron grip on the old self-system, even if
we have become aware of and even desirous of new ways of being.
This is the state wherein we can easily feel like "the old self feeling
guilty or inadequate about not being the new self!" So how do we get
to be not the old self on the new way but the new self on the new
way?

---

[180]Charles Williams, *He Came Down from Heaven and The Forgiveness of Sins* (Berkeley, CA:
Apocryphile Press, 2005), 85.

Making the Leap to the Next Level

Understanding that the ego is invested in maintaining the current self–system, we can appreciate that new input is necessary to evolution. It takes *something* beyond the current self–sense to make the actual transcending leap beyond current levels of development. Were we to remain locked in a closed system there would be nothing to catalyze change. This is another way of stating that you can't solve a problem at the same level where the problem was created. If we think of a current state of limitation, challenge, stuckness, or chaos to be the problem, then the solution will always be found at the next level beyond the problem. The pattern of evolutionary advance pulls us to the next level, where more input can be accommodated and arranged in a functional self–system. This follows what we have already seen above in Prigogine's model of self–organization in dissipative structures. The crucial thing to note now, however, is that in moving to a wider context we become able to see the old, more limited self–system from a more objective point of view than we possibly could have done while we were immersed in it.

Even if you've never thought of it in these terms, you've experienced what I'm describing here. How often do we say, with respect to some past difficulty, "Looking back at it now I realize ___?" Or, with respect to some way that we once acted out of blindness, "I didn't see it at the time, but now I see that ___?" Whenever we grow beyond the perspective we had while in the midst of a particular situation or stage in our lives, our sense of self has moved into a wider context that expands beyond the previous sense of self in some significant way. To illustrate graphically:

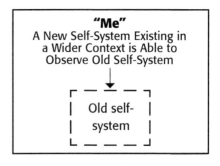

"Me"
Self-System
Enmeshed in a
Problem or
Other State of
Limitation

"Me"
A New Self-System Existing in
a Wider Context is Able to
Observe Old Self-System

Old self-
system

Please keep in mind that we are not talking here about all-or-nothing levels that would apply across the board in our lives. We are multifaceted; therefore growth and development are multifaceted. The reality of a human being's development is a complex composite, where development may be quite advanced in some areas but not so much so in others. The diagram above is simply a model for how we grow with respect to specific limitations or challenges in our lives. It shows how, when we are able to expand our context enough to become somewhat external to not only the thing that has been a problem but also *our current way of dealing with it,* we make that advance to a higher level of adaptability—which is another way of saying that we evolve.

Over time, the learning that comes naturally with the accumulation of experience will push our development onward to broader perspectives—what I am calling here wider contexts. But that process can be very slow, as many a spiritual aspirant will have noted. Add the resistance that ego puts up to major changes and we have the scenario wherein it will usually take crisis or chaos—an accumulation of input faster than the system can accommodate in an orderly way—to push us over the threshold to a truly new way of being and responding. Fortunately we do have an alternative. Knowing that advance involves moving to a broader perspective, we can deliberately cultivate that perspective as a matter of choice and practice.

We find some great advice in the Cayce readings that facilitates movement to a more expansive self-system. In fact, the entire "Know Thyself" unit in the *Search for God* material is about the capacity to know more expansive levels of ourselves by taking an objective perspective on the attitudes and actions of the current self. Each time we leap to a higher level of self-knowledge, we are able to see more and more of ourselves as we are known from an objective point of view—with a God's-eye perspective being the ultimate objective view. The overarching lesson in "Know Thyself" is that of coming to know ourselves, even as we are known from that God perspective, in order to better express Spirit in this world of manifestation. To this end, one group member asked, "How may I learn to know self as I am known?" The answer given:

Being able to, as it were, *literally*, stand aside and watch self pass by! Take the time to occasionally be sufficiently introspective of that, that may happen in self's relation to others, to *see* the reactions of others as to that as was done by self. [181]

"Stand Aside and Watch Self Go By"

The advice in the Cayce material to "watch self" pops up repeatedly as what might be considered a core practice for one who seeks greater spiritual consciousness. This is a deceptively simple practice with transformative power that goes well beyond the obvious relief that comes from taking a step back from our problems. Many readers will recognize it as the "witness consciousness" recommended and taught in many spiritual traditions. We may even see a veiled reference to it in Jesus' teachings, when we read in the Gospel of Thomas "Jesus said, 'Be passersby.'"[182] That's it. No elaboration, no illumination from the sayings before it or after it. But what is a passerby, if not someone who is a detached observer? Unlike the meditative "I am" consciousness that places attention on the essential self rather than any thoughts or observations, the witness consciousness deliberately takes an objective view of our current self–system as it reacts, chooses, and responds to various life circumstances. Standing aside to watch self should be prominent in our repertoire of spiritual practices, particularly when we face the chaos and turmoil of life, for it leads us to a state wherein we can use the power of the mind to create the most evolved response to the situation:

> Thus as we find in the experiences in the earth, one only meets self. Learn, then, to stand oft aside and watch self pass by—even in those influences that at times are torments to thy mind. Remember, *mind* is the builder.[183]
>
> . . . For again and again one must meet self, and be able more and more to stand aside and watch self and its relations and its dealings

---

[181]262–9
[182]Saying 42
[183]3292–1

with its fellow man pass by. For we meet ourselves.[184]

"Meeting self" is a phrase often used in the Cayce readings to mean "reaping karma," but we can see here an additional layer of meaning to the expression. While we are meeting our selves in the sense of facing the karmic consequences of our own past actions and attitudes, we can also meet ourselves in the sense that watching from an objective viewpoint really allows us to *know* ourselves—particularly our motivations—in a new light. Consider this Cayce reading excerpt that emphasizes both senses of meeting self:

> . . . When the activities or efforts were made for selfish indulgence and aggrandizement, they brought—and have ever brought—those very experiences in which antagonistic influences arose; and do arise in the present experience. These may be turned as it were to account in the present. For know, there is the constant meeting of self. And as has been given, if the entity will oft take counsel with self, stand aside as it were and watch self pass by, and see what have been the motivative influences that have caused the entity to choose this, that or the other, it will know as to whether or not these have been efforts on the part of self with a constructive influence or dependent upon other forces.[185]

When we are able to truly watch ourselves in the way this reading describes, it catapults us to a position outside our current stuck state. From this next-level perspective we are more open to insight concerning our motivations and can more easily recognize what needs to be changed in order for us to grow beyond current limitations. In essence, we try the next level of perspective on for size, and in so doing we *become* the next higher self, if only momentarily; for the one able to *see* the self in its limitation is not the one *mired* in the limitation. A simple self-reflective exercise for this practice appears on page 204. Whether you pause to experiment with it now or save it for the next time you are feeling stuck in a situation or behavior that impedes your evolutionary progress, you may find it to be a surprisingly effec-

[184]876-1
[185]1575-1

tive approach to bringing order out of chaos and stuckness in your life. In order for it to be most effective, however, you may want to be sure that you have first established what Edgar Cayce called a "spiritual ideal."

Stand Aside and Watch Self Go By: A Practice

Identify a situation in your own life that would benefit from your standing aside to watch self. Think of things like:

- A place where you feel stuck.

- An area of conflict in your life.

- A behavior that is less than you would ideally exhibit.

- A pattern you go through that indicates a challenged chakra energy.

- A situation where you go into overload or overwhelm.

- An aspect of your life that is chaotic.

Whatever that situation may be, think of a time when you experienced it. A recent time would be best, as that is most likely to include your most up-to-the-moment patterns of response and your memory is likely to be clearest. In the absence of a recent example, however, an older one will serve. With the situation clearly in mind:

1. As vividly as possible, relive the situation or event from inside your own skin. See it the way you see it, hear what you hear, think what you think, feel what you feel.

2. Then step outside of yourself. If there was another person or people involved, go through the same experience from inside the skin of each other person who was in any way a part of the experience or situation. Be as detailed and vivid in your imaginings as

you were when reviewing it from inside your own skin.

3. Once you have relived it from every available human perspective, watch the situation or event as if you were the proverbial fly on the wall. Pay particular attention to your interactions with any other people who may be part of the scene. Notice whatever you can notice and be aware of any new perspectives that may arise when you watch this situation from a detached but highly observant stance of "watching self pass by."

4. Pause after your observation to be aware that you are you. Notice the "I am" that you still are. Notice that you still have a sense of being *you* even as you take a higher perspective on the situation that another part of you is still enmeshed in. Spend some time just experiencing yourself as that higher perspective.

5. Then think again of the situation you have been observing and live it from inside your own skin, this time reacting and responding as the self who watched self go by.

6. Look for opportunities to act in this new way the next time the situation arises in your life.

An additional application of this practice is to review each day in the witness consciousness just before sleep, noticing any insights and embracing any adjustments in future response that may suggested from the more objective point of view. Always take a moment at the end to identify your sense of self with the one doing the observation, thus building your connection with the next developmental level of self.

The Defining Influence of a Spiritual Ideal

The capacity to stand aside and objectively analyze our own motivations implies some form of standard against which we are evaluating ourselves. Many times such standards are not only unspoken, but they remain unarticulated even to ourselves. We just carry some vague interior notion of what it means to be "more spiritual" or "more evolved" or "more conscious." And up to a point, that works reasonably well. But if we are serious about the kind of self–scrutiny implied by the exercise of standing aside and watching self pass by, we can make the process a lot more efficient and effective by asking, as the Cayce readings put it, "'What is my ideal of a *spiritual* life?' Then when the answer has come . . . seek again in the inner consciousness: 'Am I true to my ideal?'"[186]

The setting of a spiritual ideal is one of the most often recommended practices in the Cayce approach to spiritual life. One reading sums it up nicely by saying, " . . . the most important experience of this or of any individual is to first know what *is* the ideal, spiritually."[187] Distinguishing an ideal from an idea, he characterizes it as a standard or quality of motivation by which we choose to measure ourselves. "Have ye analyzed the difference between ideas and ideals?" he asked one seeker. "Ideals are set from spiritual purposes, spiritual aspirations, spiritual desires . . . "[188] An ideal is something that we hold out before ourselves, not so much the way we might set a goal, but rather the way we might set a compass direction for a journey. "An ideal means that to which the entity may, itself, ever look up, knowing itself to be gradually becoming a portion, but *never* may it be the whole . . . not an idea, that I may do this or I may do that, that I may accomplish such and such through such modes of operation! . . . "[189] In the language of contemporary spiritual thought, which often places emphasis on the importance of intention, we might say that the ideal is the overarching intention that we bring to every aspect of our lives.

We all operate under the power of our intentions, whether we have stopped to identify them or not. In that sense, we may be shaped by "ideals" that have been set by default and have come from the unconscious motivations of the ego–self. But according to Cayce, " . . . unless the ideals are creative (and creative is spiritual) they must eventually come to naught."[190] This is one reason that consciously chosen ideals are so essential to our progress. In fact, it would be hard to underesti-

---

[186]987–4
[187]357–13
[188]5255–1
[189]256–2
[190]1423–1

mate the constructive power of the ideal. It has application to our mental lives as a standard for our attitudes, expectations, and beliefs (what he called "mental ideals") as well as application to how we evaluate our behaviors and those things we attempt to bring into physical manifestation (what he called "physical ideals"). Spiritual ideals may be drawn from one's spiritual tradition; for example, "Christ consciousness" or "Buddha mind." Or they may be other evocative descriptors of what one might find to be inspirational and reflective of one's spiritual perspective: for example, "expansive love," "commitment to evolution," or "awakening awareness." The important thing is that the ideal expresses something that is deeply motivating and meaningful, something that stretches us to a higher standard of living and by which we are prepared to measure our own choices and behavior. For those who are ready to take this step, a detailed approach drawn directly from the Cayce readings on how to establish your own ideals appears below.

Establishing Your Ideals:

An Exercise Taken Directly from the Cayce Readings

The following protocol for setting ideals and using them as guidelines in your life is taken from Cayce reading 5091-3.

1. **An ideal, to be effective, should be chosen as something personally meaningful.** "For, mental and spiritual guidance should be related to what an individual entity chooses as its ideal, and what it will or should do about that ideal, not ideas but ideals."

2. **Writing your ideal down will make it much more effective as a tool for spiritual development.** "In choosing and in analyzing self and the ideal, do not merely carry these in mind but put them, as it were, upon the paper in a manifested form."

3. **Make three distinct entries on your paper:** "Write *physical*. Draw a line, write *mental*. Draw a line, write *spiritual*."

4. **Begin with the spiritual ideal, because that is the driver.** "Put under each, beginning with the spiritual, (for all that is in mind must first come from a spiritual concept) what is thy spiritual concept of the ideal, whether it be Jesus, Buddha, mind, material, God or whatever is the word which indicates to self the ideals spiritual." Take some time to ponder your highest spiritual purposes and aspirations. After some contemplation, allow a name, word, or phrase that is representative of these aspirations and purposes to occur to you.

5. **Consider the various aspects of your life and identify the attitudes that would reflect your ideal in those situations.** "Then under the *mental* heading write the ideal mental attitude, as may arise from concepts of the spiritual, in relationship to self, to home, to friends, to neighbors, to thy enemies, to things, to conditions."

6. **How would your spiritual ideal and the attitudes that flow from it manifest as behaviors or priorities in your life?** "Then write what is thy ideal spiritual, mental, material. What is the ideal material, then? Not of conditions but what has brought, what does bring into manifestation the spiritual and mental ideals. What relationships does such bring to things, to individual, to situations?"

7. **Having once set your ideals, then be willing to use these as the standards against which you measure yourself.** "Thus an individual entity analyzes itself."

8. **Make a conscious effort on a daily basis to prioritize, think, speak, and act according to your chosen ideals.** "Then set about to apply the knowledge ye have attained, for ye will get ideas and that ideal. Ye may change them from period to period, as ye study them over. For as ye apply them they become thy ideals. To be just as theories they do not belong to thee, they are still theories so far as thy personal being is concerned. It's the application of same that counts. What do they bring into thine experience? These are well if ye will apply them."

Paired with the practice of standing aside to watch self go by, the ideal becomes an especially powerful shaping force:

> As we find, then,—the entity is one *very* intuitive; easily separating self from itself—which so few may do; or, as it were, the ability to stand aside and watch self pass by. This is an experience that may be made to be most helpful, if there is first the determining within self as to what *is* thy ideal—spiritually, mentally, morally, socially or materially.[191]

When we set and then use an ideal in this way, it serves as a grappling hook that we are willing to throw up to take hold in higher levels than that at which we currently live our lives. As such, the ideal may grow and evolve as we do. But whatever form the expression of an ideal may take, it will always require an exercise of will to live up to its standards and it will always stretch us to wider circles of love and compassion. And so it is these two topics, love and will, that we will take up in the next chapter.

Still Not Sure How to Identify Your Spiritual Ideal?

If you are still not sure what your spiritual ideal is—or if the one you have tentatively chosen does not feel quite right for you—here is a very simple but very effective way to discover the ideal that arises from your own deepest values:

1. Make a list of your core life values. Your list will be as individual as you are, but the general category includes things like peace, integrity, courage, honesty, love, justice, etc. Beware of a tendency to slip into listing people or things among your core values. They may be very important to you, but they are not quite the same as life values. Values tend to be abstract rather than concrete. For example, "My spouse and children" is concrete, but "family love" is abstract. "Travel to see the world" is concrete,

but "a spirit of exploration" is abstract. Take as much time as you need to ponder this, even if that means returning to it over the course of several days. Only after you are satisfied that your list is complete (at least for now) should you move on to Step Two.

2. Choose a time when you can quietly reflect on your list of core values. Taking your values one at a time, for each one:

- Consider what that word means to you. This is not an exercise in formulating dictionary-style definitions but rather an opportunity to experience your own inner sense of that value. *Feel* its meaning inside. Feel its importance to you.

- Think of times in your life when you have experienced that value. Try to touch on what it feels like to have that value fulfilled. Amplify that feeling as much as you can.

- If you have a hard time remembering specific times when the value was fulfilled or if you do not believe you have ever known the fulfillment of that value, then feel your *desire* for that particular value to be fulfilled in your life. Let that desire resonate within you.

- Think of people (real or fictional, personally known to you or public figures) who best embody that value. Notice your images of them doing things that exemplify this value.

- Allow all of these ponderings to create a sense of what is, for you, the essence of that value. It may be something that you can't even put into words, and that's fine. You are seeking to evoke a direct, living experience of that value in your inner awareness.

3. Once you have done this for each value on your list, go back through the list again, pausing over each value just long enough to awaken its essence inside of you. Cycle through your list this way several times.

4. Now imagine a version of you and your life where every one of your values is being experienced and expressed just the way you want it to. It's like a miracle has happened and you suddenly become the embodiment of every one of these values. You find yourself naturally living these values and naturally experiencing their fulfillment in the experiences that come your way. They characterize your life and your nature. Step right into that version of you and your life. Imaginatively practice living that way. Run through a typical day. Think of challenging life areas or difficult relationships and imagine meeting them with all of your values in full expression.

5. Then let a word or phrase come to mind that describes how you are in this scenario, a word or phrase that sums it all up. It doesn't have to precisely or literally cover every aspect of your values; rather it evokes a sense of them collectively.

This word or phrase is a statement of your spiritual ideal. Try it on for size. How would it work as a reminder of all that is most important to you, or as a cue to activate the over-arching intention by which you are willing to measure your priorities, your attitudes, your behavior and your words? Take it out into your daily experience (as described in the exercise before this one) and let it have its awakening impact on your life. And remember: as we grow and develop, our core values and therefore our spiritual ideal may also change. Revisit the identification of your ideal periodically.

Chapter 14:
Love—Evolution's Radiant Core and Will, Evolution's Accelerator

And life is truth. Truth is love. Love is God. God is life.   5733-1

You have too many principles; and, mind you, principles are often shockingly egotistical and selfish. I would rather have a mountain of sins piled up against me on the judgment-day, and a crowd of friends whom I had helped and made happy, than the most snowy empty pious record in the world, and no such following.

Constance Fenimore Woolson, Anne*

So far I have not addressed what may be for many readers the proverbial elephant in the room. What about the dark side of the evolutionary perspective? No, I'm not talking about the "godless atheism" so feared by many anti–evolutionists, but something far more sinister: The specter of Social Darwinism, eugenics, or at the very least a smug elitism oozing out from behind claims that we who embrace the evolutionary perspective are somehow at the leading edge of the trajectory. Is evolution really the be-all and end-all of human progress, or is it just another mask for the ego that is always looking for new ways to elevate itself? The answer to that question may depend on what we really mean by evolution. Is it a competition for survival, position, and privilege, or has it become at this stage a refinement of the best and highest impulses that life produces? Apropos this question, Jean-Yves Leloup asks, in his commentary to *The Gospel of Mary Magdalene*, whether the commandment, "Thou shalt not kill," runs counter to our evolutionary drive:

> Isn't this the law of evolution—survival of those who are the strongest and most capable of adapting to circumstances? But

---

*Constance Fenimore Woolson, (1880), *Anne*, e-book.

which evolution? Is it the evolution of ever more neocortex cunning
in service to the reptilian core of the old brain, or the evolution of
the entire brain as a holistic instrument capable of peace, harmony
and the higher perception of which the Teacher speaks?[192]

And therein lies the crux of it. The evolutionary path cannot at this
point in our development be one of intellect only—a cerebral embrace
without the kind of personal application born of true awakening of
consciousness. The pages of science fiction and political thrillers are
rife with villains whose evolution of knowledge and intellect has left
evolution of heart and spiritual awareness in the dust. More sobering
by far, the pages of history demonstrate the disastrous results of such
uneven evolution. We need look no further than the Third Reich's sick
program for creating "supermen"—a morally and spiritually bankrupt
response to the evolutionary world view of the German idealist phi-
losophers—to see just how perverted the human response to evolution may become. When radioactivity was first discovered, Alice Bailey
predicted that scientists would soon be able to use the power of the
atom for heating, lighting, and other constructive purposes, but
warned that "men are as yet far too selfish to be entrusted with the
distribution of atomic energy."[193] Unfortunately, her prediction has
proven all too accurate.

Clearly, what we don't need is the evolution of what Leloup aptly
called a more cunning neocortex in service to the reptilian brain. We
are at a crucial juncture of human development where our potential
to wreak havoc on a planetary scale necessitates as never before that
ethical, moral, and spiritual values keep pace with evolution of science, information, and technology. We need a mass movement of
evolving heart and consciousness within the human race, or the results will be unthinkable. In order to meet this need, we must have
avenues of translation from concept and belief to lived reality. This is
why I have woven personal exercises and meditations into the narrative thread of these chapters. And it is why no discussion of Cayce's

---

[192]Jean-Yves Leloup, *The Gospel of Mary Magdalene* (Rochester: Inner Traditions, 2002),
87.

[193]Bailey, *The Consciousness of the Atom*, 93.

approach to evolution can be complete without a strong anchor in two key attributes: love and will. These are the twin turbines of our internal growth mechanism, and they are that which does indeed bring order out of chaos.

At first glance, it may seem like an odd pairing to put love and will together as I am doing. Love seems so spontaneous, flowing, and heart based, while will seems so controlling, deliberate, and head based. But that's just the point, and why it's important to treat these two attributes together. Because love and will tend to be attributes of the heart and head, respectively, it is important for each to develop in tandem with the other.

We easily recognize the hollowness that arises from attempts to grow spiritually by sheer force of will. They quickly become mechanical, arid, and devoid of the joy inherent in the unfolding of the life principle—which is surely the essence of true evolutionary advance. Will without heart creates a life of "shoulds" and "have-tos"—duty without compassion, service without connection to those served, the right acts without the inner correlates that give rise to their rightness. Will to do "spiritual" acts without the love that gives them life is easily co-opted by the ego that thrives on building monuments to self—the virtuous self who is so conscientious, so faithful in spiritual discipline, so devoted to growth. As we have already seen, this role of the Serious Spiritual Aspirant may be the wily ego's sneakiest mask of all.

Love without will, on the other hand, easily dissipates in aimless intentions that lack fruition. Yearnings to serve, to fulfill a mission of love in the world, are impotent without the structuring of priorities or behavior that gives them form. Without will, even the best aspirations can become a self-involved internal affair—visioning and dreaming without follow-through. Love without will is easily hijacked by the ego into absorption in feelings of frustration or blaming the people and conditions that interfere with love's expression in the world. The Aggrieved Person with Heart is yet another of ego's stunningly cunning false selves.

So, with these things in mind, let's examine the attributes of love and will, one at a time, while remembering that each will find its best expression only when joined with the other.

Will

Will is not a very popular focus in most contemporary spiritual work. We have been steeped in a world view that says, "If you heal from your inner wounds and release your unconscious blockages, you will naturally, automatically be the radiant being of light and love that you really are at core." And so we continually seek healing and release of our blockages and wonder why our progress on the path is not any greater than it is. My point here is not to dismiss the very real need that many of us have for inner healing, nor to deny the benefit of releasing those things that may block us at an unconscious level. Both may at times be indispensable to our wholeness, and as such may constitute a prerequisite to the kind of development that leads us beyond our blind spots. Nonetheless, all of the healing and releasing in the world will not, in and of themselves, bring true evolutionary transformation. Why? Because much of what stands in the way of evolution is the simple human preference for ease and comfort.

At the close of the last chapter we saw how important it is to hold ourselves accountable to a deliberately chosen set of ideals. This is largely because it is human nature to revert to what taxes us least, unless there is a clear, motivating standard before us, something which reminds us that the sacrifices of ease and comfort which we are called to make are truly worth it in the big picture. Setting ideals is a foundational act of will according to Cayce, who said that whether we are ruled by circumstances and environmental triggers or whether we are ruled by will depends most " . . . upon what the entity or soul sets as its standard of qualifications to meet or measure up to, within its OWN self . . . " and how willing we are to be guided by that standard when we make the decisions of life.[194] This sounds pretty simple when we are reading a book or attending a retreat that fires us up spiritually. But in day-to-day life, as most of us have discovered, it can be a very different story. At the core, what most of us want is to live a nice life, be happy, and be able to feel good about ourselves. As C.S. Lewis once said regarding what we give to God, we tend to think of it like paying our taxes: we hope there is some left over for us once we have paid

---

[194]590-1

what is required of us.

It takes a significant commitment of will to push past those thresholds we looked at in the last chapter, where inertia tends to keep us locked in place. And let's face it—it's just not *fun* to develop the attribute of will. By its very nature, it's work. And for most of us, it's hard. It's not hard so much in the sense that any one act of will is difficult. It's hard in the sense that exercise of the will requires repetition and diligence. It is axiomatic that will comes into play when its exercise is most distasteful! After all, if you were doing something easily and automatically, it wouldn't call for will, would it? But will is like any muscle that needs development. If you have a functional arm, you have a bicep. But how strong that bicep is depends on how much lifting you have done. Or think about the common need for those who have been bedridden to rebuild capacity for even the basic demands of daily living. An unexercised will is like the atrophied muscles of someone who has been confined to bed for a long time. The only way to build a muscle is to make it do at least a little more than what feels easy and comfortable. The same is true for will.

Once again, it is consciousness of our ideals that can make the difference between satisfying developments in our lives or the malaise that we experience when we surrender to spiritual sloth:

> Know, however, that it is what the will does about that which is set as its ideal in a mental, in a material or in the physical experiences as well as the spiritual—and then having the courage to carry out that ideal—makes the difference between the constructive and creative forces or relationships and those that make one become rather as a drifter or a ne'er-do-well, or one very unstable and unhappy.[195]

Haven't we all experienced the truth of this at one time or another? As challenging as it can be at times to exert the will, when we do so in alignment with consciously chosen standards for ourselves, we experience greater levels of mental, spiritual, and even physical well-being.

According to the Cayce source, such development of the will is cen-

---

[195] 1401-1

tral to our evolution. It is what makes for the individuality of the soul.[196] It is the attribute that distinguishes us from the rest of the animal kingdom[197]—and not just because it is a tool that enables us to meet the developmental thresholds that are unique to a human being. Will is more than a means to an end. It is an expression of our deepest Selves and as such, its development is an end in itself. " . . . The will is a portion of the soul-entity, a part of . . . creation itself . . . ," we're told in one reading. That same reading goes on to say that just as the "atomic structures" within our bodies operate in relationship to one another, so too do each of our wills—in relationship with others' wills—influence evolution and creation.[198]

In short, will is a core attribute of the true Self. To those who have practiced some of the forms of meditation described in Chapter 6, where we rest in that aspect of consciousness that transcends the thoughts and feelings that may arise *in* consciousness, this will become obvious. When we experience ourselves as the awareness that makes thought possible or as the field or container within which thought happens, we touch a core self who is unbound by conditions or conditioning, who is unmoved by the fears, anxieties, or drives of ego, who is utterly *free*. That Self—who is none other than the "I am" present in every moment—is the chooser, the unfettered will. And just as meditation on the core awareness that is the Self strengthens its manifestation in our everyday choices, priorities, and behaviors, so too does the conscious exercise of will strengthen will's presence in our everyday lives.

When we feel that we lack "will power," this is only a reversible atrophy of our functioning "will muscle." This means that even the frustrating tendency that many of us have to relapse repeatedly in maintaining good habits actually serves a constructive purpose in developing our capacity of will. That might sound a bit counter-intuitive on the surface, but consider this: Every time we make the effort to re-instill a good habit (it doesn't matter whether we are talk-ing about health disciplines like good nutrition and exercise or spiri-

---

[196]1373-2
[197]909-1
[198]1473-1

tual disciplines like meditation and chosen alterations of behavior), we have to overcome the inertia we experience in re-starting the habit. And it takes more "will muscle" to overcome inertia than it does to maintain momentum once the habit has been established. This is the reason why personal trainers instruct their clients to lift weight slowly and deliberately rather than use fast, swinging motions on the exertion or allow the weight to fall back into position on the releasing side of the movement. One style uses muscle effort throughout the repetition while the other allows momentum to make the job easier, thus working the muscle less. By the same principle, each time we have to fight against inertia to reestablish a good habit, we use more "will muscle" than we do while relying on momentum to keep it going. This is important because in order to progress in our evolution, we need "will muscle" strong enough to withstand the inevitable obstacles life throws our way and not let them derail us. In other words, we're learning to keep our spiritual commitments even when it is not easy. Obviously, the longer we stay away from use of the "will muscle," the more it atrophies; so I am not recommending relapsing as a spiritual strategy! But neither should we allow a consciousness of futility to discourage us from repeatedly attempting to reestablish the same good habits of spiritual practice. There is a reason, after all, that our spiritual work is called *practice*. It takes repetition and patience with ourselves, even and perhaps most of all when we are inclined to think that we are failing. As the Cayce readings remind us, " . . . You only fail if you quit trying . . . "[199] Will is the faculty that is exercised and developed each time we renew our efforts.

In truth we have unimagined potentials of will and knowing this is can be a powerful motivator. New Thought writer William Walker Atkinson put it quite compellingly when he said:

> The majority of us have little or no conception of the reserve mental energies and forces contained within our being. We jog along at our customary gait, thinking that we are doing our best and getting all out of life that there is in it—think we are expressing ourselves to our utmost capacity. But we are living only in the first-wind mental

[199]3292-1

state, and behind our working mentality are stores of wonderful mental energy and power—faculties lying dormant—power lying latent—awaiting the magic command of the Will in order to awaken into activity and outward expression. We are far greater beings than we have realized—we are giants of power, if we did but know it. Many of us are like young elephants that allow themselves to be mastered by weak men, and put through their paces, little dreaming of the mighty strength and power concealed within their organisms.[200]

Cayce would concur, repeatedly insisting that there is no force or influence that surpasses the will because will is of the same force that powered the creation of all that is. It is the evolutionary drive imbued with choice. And whenever that choice is aligned with the divine purpose, it will be an unfolding of love.

Love

We're not used to thinking of evolution as having much to do with love. In fact, most of us have been taught just the opposite. The Darwinian principle of survival of the fittest and the dog-eat-dog mentality of Neo-Darwinism conjure up images of the strong and aggressive obliterating the weak and defenseless. Yet as we have already seen, an equally important thread of cooperative force has enabled evolution at least as far back as when the first bacteria colonized into multicelled organisms. Bruce Lipton champions this cooperative side of evolution, calling the study of it the "New Biology." He describes us as standing on the line between Neo-Darwinism, that sees life as an "unending war among battling biochemical robots" and the New Biology, "which casts life as a cooperative journey among powerful individuals who can program themselves to create joy-filled lives."[201] So while we cannot deny that evolution is partially a tale involving death and dissolution (as the last chapter made clear), it is also a story of ever more

---

[200]William Walker Atkinson, (1907, pp. 13–4), *The Secret of Success*, retrieved as free PDF from scribd.com.

[201]Lipton, *The Biology of Belief*, 29.

complex, cooperative interconnectedness—or, as we may also call it, love.

The Cayce readings call love a law, casting it as an indispensable ingredient to our evolution. In saying this they are not alone in the world of spiritually oriented evolutionary thought. Rudolf Steiner said that the key to future evolution is in realizing that evolution itself is the "sowing of seed which must ripen into love" and that "the greater the amount of love-force, so much the greater will be the creative force available for the future."[202] Henry Drummond characterized love as the supreme law from which all other laws derive. Ken Wilber identifies love as the force behind each leap to a new level of organization and complexity in our past and future evolutionary history. In calling love "the attractive, cohesive force in and of God," Alice Bailey postulated that the force which holds atoms together was none other than the love that emanates from the core of all that exists.[203] Teilhard de Chardin said essentially the same thing in asserting that if there were no force inclining molecules to unite, it would be impossible for love to appear higher up the evolutionary chain.

We have already seen how unity consciousness is the next major evolutionary potential for humanity, and we have seen how our personal and collective advancement in consciousness is characterized by care and compassion extending to wider and wider circles beyond oneself, one's family, one's ethnicity, or one's nation. This is the construction the Cayce readings put on Jesus' central teaching to "love the Lord your God with all of your mind, heart, soul, and body" and to "love your neighbor as yourself." In the Gospel account, Jesus is challenged with the follow-up question, "And who is my neighbor?"[204] Quite tellingly, this is when Jesus gives the parable of the Good Samaritan—someone who reacts in kindness and generosity to a person decidedly outside his own ethnic and religious boundaries. The message is unmistakable that our neighbor is not necessarily the person closest to us but rather *any* person we may come upon as we walk the road of life. There is simply no meaningful way to talk about the next

---

[202]Steiner, *An Outline of Occult Science*, 117.
[203]Bailey, *The Consciousness of the Atom*, 83.
[204]Luke 10:25-37

evolutionary leap without framing it in terms of an expanding love that calls us beyond our present boundaries, for the evolutionary trajectory of consciousness is leading toward greater unity with all others as part of one's own Self.

This love that flows as the expression of unity is an affirmation of the true Self, and it flows with a sense of freedom rather than coercion. I emphasize this point, because in this day and particularly in the American culture that has a reputation for admiring rugged individualism, it is not uncommon for skeptics to fear that this talk of unity hides a secret agenda to erode the rights of the individual. In this regard, Teilhard de Chardin makes an important distinction between the spread of unity consciousness and a pernicious imposter—collectivism. Likening collectivism to a crystal rather than a living cell or the anthill instead of brotherhood, he said that "so long as it absorbs or appears to absorb the person, the collectivity kills the love that is trying to come to birth."[205] Annie Besant may have meant the same thing when she said "man's will may not be forced, else were the divine Life in him blocked in its due evolution."[206] Cayce chimed in on this theme in pointing out that from the time when the Spirit of God moved to bring order out of chaos and souls were charged with subduing the earth, " . . . man—with his natural bent—not only attempted to subdue the *earth*, but to subdue one another.[207] Social and political structures designed to control our behaviors may be necessary up to a point to maintain social order, but they can never create oneness, for true unity consciousness is a product of that divine life that must bubble up from within the hearts and minds of human beings.

By these examples we can see that such love is not so much a particular emotion as it is the organic awakening of the one Consciousness in which we all live and move and have our being. The ultimate love that is slowly awakening on the leading edge of evolution transcends all dividing lines, for it is nothing less than the radiant core of existence. Yet it is still most practical to begin wherever we are; most of us love better in the specific than in the abstract. In fact, the genu-

[205]Teilhard de Chardin, *The Phenomenon of Man*, 267.
[206]Besant, *Esoteric Christianity, or The Lesser Mysteries*, 79.
[207]3976-8

ineness of an abstract love for everyone and everything that seldom finds its way into one-on-one interactions would be suspect, to say the least. As Thomas Jefferson once said, "A great deal of love given to a few is better than a little to many."[208] This is true, but it is also true that genuine love directed toward specific people will tend to generalize outward from there if we provide a climate in which love can grow. I think back on how the arrival of my son and the consequent opening up of mother-love within me opened my heart to all children in a way that I had never experienced before loving my own child. This is why deliberate acts of engagement with people from a religion or culture or political stance unlike one's own can have such powerful impact on expanding love and compassion. At levels deeper than we might have imagined, bonds of oneness underlie the differences that dominate on the surface of things. In building connection with specific representatives of a group we consider to be on the other side of the divide from ourselves, we tap that underlying oneness. It is more than a change in our attitude; it is an awakening of nascent unity consciousness.

Like will, love can be strengthened and its reach widened by the practice of it. Anything that reminds us of the interconnectedness of not only all souls but of all living things and all reality will help to awaken latent reserves of love within us. Even the most simple practices can have a profound impact. I remember feeling bewildered, when I first met my husband, at his practice of passing up the best parking spaces so that others could have them. What I see now is how strongly this contrasts with the everyday mindset among even spiritually motivated people. How often is getting the best parking space used as a practical exercise in "Learn to Manifest What You Want 101?" We don't even think of the myriad ways we subtly reinforce a consciousness of "me first" separation or how easily we could cultivate love by taking a different approach in these everyday opportunities to interact with others on the highway or telephone, at work and at home, in the grocery store or shopping mall. In virtually every encounter with another human being, whether live or virtual, we can practice loving our neighbors as ourselves—that is, remembering that our

---

[208]As quoted on goodreads.com

neighbors *are* ourselves encased in another skin and wanting the best for them as we do for ourselves. If you have ever found yourself smiling and feeling joy as you watched a game show contestant win big, in that moment you were loving your neighbor as yourself. Your oneness with that stranger was sufficient for her good fortune to be your joy. That capacity is strengthened when we use our will to enact loving behaviors or deliberately remind ourselves of oneness during all of our encounters with other people. (A starter list of ideas for cultivating love and will appears below for those who are drawn to this discipline.)

Everyday Disciplines to Cultivate Love and Will

Below are just a few simple practices related to the development of will and the increase of love. This is by no means a definitive list. Rather, it is meant to spark some of your own ideas about how to awaken your experience of unity with others and your capacity to exercise the will. These exercises do not replace those acts of love and service that we typically associate with charity, volunteerism, and other forms of helpfulness. Rather, they are meant to foster the *consciousness* undergirding such avenues of service. It is a good idea to set your spiritual, mental, and physical ideals (as described in the last chapter) as a foundation for these practices.

- In situations where it may be most natural to find a place in the fastest-moving line, open your awareness up to the others around you who are also seeking to get through the line as quickly as possible. Remember that they are parts of you and allow their smooth experience with the lines to be as important as your own.

- When you sit down to meditate, take a moment to hold the intention that you are doing so on behalf of all humanity.

- Choose one place where you have been putting off making a desired change in your habits. Make a commitment to use this as an opportunity to develop your capacity of will. Whenever you are tempted not to perform the desired good behavior, remind yourself that you will do it—not because you feel like it but because you have decided you will. Hold the image of a muscle that builds with weightlifting. As you use will to do the desirable behavior, actively imagine it as a weightlifting exercise. Add the awareness that when you exercise your will in this way, you are helping to create leverage for countless other people who share your difficulty in implementing this desirable behavior.

- When watching a television program that involves people being themselves (news and interview programs, reality programs, anything that is not an acted story), stop to be aware that the image on the screen is a real person and that that person is somewhere right now, having an experience of one sort or another. Feel that person as another aspect of yourself that is simply manifesting in another place and physical form.

- When you meditate and move into awareness of the core "I am," before concluding the meditation, deliberately feel that Self's utter freedom to make choices in your life, independent of past conditioning or experience. Make a choice in that moment, in that consciousness.

- When you lose an item that you care about, imagine someone who needs it or who will enjoy it being the one to find it. Practice allowing their experience with the item to be a perfect substitute for your own enjoyment of it.

- Before making any comments in a group discussion or via social media, stop to ground yourself in your best understanding of unity and our collective evolution. Contrast that with what your ego seems to need in the moment. Make your decision about whether to comment—and, if so, how to comment—according to whether it serves ego or unity and evolution.

- Observe another person doing something or exhibiting a trait that you find positive, but have not yet mastered in your own experience. Remind yourself that the other person and you share a common, unified consciousness at a deeper level and open up to the strengthening that comes to you from the other person's attainment.

- When you observe another person doing something or exhibiting a trait that you find negative or destructive, remind yourself that you and this other person are part of the same whole. Claim that person as part of you and send healing thoughts the same as you would do if a part of your body were in pain or not functioning properly.

The opportunity to experience the oneness is literally everywhere and in every human endeavor. It can take us unawares and engulf us in love that does indeed carry a profound emotion within it, even if the love itself is not primarily emotional in nature. When we experience it, we experience God. Over the years I've had a handful of such experiences, each one seeming to occur spontaneously and yet in its own way popping up as a manifestation of the oneness that I had been trying to cultivate in my awareness. One experience in particular stands out for its simplicity. It happened more than ten years ago in a discount department store. As I pushed my cart of household supplies down the aisle, my eyes suddenly lighted on a woman standing in the lamp department. She was holding a small table lamp out at arm's length, her head inclined as if to get the best possible view. The glow of pleasure on her face as she looked at this treasure and (as I imagined) pictured it on some table or dresser in her home, still stands out in my mind like a little tableau that might be titled "Life's Little Moments of Happiness." No sooner had I observed her than I was overwhelmed with joy at her pleasure, as well as deep love for her. As I went on toward the checkout counter blinking tears out of my eyes, I knew that I had been swept into a "God's-eye-view" of the scene. I had tasted true oneness as I felt such love for a stranger and such deep joy over her simple pleasure.

This love was irrational in that there was absolutely no reason that she, rather than the hundreds of other people in the store, caught my attention in this way. I was not currently interested in buying any new lamps; she did not remind me of anyone I knew; nor was there anything particularly striking about her appearance or manner of dress to catch my attention. The intense rapport I suddenly felt with her hit me as a purely random event. There was no conscious thought of building unity consciousness, or any other spiritual thought for that matter. I was in the store to buy some needed supplies, and my mind was not on anything that predisposed me to a sudden influx of oneness. The love I felt for her was totally unconditional in that I knew nothing whatsoever about her. In that moment I loved her deeply just because she *was*. Significantly, it was simultaneously a moment of deep joy for me. It just *feels* good to love another human being without needing anything at all from that person, not even an acknowledgement of your love.

When we speak of "unity consciousness" as the next evolutionary development, perhaps the term doesn't adequately capture the experience of love that accompanies each incremental realization of oneness. But when we feel it, the ultimate inseparability of love and oneness is unmistakable. Even the tiniest taste of it confirms unity consciousness as an evolutionary ideal worth aspiring to, and we can only try to imagine what life will be like when such love is more than a startling episode that pops up now and again. One thing does seem certain: The love that is evolution's radiant core will be brought to manifestation in the affairs of human beings only through deliberate acts of will. Such acts will be as individual as we are, but they will always stretch us to greater levels of wholeness within ourselves and greater levels of unity with all of life. As that occurs, evolution itself takes a giant leap.

Giving Our Best Love and Will for the Sake of Evolution

And so we return to the idea that evolution cannot, will not take us beyond our current crises as a species unless an awakening consciousness of love leads the way. When we embrace the evolutionary perspective, we acknowledge a claim on our love and a responsibility to use our will in ways that further evolution—not because we are paragons of enlightened living but because we recognize that we are each representatives of the human race. We share our weaknesses with untold numbers of other people, and we hold the untapped potential of humanity in our hands. We have the opportunity to leverage the collective consciousness when we work on a weakness or develop a strength within us. We are influential beyond what most of us ever imagine. Seeing ourselves in this way not only enlarges our motivation beyond the scope of the purely personal, it bonds us with humanity and thus increases our love. This is what it means to be agents of transformation, carrying the evolutionary priority out into the world.

PART FOUR
GOING OUT IN SERVICE TO THE WORLD

Then, we would give that not only must the body-mind turn to the spiritual promises that are a part of its mental and spiritual self, but the environment must be changed; so that the spiritual promises may be put to active service and work to replace the habits with the habits of doing good, doing right, doing justice, being merciful.   1427-1

CHORUS OF THE PITIES:
We would establish those of kindlier build,
In fair Compassions skilled,
Men of deep art in life-development;
Watchers and warders of thy varied lands,
Men surfeited of laying heavy hands,
Upon the innocent,
The mild, the fragile, the obscure content
Among the myriads of thy family.
Those, too, who love the true, the excellent,
And make their daily moves a melody.
                    Thomas Hardy, *The Dynasts**

---

*Thomas Hardy, *The Dynasts* (London: Macmillan, 1918), 3.

Chapter 15:
Tending the Garden

... Each entity, each individual—today, has its own vineyard to keep, to dress—For who? Its Maker, from whence it came! What is to be the report in thine own life with those abilities, those forces, as may be manifest in self...?   364-10

You shall lay down the saw and the plane to take upon yourself the regeneration of the world.   James Allen, *As a Man Thinketh**

*T*he dominant creation myth in the Western world casts us as gardeners of a developing world. In contrast to popular treatment where the Garden of Eden is taken to represent a paradise lost, if we look closely at the story as told in Genesis, we find that human beings arrived on a planet that was not yet complete. We are told that after the initial appearance of the heavens and the earth, "no shrub of the field had yet appeared on the earth and no plant of the field had yet sprung up, for the Lord God had not sent rain on the earth and there was no man to work the ground."[209] Did you get that? The arrival of the gardeners was as essential as rain in order for the earth to continue its development!

This places the story of Eden in a light far more compatible with the evolutionary view than with the view that we are still trying to regain our original, perfect estate. A new garden is good but not perfect. It is incomplete, a place where things must be planted and carefully tended. Only in time will they grow into what they will be and only in due season will they bear their fruit, with the fruit of each season yielding seeds for fruit yet to come. This planet of ours has been shifting and changing and erupting and reforming for all of its history. Only a very short-term view that defines "normal" in terms of very recent history would assume that we are not making progress or that upheaval is a

---

*James Allen (1902, p. 62), *As a Man Thinketh*, e-book.
[209]Genesis 2:4-5

sure sign that the end is coming. We may not know exactly where the forces of evolution are leading, but surely we are part of a moving, developing manifestation.

When we don't feel the reality of that movement and development, it's analogous to the way it doesn't feel like we're moving when we look out the window of a building. Despite the subjective sense that we are standing still, we are right now spinning at a speed of about 1,000 miles per hour as the Earth turns on its axis, and we are circling our sun at a dizzying 66,000 miles per hour. That rate of speed would get us from Washington D.C. to San Francisco in three minutes. And if you're not motion sick yet, the solar system is circling around the center of our Milky Way galaxy at a speed of about 483,000 miles per hour. Yet it has made the complete circuit only twenty times since the sun and earth were first formed—and all of recorded human history has seen us move only the slightest bit around that circumference. Nor is this Milky Way Galaxy standing still. It is spinning like a giant pinwheel—and it is moving through space at a rate of 1.3 million miles per hour. Does this put any perspective on the immensity of the project we are involved in?

Caring For a Garden in Upheaval

This garden requires a very long time period to bring its growth to fruition, and this has ever been a source of frustration to those who hope for a better day. As we look around at the numerous problems that face us in the world, it is understandable if at times we wish we could flee this garden. The weeds of poverty and disease and oppression can seem overwhelming. Worse, the metaphorical political, social, medical, and religious herbicides in our garden sheds all too often end up only polluting our garden even more. Throw in the competing demands from our personal lives or shake things up further with a natural disaster, and it's easy to see how even the best-intentioned would-be gardener is tempted to throw down the hoe in despair and wait for a rescue team to arrive from some higher plane.

As a case in point, I write these words as the ravages of Hurricane Sandy dominate the news. Last evening, as we watched the images of an entire neighborhood in Queens, NY burned to the ground, subways flooded, and New Jersey coastal towns that I remember well from my childhood reduced to beach rubble, I turned to my husband and said, "I wish I could believe in December 21, 2012." That yearning for someone, some thing, some event to just make it all okay was a primal emotional response for me in that moment, as it is for many others. Maybe you are one of them. It's at these times that the mythic God often enters the public discourse, with the disillusioned asking "How could God let this happen?" and the pseudo-pious re-interpreting the event as a visitation of God's righteous wrath upon the collective sin *du jour*. But when we no longer have the mythic God to petition or blame or credit, it can feel pretty lonely and frightening when so much destruction and loss confront us. It was hard to feel particularly evolutionary as I watched the endless footage of total disaster.

Then something else seeped into my awareness as the news report went on. Yet another mayor was talking about the resilient people of his town and how they would rebuild. The first few times I'd heard this brave assertion, it just sounded like so much whistling in the dark. But in the aggregate it began to get through to me. It would take time, of course, but people *would* rebuild as they always have done. I'd also seen some admirable examples of politicians from both major political parties rising above pre-Election Day rhetoric to support and give due credit to one another as they joined in common humanitarian response to the disaster. There it was: that forward-moving direction, that rising above habitual limitations, that expansive quality that is the hallmark of the evolutionary advance. In a flash that was as brilliant as the earlier one was dismal, I saw that even though I could not include the mythic God in the equation for this event, God was nonetheless emerging in the human consciousness that responded to it.

Now I'm not so naïve as to think that it will unfold from here as an inspirational tale of how disaster triggered an evolutionary leap. Just as we each tend to slip back into relative unconsciousness after our times of momentary illumination, it is likely that the same will be true of those who are at this moment operating from keenly awakened care and compassion. The days ahead are sure to bring stories of both the best and the worst of human consciousness in action, just as they did following the 2004 Indian Ocean tsunami, Hurricane Katrina, and the earthquake in Haiti (In fact, just now as I took a coffee break and turned to CNN, a story about looting was juxtaposed with one about tireless rescue efforts.) Of course by the time you are reading this, Sandy will have receded into the past for all but those directly affected, and I have no crystal ball to know what other events may be looming large when any particular individual may be reading this. Nor do I know what economic, political, or social consequences may unfold from Sandy and other natural and man–made disasters to come. What matters for our consideration here is what you and I do with that spark, that evolutionary drive forward that arises in our personal and collective experience and compels us to work the rich soil of the earth just when we may be most tempted to give up on it.

Cayce, perhaps because of his tendency to borrow biblical imagery, often used this agricultural metaphor to frame the ideal response to the challenges and opportunities of his contemporaries. " . . . The harvest indeed is ready, but the laborers are few . . . "[210] In this particular reading he went on to urge the recipient to seize an opportunity to disseminate ideas and be an influence that would have effective impact on others. The specific advice may have varied, but repeatedly in these readings we find a call to action and influence in the world rather than merely tending to personal spirituality. The call is as relevant today as it was then. As people living through a time of war and worldwide economic uncertainty, we may well relate to this exchange, which took place in 1943, in the midst of World War II:

> (Q) Is there going to be a great spiritual change immediately following this war? Its effect on economic conditions in this country?
> (A) That depends upon what *you*—as millions of others do about it. Do ye choose that such should be? Do ye choose this as the opportunity that people shall be warned that the day of the Lord is at hand and let every man forsake the old ways and cleave to that which is good? This can only be answered in thyself.[211]

The responsibility this reading places on ordinary people to guide the outcome of world affairs is decidedly evolutionary in flavor. But

---

[210]1472–13
[211]3213–1

this excerpt also introduces a rather problematic element for our consideration. What does he mean by "the day of the Lord is at hand?" Is this some kind of prophetic utterance? If so, it would appear to be at odds with prevailing evolutionary thinking, which insists that the future is an unfolding matrix of many complex factors rather than a preset destiny. Other similar excerpts such as this one would add only to the sense that there is a great divide between the Cayce perspective on prophecy and the evolutionary viewpoint:

> (Q) What is meant by "the day of the Lord is near at hand"?
> (A) That as has been promised through the prophets and the sages of old, the time—and half time—has been and is being fulfilled in this day and generation, and that soon there will again appear in the earth that one through whom many will be called to meet those that are preparing the way for His day in the earth. The Lord, then, will come, "even as ye have seen him go".
> (Q) How soon?
> (A) When those that are His have made the way clear, *passable*, for Him to come.[212]

There is no getting around the eschatological, "end times," tone of this message; it would be disingenuous to ignore this admittedly significant aspect of the readings' take on world events. But this need not drive a wedge between the Cayce philosophy and the modern evolutionary movement. For as we'll be seeing, Cayce's viewpoint is not your typical end-of-the-world, "Jesus will take us all to heaven" eschatology. Our first indication of this comes from the second answer above, which identifies human preparation rather than externally determined divine timing as the trigger for what is known in many Christian circles as the "second coming." Beyond that, a study of the way the term "day of the Lord" was used in the Cayce readings yields a view that is surprisingly consonant with the modern evolutionary view, biblical phraseology notwithstanding.

---

[212]262-49

"The Day of the Lord":
Personal and Collective Evolutionary Leap

We find the phrase "the day of the Lord" in about sixty Edgar Cayce readings, so obviously it is not a minor note in the Cayce canon. That makes it particularly important to understand what he meant by the term; and in order to do so, it may be helpful to take a brief look at the particular line of Christian thinking that Cayce was steeped in from birth. As a deeply committed member of the Christian Church, Cayce would have been quite familiar with the views of its founding leader, Barton W. Stone (1772–1844).* Stone was quite unusual in his day for his rather progressive thinking on many issues, including a radical focus on God's love rather than sin and judgment, a rejection of creeds as litmus tests for one's Christianity, and a view of the atonement that focused on the elevating influence of Jesus' willing surrender of his life rather than a substitutionary blood sacrifice. Longtime students of the Cayce material will instantly recognize compatibility between these positions and the flavor of the readings.

Stone's thinking regarding prevalent nineteenth century expectations of Christ's imminent return is of particular significance for our understanding of Cayce's approach to prophetic epochs, for it shows us a formative influence on the young Cayce's very active theological inquiry. Stone, like many in his day, was aware of Baptist preacher William Miller's calculations that Christ would return in 1843. Although never casting his lot with Miller, who has been colorfully described as "the poster child for all forlorn efforts to predict the end of the age,"[213] Stone also thought Christ's return was likely to be soon and

---

*By Cayce's time of birth, the Christian Church, under the leadership of Barton Stone, had merged with the Disciples of Christ, under the leadership of Alexander Campbell, with individual churches from both branches tending to retain their respective names. In Cayce's native Kentucky, the influence of Stone was dominant. The two groups had come together around their shared ideals and originally intended to be a non–denominational federation of Christians seeking unity that rose above petty doctrinal squabbles. The movement nonetheless became a *de facto* denomination as it steadily gained adherents. It wasn't until the 1960's, however, that most Christian and Disciples churches acknowledged this reality and officially became the denomination now known as the Christian Church (Disciples of Christ).

[213]Jerry A. Gladson, "Echoes of Millerite Millenarianism among the Founders and Heirs of Brush Run," retrieved from brushrunchurchbicentennial1811–2011.org.

he followed the Millerite movement with interest. When his predictions for Christ's return some time between March 1843 and March 1844 proved untrue, Miller went back to his calculations and reset Millerite expectations for October 22, 1844. That, as we know, was another failure in the art of interpreting prophecy. So great were the dashed expectations of the many Millerites, thousands of whom had left their lives behind to gather in groups large and small across the entire eastern United States, that the event came to be immortalized among them as "The Great Disappointment."

Stone died less than a month after The Great Disappointment, but his mature views on such attempts to pinpoint prophesied outcomes were published posthumously in his journal *The Christian Messenger*:

> We have long observed, that when once the mind becomes intensely fixt [sic] on this subject [prophetic predictions], it seems to relax its hold on every other, and is oftener floating in the unexplored regions of fancy, than of truth; and loses the spirit of pure devotion, and contracts a zeal for opinions, and inspires too often an unholy opposition against those who differ. . . . Our firm conviction, from observing the signs of the times, [is] that some mighty revolution is just ahead, and that it behooves all men to be ready to meet it. But, [as to] when, how, or what that revolution may be, we confess our ignorance.[214]

When we consider that at the time Stone wrote this, the Civil War was right around the corner (though southern-born and bred, Stone was an avid abolitionist) and that the tumultuous twentieth century—with not only its wars but also the coming of electricity, automobiles, flight, and the atomic age—was a just a little more than fifty years away, it is fair to say that he was correct in predicting imminent revolution. We should also keep in mind that during his lifetime the Industrial Revolution had completely altered a way of life which had prevailed for hundreds of years. No wonder Stone, like many of his contemporaries, was primed to expect revolutionary changes. In this, his ultimate position on prophecy, we find great resonance not only

---

[214]William Miller, *The Christian Messenger* (November, 1844).

with statements that later appeared in Cayce's readings, but with expectations within our own time as well. Who could deny that a "mighty revolution" is just ahead? And who is cocky enough to predict with any certainty just what it may be or how it will happen? Against this backdrop, we can more fully appreciate the nuances that allowed Cayce to speak of an imminent "day of the Lord" and urge people to work toward it, yet at the same time link it inseparably to human willingness to awaken in consciousness.

Echoing some of Jesus' teachings that the kingdom of heaven is "at hand," the Cayce source locates the potential for "the day of the Lord" across all time periods. It is most definitely not a single, onetime event that we must wait for. Some readings reference declarations of the day of the Lord in New Testament times as valid utterances. Some point to it as an event to come in the near future. Most treat it as an ever-present possibility—for example, " . . . as the call has *ever* been, 'Harken! For the day of the Lord is at hand—make thy paths straight!' . . . "[215] and "For, remember, as has been given, Today—*today*—now—if ye will accept, if ye will set thyself in order—is the acceptable day of the Lord."[216] Perhaps the quintessential expression of this point comes in this:

> Think never that the opportunities have passed; for ever is there set before thee a choice to make, and has always been given "*today* is the acceptable year, the acceptable day, of the Lord!" It is never too late to begin, even in an experience; for Life in its experience is a continued, a continuous effort . . . [217]

Most telling here is the reference to Life as a "continuous effort." Though he may not have used the language of evolution here, the concept is implicit. The day of the Lord as Cayce describes it is not an externally generated historical event, but an awakening to and an application of the divine within each soul.[218] Further, we are told that such awakening is not likely to come until we love God better than

---

[215] 1587-1, emphasis added
[216] 404-14
[217] 909-1
[218] 254-83

ourselves. " . . . Then is it the day, the hour, of the awakening in thine self! . . ."[219] The day of the Lord is also described as " . . . the white light of health, help and happiness . . . " that can come even at times when fear threatens to overtake us.[220]

If we look beneath the traditional biblical language of the readings, we find that the day of the Lord is a call to service as instruments of divine manifestation in the earth:

> . . . What, then, is the standard? "*Others*, Lord, not myself but others, that the glory of the Father may be manifested in the earth; and as the day of the Lord approaches that many may be ready and willing to answer, 'Here am I, use me.' 'Here am I, use me.'"[221]

The collective historical significance of such service comes in the promise that it could catalyze widespread spiritual awakening. Hence, numerous people were told that their path of service involved "hastening" the day of the Lord or helping to bring it to manifestation.

The form such contributions might take varied from person to person, but they were usually some combination of living one's ideals and being able to articulate a hopeful message to others. Expanding on a theme that is prevalent in the Cayce readings, the emphasis is on unity in diversity and the strength that comes from a variety of contributions that, together, serve the creative advance. "Concerted" effort is to be desired, but we should take our cue from nature, where no two blades of grass or leaves on a tree are alike, and where even no two roses on the same vine are alike. These differences, when combined, the readings say, give " . . . a better, a greater manifestation of that Creative Force, that Universal Energy we call—*ye* call—*God!*"[222] One person was told that his ability to " . . . correlate truths . . . " could " . . . make the fast approach of that Great Day of the Lord."[223] A reading requested by the parents of an eleven-year-old girl told her that she

---

[219]262-59
[220]1472-13
[221]254-91
[222]1159-1
[223]900-15

would have " . . . opportunities to serve and to bring to others knowledge of the truth of the day of the Lord." She was told to care for her body and mind as preparation for such service and to keep them spiritualized according to her ideals and purposes. Her parents were advised to provide her studies in voice and journalism.[224] From this we can see that both personal disciplines and the development of practical skills are all part of the commitment to an evolutionary lifestyle.

One thing was clear: If a mass realization of that state Cayce called the day of the Lord is to come about, it will require us being " . . . one in mind, in purpose, that the day of the Lord may draw nigh unto each, and that ye may have the greater love, the greater patience one with the other."[225] Here we find intimations of unity consciousness. It will also require a change in consciousness that spreads well beyond the domain typically considered to be the "spiritual" aspect of life; it will need to influence our ways of living in the world, right down to our business models. This bit of advice, given during the depths of the Great Depression, has much relevance for us today as we wrestle with worldwide economic woes:

> . . . more and more must there be the necessity of business and business relations on every hand to have an ideal. The sooner the necessity is recognized in the minds, the hearts, the souls of individuals that carry on *in* the commercial or business world, the sooner will there come that regeneration which will make for the drawing together of those who may make the day of the Lord at hand; for in Him we live and move and *have* our being. Business must have an ideal, a soul.[226]

As much as we all might wish it to be otherwise, Cayce's pronouncements about an imminent day of the Lord were not about someone swooping down to save the day. They were a call to evolutionary action in the world. And this is true not only of the readings explicitly referencing the day of the Lord; it was a consistent theme whenever

---

[224]2572-1
[225]262-96
[226]257-88

world affairs were addressed. During the Great Depression, when Cayce was hurting as badly as anyone, his readings threw responsibility to address collective challenges right back on us:

> . . . Think not as to who will ascend into heaven to bring down comfort and ease to thine own aching heart, or who will go over the seas to bring that which may be of a recompense within thine own experience, but lo! ye shall find it in your own heart![227]

On eve of World War II, we find the very same message. Responsibility lies with each one of us to turn the tide when destructive forces threaten, and only a movement of heart holds the answer to our collective woes:

> "What then," ye ask, "is to be the outcome? What is there that I can do about it?" Let thy daily life be free from criticism, from condemnation, from hate, from jealousy. And as ye give power to the Spirit of Peace, so may the *Prince of Peace*, the love of God, manifest. So long as ye turn thy thoughts to the manners and means for meeting and overcoming those destructive forces, ye show forth that which may bring to the world that day of the Lord. For the promise is that in the latter days there shall be the purposes in the HEARTS of men, everywhere![228]

These last two excerpts are drawn from an extraordinary collection within the Cayce material that is called the "World Affairs readings." Taken as a whole, these may well be considered the Cayce readings' evolutionary manifesto.

The Cayce World Affairs Readings, Evolutionary Manifesto

A collection of twenty-nine readings that take us from the pit of the Great Depression through the build-up to World War II and into the

---

[227]3976-14
[228]3976-23

war years themselves, the World Affairs readings have much to say
about individual responsibility in any time of crisis. They cast the
hardship of the Great Depression as a time " . . . when each soul must
turn to that thought within of what is its relation to the Creative Forces
in its experience . . . "[229] It is both fascinating and challenging to think
that the same might be true for our own uncertain economic times. As
the world economic situation grows more and more serious, should
we each be thinking more about how we stand with respect to that
great evolutionary drive toward creation of new forms? The 1930s depression—perhaps much like our own time—was about the loss of ideals in the world:

> " . . . The world, *as* a world . . . has lost its ideal. Man may not have
> the same *idea*. Man—*all* men—may have the same *ideal*! . . . that
> can only come with all having the one ideal; not the one idea, but
> 'Thou shalt love the Lord Thy God with all thine heart, thy neighbor
> *as* thyself!' This [is] the whole law, this [is] the whole answer to the
> world, to each and every soul. That is the answer to world conditions
> as they exist today."[230]

Characterizing the depression as the inevitable consequence of what
happens when we forget to heed this admonition, the readings said
that each person would have to turn within and decide what he or she
was going to do about it. This reflects a radical level of self-responsi-
bility in our approach to world conditions, a major theme throughout
reading 3976-14. For example,

> Hence each would ask, then: "What must I do about it; not what
> shall this, that or the other ruler, other office holder, or the other
> individual do" but each should ask, "What must I do about the
> economic conditions in which we find ourselves?"

Despite the near–universal tendency for us to point to greed in business or failed government policy or the off-kilter values of other

[229]3976-14
[230]3976-8

people when we see the world in crisis, these readings are adamant that we are to correct these failings first within our own consciousness (continuing to excerpt from 3976–14):

> So, in the experience of those that have sent and made the conditions are greed, selfishness; that has been practiced in the minds, in the lives, in the experience of the nation. Think not any soul, "Yea, that is true for the other fellow." But it applies to Jim, to Tom, to those in ordinary walks of life, to those who have been given those powers in high places, those that have wealth about them; *they* are the oppressors; yea, look within thine own heart! Hast thou not practiced the same? . . .

In true evolutionary spirit, this same reading reminds us that, as we cultivate the higher consciousness of love within ourselves, we can have decisive impact on the whole:

> . . . For, as it has been given, "Yea, though there be only ten just men, they may save the city; they may save the nation; they may save the world," if they will but *practice* in their daily experience that which has been the command from the first: "Thou shalt love the Lord thy God with all thine heart, and thy neighbor as thyself."

Conversely, our failure to live up to the very best we are capable of becomes a weakness affecting every group that we are a part of, from family to nation:

> . . . No government, no nation, no state, no city, no family—yes, no individual—is stronger than the weakest habit.[231]

> (Q) Is America fulfilling her destiny?
> (A) Rather should the question be sought, my children, are individuals fulfilling those channels to which they have been brought through their own application of the knowledge within themselves.[232]

---

[231]3976-17
[232]3976-15

The evolutionary manifesto of the Cayce World Affairs readings makes it clear that changes of enormous proportions are in the offing:

> It is also understood, comprehended by some, that a new order of conditions is to arise; that there must be many a purging in high places as well as low; that there must be the greater consideration of each individual, each soul being his brother's keeper. There will then come about those circumstances in the political, the economic and the whole relationships where there will be a leveling—or a greater comprehension of this need.[233]

But this change is not one that we are to passively wait for. We each have a choice to make:

> " . . . Declare ye today *whom* ye will serve! As for me and my house, we will serve the living God." If there is sufficient, then, of those that will not only declare this in mind and in purpose but by deed and word of mouth, there may come then an enlightening through that which has been promised of old; that the young men shall dream dreams, the old men shall have visions, the daughters or maidens may know the spirit of truth,—yea, that all may come to the greater knowledge of the indwelling of the Prince of Peace.[234]

Our role as agents of evolutionary transformation is a sacred trust, for we are asked to be the channels through which Spirit can flow freely into the affairs of this world. It would seem that it is just not going to happen unless enough of us get on board to make it possible:

> As the Spirit of God once moved to bring peace and harmony out of chaos, so must the Spirit move over the earth and magnify itself *in the hearts, minds and souls of men* to bring peace, harmony and understanding, that they may dwell together in a way that will bring that peace, that harmony, that can only come with all having the one Ideal . . . [235]

---

[233]3976-18
[234]3976-26
[235]3976-8, emphasis added

Back in Chapter 5, we examined the question of "Why me?" when it comes to taking up the evolutionary cause and dedicating ourselves to it. In the World Affairs readings, we are challenged once again to see this cause not as an optional add-on to the spiritual path, but as a requirement arising from the simple fact that spiritual knowledge brings spiritual responsibility. That responsibility began to form when we first picked up spiritually themed books to read. It grew with each conference we attended or each discussion group we joined. It knocks on the door of our hearts each time we enter meditation. The urgency grows as the world hurtles toward bigger and bigger changes:

> . . . as the time or the period draws near for these changes that come with the new order, it behooves all of those who have an ideal—as individuals, as well as groups or societies or organizations, to be practicing, applying same in their experience—and their relationships as one to another.[236]

The cost of delay is real, this reading insists, "For unless these are up and doing, then there must indeed be a new order in THEIR relationships and their activities."

The Future Is in Our Hands

In a World Affairs reading sought specifically for the Association for Research and Enlightenment's Eighth Annual Congress in 1939, the request was made of the sleeping Cayce to "comment fully on the conditions which exist in each of the principal countries." Instead of providing that information, the reading threw it back on exhortations made in a previous reading:

> . . . *now*, the conditions or the circumstances throughout the nations of the world, or in the earth, are a challenge to every thinking person; that ye are not alone to pray for peace but are to PURSUE peace—by *living* the second phase of the divine injunction, "thy neighbor as thyself."[237]

---

[236]3976-18
[237]3976-22

And so it is with us. The great opportunity of modern life comes in the fact that each of us can bring unprecedented spiritual consciousness into the world by living it. Until fairly recent times, enlightenment has been the prize primarily for those who are sequestered from the world, those who are able to enter monastic life, and pursue spiritual consciousness relatively free of distractions. In a workaday world where most people had to toil incessantly just to provide for their basic needs, precious little was left for the luxury of what we today call the spiritual path. Yet, if evolution is leading toward full integration of Spirit and matter, that means learning to be conscious while fully engaged in "real life." Only in the modern era did this become possible for great numbers of ordinary people. I think this is why Cayce emphasized the application of spiritual law to our relationships, home life, community life, and planetary citizenship. For spiritual consciousness to manifest functionally within the world, it must awaken *within* the world. This is best accomplished through what is called in Buddhist traditions the path of the "householder." It is undeniably a harder path, for we must find the right priority for spiritual discipline amidst many priorities competing for our attention. What spiritual aspirant has not discovered how much easier the path is while on retreat? Who among us has not despaired over how that post–retreat spiritual glow diminishes once we are back home juggling job, family, finances, and the ever–tempting allure of our entertainments? Yet in that juggling we may find the highest calling of all.

While we may never know the full extent of the debt of gratitude that we owe to those who have long upheld our collective consciousness from their places of spiritual retreat, the next step can't possibly come until we also learn what it is to be fully in the world and yet not spiritually incapacitated by it. The abysmal record of supposedly enlightened teachers who fall victim to their shadows and get caught up in sexual abuse or excess, megalomania, materialism, drinking or drugs is testimony to what can happen if awakening to higher states of consciousness is not tempered with ongoing real–world application of spiritually established ideals and purposes. Teilhard de Chardin spoke of how " . . . India allowed itself to become drawn into metaphysics, only to become lost there." He goes on to say that we can never make too much of our indebtedness to India for the philosophy and mystic influences it brought, but that in the evolutionary scheme of things the "passivity and detachment" that such spirituality brought was not what builds worlds. When the phenomena of this world are regarded as illusion, he points out, there is little left to "animate and direct human evolution."[238]

We need to keep in mind that while evolution as a whole has a forward-moving trajectory, not every developmental strand within it automatically advances. Even in Darwin's writings there are numerous examples of retrogression. From exotic pigeons that reverted to gray, to cultivated roses and strawberries that revert back to earlier, less desirable forms, to domestic animals that go feral, nature is replete with examples of regression toward an earlier form. More sobering still is the fact that most environmentalists would agree that we are in the midst of the fifth mass extinction this planet has undergone. While this tells us that mass extinctions are nothing new to earth's history, the others were caused by a cosmological event, such as a comet. We humans have the dubious distinction of being the first species to cause a mass extinction. This alone should make it clear that we are not riding the evolutionary escalator up to our next level; it is more like a flight of stairs that we may walk in either direction.

Humanity, now that it is conscious, must consciously choose advance. That is the burden inherent in our gift of consciousness. There are no built-in guarantees that this time of great awakening will succeed. World history makes it abundantly clear that even as civilization as a whole has moved forward, individual societies have risen to great levels of learning and culture only to fall away into ignorance and depravity. We must be careful lest an overconfidence in evolution makes us apathetic about the very real perils we face. As Gopi Krishna warned,

Insensibility to the present grave crisis, even on the part of the learned, is a sign that the mental stasis that has occurred. A state of apathy toward acute problems of life is a prominent symptom of senescence. An attitude of this nature among intellectuals is fatal to the balanced and harmonious progress of the race.[239]

---

[238]Teilhard de Chardin, *The Phenomenon of Man*, 209–10.
[239]Krishna, Gopi, *Kundalini: Empowering Human Evolution*, 47.

Cayce seems to have been sensitized to the same concern, stating that " . . . It is not that which man does or leaves undone, but rather indifference toward the creation that makes or loses for the individual entity. Then let's be up and doing . . . "[240]

The rich soil of the earth requires gardeners to tend it. If we shrink from our opportunity now to be "up and doing," sinking instead into the morass of apathy and indifference, evolution itself will not stop; another race may rise to carry on the task at some distant point in the future. Even if we destroy the Earth, another set of gardeners may carry on in another corner of the manifest universe. But what would that say about us as human souls and the opportunity we have squandered? As one Cayce reading reminds us,

> . . . Remember, God hath delivered to thee—as to every other soul—that as pertaineth to heaven, to earth and to hell. What do we do with it? It depends upon the spirit ye entertain, for ye become co-creators with the Father—in bringing what? in the earth.[241]

From this reading and others like it, we are reminded that we would do well to remember to keep the "co" in our concept of what it means to be a co-creator. We turn to that topic next.

---

[240]3744-4
[241]2602-3

Chapter 16:
Keeping the "Co" in "Co-Creator"

> . . . For thy pattern is set and ye are a free-willed soul. Ye may either use or abuse the privileges given to thee. From whence? The source of all life, and life in every form—whether it be in the vapor, the chemical motivative force as accredited to the vegetable, mineral or even the animal kingdom—is of one source, God. Make thyself, then, put thyself, be thyself, in companionship with Creative Forces. For the purpose is that each soul should be a co-creator with God.   4047-2

> The moment God is figured out with neat lines and definitions, we are no longer dealing with God. We are dealing with somebody we made up.
>
> Rob Bell*

I come to this chapter with a certain amount of trepidation. On one hand, it seems to me audacious to imagine that *we* are the creators or evolvers of our world, independent of an underlying divine intention and presence that is greater than we are. I am convinced that the Cayce material is correct in asserting that we are *co*-creators with God. But on the other hand, I am increasingly unsure of just who or what God *is*. How can we even talk meaningfully about the great mystery that has been given the name God, let alone understand what it means to "co–create" with this God? To make matters even more complex, Cayce moves with shocking ease from sophisticated–sounding references to God as "Creative Force" to mythic–sounding references to God as a loving Father. What are we to make of this?

It is important for me to come clean at the outset and admit that the older I get, the less I know about God and the farther away the comfortable God of my youth becomes. I find that alternately frightening and encouraging. It encourages me because it suggests that my concept of God is probably evolving; and evolution of understanding, just like evolution of consciousness, values, love, and will, is a hard-

---

*Rob Bell, *Velvet Elvis: Repainting the Christian Faith* (Grand Rapids: Zondervan, 2005), 25.

won prize. Old understandings are hard to shake, and when they are shaken, it can be even worse; for when the God you once believed in becomes unbelievable, it's very tempting to reject all theism. The time between letting go of an understanding that you no longer find supportable and the gelling of a new understanding can feel pretty lonely and disorienting. Usually it feels like a leap into nothingness, and that is frightening.

I find a further complicating factor in my attempt to tease out the Cayce readings' perspective on co-creation arising from the fact that as my understanding of God continues to change over time, it becomes increasingly difficult to describe in words. Nonetheless, we must use words in any discourse aimed at examining just who or what it is that we are to co-create with. There is no getting around the fact that whenever we consider "co-"doing anything, we are talking about relationship with *someone*. In essence, therefore, it comes down to the question of whether we co-create in relationship *to* impersonal force or in relationship *with* a personal presence in our lives. This will be the locus of this inquiry, with special attention given to the question of whether there is room for a personal God in the path of the evolutionary. First, however, I want to be very clear that when I make a case for God having personal attributes I am not suggesting that God is anything like what I have come to call the "Santa Claus God."

The Santa Claus God

The Christmas when I was five years old, Santa Claus brought me a baby doll that I loved with a passion for the remainder of my childhood. All of the girls that year wanted a Tiny Tears doll, and I was no exception. (There had been quite an advertising blitz that year!) On Christmas morning, the doll I found under the tree was not Tiny Tears, but when I looked into her beautiful blue eyes, it was love at first sight. I named her Nancy. How could I have been so silly as to have thought I wanted a Tiny Tears? Nancy was superior to Tiny Tears in every way. Santa knew best. Santa knew me better than I knew myself. You see, Santa was God.

This isn't simply a construction I place on those events as I look back. It is an accurate description of what I believed at that time. I distinctly remember when I'd reached that conclusion during a conversation with my mother earlier that year. I was asking her questions about God and Jesus. They dealt with things about whether they knew what we were thinking and what we did or questions about where they were and where they came from. As I tried to digest my mother's answers and relate it to something I understood, I said, "Then God is just like Santa Claus!" I could sense that my epiphany caused Mom some distress; I could feel the discomfort that exuded from her as she tried to tell me that Santa wasn't like God. Poor Mom! I think she felt that she had somehow blundered and unintentionally given me ideas that were not properly reverent. But as I pressed my point about all of the matching characteristics between the two, she couldn't really explain to me how God and Santa were not the same. So I held to my conviction. I loved Santa dearly and my child's mind saw no dishonor to God in allowing Santa into the ranks of the divine. But—to borrow from the New Testament—"When I was a child, I talked like a child, I thought like a child, I reasoned like a child. When I became [an adult], I put childish ways behind me."[242] Or did I?

Like many theists, I outgrew the most blatantly childish version of the Santa Claus God as a natural consequence of maturity. But to shed the vestiges of the Santa Claus God is the work of a lifetime, and most of us, if we believe in a personal God at all, would do well to remain alert to signs of a lingering, covert belief in the Santa Claus God. A God who is nothing more than a superperson, one who provides both the goodies and the punishments of life, one who is "out there" somewhere, at the heavenly equivalent of the North Pole—all of these concepts can exert a subtle influence on our thinking long after we have outgrown the old man in the sky with a beard. Of course God doesn't have a body, but He's still the one making everything happen "down here." God is everywhere—unless, of course, you are talking about that particularly obnoxious person next door or someone who is "unsaved." God doesn't cause earthquakes and floods, because He loves us—but when a storm blows out to sea or a loved one recovers from a dire illness, God is so good to us! Even long after our views of God have matured beyond childhood, they may still have a long way to go be-

[242] I Corinthians 13:11

fore they have fully grown beyond assumptions that are rooted in mythic childhood characterizations. These assumptions often operate at the stealth level, until some life crisis in which "God" lets us down catalyzes either a leap forward in our understanding or the abandonment of belief in God altogether. A number of years ago, I was talking to someone very dear to me who had just endured another heartbreak in a string of deep disappointments. In her pain and anger over it all, she vehemently declared, "I don't believe in God anymore." It was then that I first found myself talking about the Santa Claus God, doing my best to make a case that it was not God she no longer believed in, but rather her *concept of God* as someone who was pulling the strings in her life, causing things to go well or poorly, blessing or cursing her by turns.

A child believes that Santa lives at the North Pole, makes all the toys, and somehow gets to the house of every child on Christmas Eve. In earliest years, there is no reason to question such an idea. Then, for most children, the first chink in the story comes when they really think about that trip around the world. That's just not possible for one person to do! Then we learn about time zones and figure, okay, Santa still might make it around the world if night lasts *that* long. We use our growing knowledge of the world to shore up our crumbling faith in Santa. Then comes the day when the jig is up. We know too much; our rational understanding has finally outstripped the ardent desire to believe. For me it came the day I found the carton from a doll house I'd received the previous Christmas in my father's closet. Our Santa toys were never wrapped or in manufacturers' cartons because of course the elves would not put their handiwork in a box that says "Mattel" on it. But here was a manufacturer's box. The elves hadn't made my dollhouse after all. The presence of that box forced me to face what I had willfully refused to see as long as I could find any rationalization for Santa's existence. From that one realization of "this cannot be," the whole myth came tumbling down. Santa took the Easter Bunny with him.

Oddly enough, many people's thinking about God only progresses to a stage roughly analogous to the time zones rationalization about Santa's midnight trip around the world. Then when they find their equivalent of that dollhouse box—maybe incontrovertible evidence that God did not create the world in six days 6,000 years ago, maybe the realization that it's totally illogical to think that God causes all the blessings in life but is somehow off the hook when bad things happen, maybe just a maturing intellect that finds the mythic God no longer supportable—a crisis of belief sets in. No wonder so many people give up believing in God entirely. When their knowledge and understanding grow up—about science, about human nature, about history—in short, when their understanding about life matures—if the concept of God stays rooted in childhood, the straw man comes tumbling down and theism is no longer tenable for the adult intellect.

Worse yet, the Santa Claus God has a decidedly dark side. The benevolent old gent who brought me Nancy also makes his list and checks it twice. He knows who's naughty and he knows who's nice. And he leaves coal in the stockings of those who are not good. To co-create with the Santa Claus God can degenerate into being the helping elves who deliver that coal. Think fundamentalists of every stripe, from those who fly airplanes into skyscrapers to those who bomb abortion clinics. Historically, belief in the Santa Claus God was behind the inquisition and centuries of witch burnings, hangings, and duckings. To this day, most of those who reject science do so in service to the Santa Claus God. Understandably then, the Santa Claus God is a distinct liability from the evolutionary perspective.

Yet, must we abandon all notions of a personal God? There are countless other childhood beliefs we grow beyond as our understanding grows, but we don't throw the baby out with the bath water. Many young children think that television involves little people inside the box. We don't say "I don't believe in TV anymore" just because we come to realize there are no little people in there. As children we may have thought that the sun and moon were traveling around the earth, or maybe even following us. We didn't decide that the sun and moon have let us down or have no relevance to us anymore just because we discover they don't revolve around us. Yet thinking adults repeatedly do the equivalent with respect to God.

To be aware that your *concept* of God is woefully inadequate to the *reality* of God does not require the abandonment of all theism, nor does it require relegating God to the category of the strictly impersonal. It does, however, require willingness to leave our concepts open to ongoing growth. Any time we find ourselves falling into the trap of making God in our own image, we would do well to remember just how great is the distance between our currently limited consciousness and the ineffable consciousness that is God. My favorite treatment of this point comes from a fictional dialog written simply enough for a child to understand: In the Narnia novel *Prince Caspian*, when Lucy returns to Narnia after having been back in our world for a year, she meets the leonine Christ-figure Aslan, who had been the principal character in her earlier adventure into Narnia. As she hugs him, Lucy says, "Aslan, you're bigger." Aslan replies, "That is because you are older, little one." At first Lucy is confused and asks, "Not because you are?" "I am not," Aslan explains, "But every year you grow, you will find me bigger."[243] We, too, as we grow in consciousness and in understanding, should expect our notions of God to grow.

And with each increment that God grows beyond our previous understandings, more is required of us. It might seem counterintuitive, but the more our concept of God expands, the greater our co-creative responsibility becomes. This is because we realize that things we once blamed on God are our own problems to rectify and things we expected the Santa Claus God to do are just not going to happen unless we step up to the plate.

Stepping Up to the Plate

Andrew Cohen, one of the leading voices for the contemporary evolutionary movement, says in his book *Evolutionary Enlightenment*, "Throughout history, when we've been in need, we've prayed to God for help. But now, at the beginning of the twenty-first century, God needs *our* help."[244] Wow. Even though I thought I'd outgrown the Santa Claus God years ago, this statement really set me back on my heels. It was like being confronted with a cosmic-proportion case of having to take care of the parent you once relied upon to take care of you! I have to admit that Cohen's statement triggered resentful thoughts, ones that

---

[243]C.S. Lewis, *Prince Caspian* (New York: HarperCollins, 1951), 141.

[244]Andrew Cohen, *Evolutionary Enlightenment: A New Path to Spiritual Awakening* (New York: SelectBooks, 2011), 48.

revealed vestiges of the Santa Claus God lurking in the recesses of my unconscious. Things like, "God started this mess and now we're stuck with cleaning it up?" Or, "It seems to me that if God wanted to experience manifest form, God could have come up with a less painful way of going about it." Of course, I could just reject outright the premise that God needs me. The problem is that Cohen's statement is unavoidably true. We are the proverbial hands and feet of God. Without flesh-and-blood delivery systems, God's love becomes a mere abstraction in many cases. And although Cayce might not have put it as bluntly, certainly his readings would agree that great responsibility rests with us; they are replete with exhortations to manifest God's love in the earth. The overarching purpose specified in the readings for the work to carry on the Cayce legacy appears over the doors of the A.R.E. Library and Conference Center so that all who enter may see it: " . . . To make manifest the love of God and man . . . "[245]

To reject the claim that God needs us as much as we need God is to retrench in some version of the Santa Claus God, one who is supposed to take care of us in our helplessness, rather than move onward to mature partnership with the forces of the divine in this world. But is this a one-way street? When we agree to "help" God, does God bring anything to the table? Can we call on God for help as well? Once we have left the Santa Claus God behind, is God even a "someone" anymore, someone upon whom we can call, or are we on our own? The position of the Cayce readings on this point is reassuringly clear:

> . . . The startling thing to every soul is to awaken to the realization that it is indeed a child of God! That is startling enough for any man, any woman, any being, in this sin-sick world! And yet it is the heritage of every soul to awake to that consciousness that God indeed is mindful of the children of men, and calls ever, "If ye will be my children, I will be thy God." This is the message, then, that you shall carry; for there is a loving Father that cares. That is thy message![246]

---

[245]254–42
[246]254–95

After all that has just gone before concerning the Santa Claus God, what are we to do with this reading and countless others like it that use the "Father God" metaphor? Is there any way to defend this terminology against charges of blatant anthropomorphism? I think we can, but first I must emphasize that this *was* a metaphor—used perhaps as a point of interface with the religious culture of Cayce's time—because I don't think anyone who knows the overall content of these readings would seriously think that they were putting forth a God who is a kindly old father "out there" somewhere. Rather, it was central in the Cayce material to assert that the same God–force that created individual souls out of a desire for companionship continues to extend the personal attribute of care toward each of us. God is "mindful" of us, the readings say in numerous places; and even if such caring and mindfulness in Creative Force itself is beyond the grasp of our three-dimensional minds, we can use the metaphor of a loving progenitor who is ready to nurture, guide, encourage, and love us. In fact, this point is so central in the Cayce work that the folly of attempting to work independently of God is repeatedly brought out in readings like this one:

> And the abilities are here to accomplish whatever the entity would choose to set its mind to, so long as the entity trusts not in the might of self, but in His grace, His power, His might. Be mindful ever of that, in thy understanding in thy own wisdom, much may be accomplished; but be rather thou the channel through which He, God, the Father, may manifest His power—in whatever may be the chosen activity of the entity.[247]

This is consistent with the reading, used in the epigraph for this chapter, which says that our free will is a privilege that comes from God, the one source of all life, and that we should put ourselves in "companionship" with the Creative Forces. And therein lies the great mystery whereby God is personal enough to be companionable with and yet (as described in this reading) is also the same impersonal life force found throughout the cosmos from vapor to mineral to plant to animal manifestations.

---

[247]3183-1

The Impersonal Personal God

From the perspective of the Cayce readings, there is an intensely personal aspect to the Ultimate Reality that is also characterized as Creative Force. It's hard to wrap our minds around that without reverting to mythic, "daddy in the sky" concepts of God, so it's often easier just to favor the nonpersonal concept and use terms like "the Universe," the "All in all," "the Ground of Being," "Creative Energy" or "Creative Force" if we want to talk about the God factor in evolution. But even if we favor these nonpersonal terms, we still need to keep in mind that *every* description of God is ultimately a metaphor. "Creative energy of the universe" is admittedly less anthropomorphic than "God the Father," yet when I think of God as Creative Energy (which I often do), if I carefully examine what's going on in my mind, I find images of swirling nebulae and stars and planets. Only a moment's reflection will tell me that these celestial bodies are not God. They, too, end up to be merely metaphors—my mind's way of representing an incomprehensible, unknowable Ultimate Reality.

If you think carefully about your preferred nomenclature, you are bound to discover the same thing—concrete images hiding underneath even the least mythic descriptions of God. I am reminded of C.S. Lewis telling about a friend whose parents, in an effort to avoid mythic, anthropomorphic images of God, taught her that God was "perfect substance." The problem, however, was that in this child's mind "perfect substance" never failed to conjure up images of a sea of tapioca pudding, something she greatly disliked![248] I am not in any way denigrating or quarreling with these alternative metaphors for God. They are certainly more sophisticated than the concepts of God that we may have left behind in childhood. The point rather is that all metaphors for God have their inherent limitations, yet we must use them if we are to think or speak of God at all. Nor does the fact that all personal metaphors for God are severely limited mean that God does not have personhood.

Even a casual look at biological life will show us that the personal dimension grows rather than diminishes as life forms complexify. A

---

[248]C.S. Lewis, *Miracles* (New York, Macmillan, 1947), 90.

plant has less "personhood" than a jellyfish; the jellyfish has less
personhood than the cat that right now purrs in my lap; and (although he might not agree with this), the cat has less personhood
than I do. Why should we expect the progression to reverse when it
comes to the leap from human to God? My cat may not be able to
imagine the inner world of my mind, and for all I know he makes the
reductionistic error of thinking I'm a large, rather strange-looking version of his own kind. But even if that is the case, the cat's failure to
conceive of a personhood beyond whatever his own inner world may
hold does not make me any less a person. Just as my greater consciousness gives me more personhood than my cat may be able to
comprehend, it is reasonable to expect that God, as ultimate consciousness, is more, rather than less, personal than we are, our inability to
conceive of *how* God has personhood notwithstanding.

The challenge is to somehow incorporate a view of God that includes personal attributes with one that allows God to be the unimaginable, undefinable Ultimate Reality. While we may be far from
wrapping this conundrum up in a neat package, some elucidation of
this point comes in Cayce's response to questioner 1185 (to use her i.d.
number) who asked whether, in praying, we were to address " . . . our
own I Am Presence as our All-knowing God-Self . . . " The response
began by saying "It is that Presence. But there is confusion here," and
then went on to explain where the confusion lay: "The I Am Presence,
that is all-knowing within self . . . must be motivated *by* the Father,
God . . . " By way of further explanation, the reading likened the relationship between our inner *"I Am Presence"* and God to the way that
Jesus said he was "in the Father."[249] Clearly, then, the inner "I am" presence is not identical with God, for it needs "motivation" by "the Father"
in order to be effective in prayer. This is reminiscent of Jesus saying, "I
do not speak on my own authority. Rather, it is the Father, living in
me, who is doing his work."[250] It is also the same idea we looked at in
Chapter 6, when exploring how the inner "I am" is an expression of
the universal "I am" without being the *totality* of God and again in
Chapter 9, when we considered how we can know ourselves to be one

---

[249]1158–12
[250]John 14:10

with the whole and yet not the whole.

Cayce, at least, was clear that prayer involves more than simply our own "I am" presence. But Mrs. 1158 apparently still did not have the clarity she sought, for her next question was, "If God is impersonal force or energy—" She didn't even get to finish her question. The response interrupted her with, "He *is* impersonal; but as has just been given, so *very* personal! It is not that ye deal only with *impersonal*—it is *within and without!* It is *in* and *without*, and only as God *quickeneth* the spirit within, by the use, by the application of the God-force within to mete it out to others . . . [does prayer take effect]." Now if you find this response less than elucidating, so did Mrs. 1158, for she went on to ask how God could know the personal needs of his countless children and work to fill those needs. Notice the familiar signs of the Santa Claus God influencing the assumptions behind this question. To her, as to many people, "personal God" equaled "exterior God who is out there listening and dispensing answers to prayer." In response, the reading attempts to redirect her to a different understanding of God's personhood, first by pointing to God's presence everywhere as the spirit of life and then saying:

> . . . As the spirit of same [life] is manifested in the body, it becomes not only in the *personal* manner and way the supplying influence but that as from without, by "Seek and ye shall find," by attuning to same just as ye would attune thy radio to the *great station* of life and God Himself! It supplies and pours out to those that seek—seek— to know His ways![251]

The universal, impersonal life-force that is God "pours out" into personal manifestation in direct response to our seeking. It's almost as if God's personhood grows as God becomes personal to us and within us. We find a very similar idea in the writings of Teilhard de Chardin, who said that "The only universe capable of containing the human person is an irreversibly 'personalizing' universe."[252] As the "floating, universal entity from which all emerges and into which all falls back

---

[251]1185-12

[252]Teilhard de Chardin, *The Phenomenon of Man*, 290.

as into an ocean, God is impersonal," he says. But it is also true that consciousness is becoming self-aware in the process of evolution, and with growth of self-awareness comes movement in the direction of greater personalization.[253]

In considering these very similar points from Cayce and Teilhard de Chardin, one subtle but very important point should be kept in mind. They are not saying that God's personhood is nothing more than our collective personhood. Remember, Cayce speaks of us needing "motivation" from the Father God and suggests that we are like radios that must tune to the "Great Station" that is life itself. Teilhard de Chardin says that the personal and the universal grow in the same direction and culminate in each other. The personhood of God is the product of a relational dance between impersonal and personal, universal and individual, being and becoming.

We might say that God becomes personal in the very act of creation. Here is why: As the Something beyond all time, space, and manifestation, God is beyond attributes and descriptors. Logically there is no personal quality to that which is beyond all qualifiers. This is the impersonal God. But in bringing forth focal points of consciousness (that would be us) and in manifesting a world of form, God takes on attributes and becomes personal—personal in the sense that aspects of God's own totality now have consciousness that can be relational to one another and to the Whole of which they are a part. The Cayce readings took the thought-provoking position that the very fact that we have consciousness in a material plane is " . . . proof of a loving Father-God being aware of the entity's abilities, possibilities, virtues and faults."[254] Elsewhere we read, " . . . The entity should realize that the fact that it is aware, or is conscious of itself in material experience, is proof that the universal consciousness, or God, is aware of the entity and has need of the entity . . . "[255] We might rephrase this by saying that the very existence of focalized points of relational consciousness within God makes God relational to all centers of consciousness within God and to the totality of God's manifestation. This is how Teilhard de

---

[253]*Ibid*, 260–61.

[254]2905–3

[255]5343–1

Chardin could call God "hyper-personal" and could describe God as the "source of love and the object of love" "at the summit of the world above our heads."[256]

How could it be otherwise, if we are truly to co-create with God? Could a God without personal attributes respond to us? Would it even be possible to partner with a thing? How could we actively co-create with an impersonal force that has no cognizance of us personally? Without falling into anthropomorphic Santa Claus God images, we might say that the universe itself is kindly disposed toward us and eager to partner its creative-evolutionary drive with our own creative-evolutionary capacities. Thus, when we come to recognize our own evolutionary impulse, our first choice is whether to accept that partnership.

Partnering With the Divine

So great is our co-creative capacity, according to the Cayce source, that we " . . . are a part of the controlling influence of the universe . . . "[257] And because we have free will, we can create in alignment with God or we can create in opposition to God. " . . . For ye live, ye move, ye have thy being from the spirit of truth. Yet the will of an entity is either the co-creator with the Creative Forces (or God) or in opposition to such in a material world."[258] The choice is ours and the stakes are high, if current world conditions are any indication. How can we afford not to align our creative power with that of God? More to the point, once having arrived at this conclusion, how do we bring such alignment about? While there is much room for caution here (after all, there are few things more frightening than a person convinced that he is carrying out God's will) and we should be skeptical of formulaic answers, we can start with relationship as the foundation of the co-creative partnership, for to be in a co-creative state is to be drawn into relationship with God.

In all relationships, communication is the key, and this is certainly

---

[256]Teilhard de Chardin, *The Phenomenon of Man*, 266.

[257]2560-1

[258]3412-2

true of our co-creative relationship with God. Learning the art of communication with the divine is essential to the evolutionary path
mapped out in the Cayce material. Again, we come up against the
dilemma of how to think and speak meaningfully about such communication without invoking images of a daddy-God in the sky; yet
there is no mistaking the readings' position that such communication
is our birthright. " . . . Fear not to speak oft with thy God. BE on
speaking terms with thy Father."[259] Great intimacy is implied by exhortations to " . . . speak oft with thy Lord as ye would speak to thy
brother . . . "[260] In developing and maintaining a relationship that directs our co-creative capacities, the motivational tone is not to be one
of narcissistic focus on self, but rather empowerment for service. "Then,
speak oft with thy Maker. And let thine meditation be: Lord, use thou
me in that way, in that manner, that I—as thy son, they servant, may
be of the greater service to my fellow man . . . "[261]

Perhaps most mind-boggling of all, we can actually put ourselves
under divine mentorship as we learn to cultivate the relationship with
God within our own beings. One questioner asked in his reading
whether his current guru would remain his teacher or lead him to
another teacher. The reading's response was to advise him not to think
" . . . who will come from heaven that ye may have a message, or from
over the seas that ye should hear, for lo, it is within thine own heart,
apply it! Speak oft to thy Maker and in Him ye may find the light
within."[262] This advice to find God within rather than to seek external
oracles is a prominent theme in the Cayce material, which suggested
that the idea that we can find God within " . . . is as new today as it was
in the beginning of man's relationship or seeking to know the will of
God . . . " We are advised to "call on Him" within the inner self and to
know the body as " . . . the temple of the living God. There He has
promised to meet thee."[263]

If our educated, scientifically sophisticated minds are still challenged

[259]473-1
[260]3508-1
[261]440-8
[262]5265-1
[263]281-41

by such images of cozy, intimate chats with the Force behind the Big Bang, it is understandable. Even after the explanations given to our old friend Mrs. 1158, she was back nine days later with her original line of questioning, only to be told pretty much what she had been told the first time, that as God is active through us in the manifest realm, the divine takes on personal attributes:

> (Q) Is it correct when praying to think of God as impersonal force or energy, everywhere present; or as an intelligent listening mind, which is aware of every individual on earth and who intimately knows everyone's needs and how to meet them?
> (A) Both! For He is also the energies in the finite moving in material manifestation. He is also the Infinite, with the awareness. And thus as ye attune thy own consciousness, thy own awareness, the unfoldment of the presence within beareth witness with the presence without. And as the Son gave, "I and my Father are one," then ye come to know that ye and thy Father are one, as ye abide in Him.[264]

Admittedly this—the idea that God is the divine personal presence that both indwells and transcends us—while at the same time being the universal, impersonal energy that comprises all that is—is a paradox among paradoxes, a mystery within mysteries. Yet this is the very cornerstone of the co-creative relationship we have with God. As such, it is a paradox worth holding, a mystery worth plumbing. But perhaps this is best done not with the intellect alone. When the mind is challenged by concepts that reach beyond what we can easily incorporate into our finite, three-dimensional models, we can sometimes better enrich our understanding through the avenue of direct experience. Those who would like to pursue this further may find the questions and suggestions under "Opening to God's Presence," on page 264 helpful.

---

[264]1158-14

Opening to God's Presence

In the light of the concepts you have just been reading and thinking about in this chapter, spend some time reflecting and/or journaling on the questions below. Rather than feel that you have to cover every question, spend time with the ones that have the most relevance for you or the ones that stir the strongest feelings.

1. What does it feel like to think that God might need you as much as you need God?

2. What are the things you feel are needed most in the world right now, if we are to advance along the evolutionary trajectory?

3. Bearing in mind that God can only act in material ways through physical, material emissaries, how can you be God's way of meeting some of the needs you just enumerated?

4. How does it feel to think that it's up to us, and us only, to meet the challenges of our day (both personally and collectively)? How does it feel to think you are like a radio that can tune in to Godself in order to find strength and guidance?

5. What do you need from God in order to do your part?

6. In terms of your contribution to the evolutionary advance, where are you uncertain about which way to go? What kind of guidance would be helpful?

7. What does it feel like to think of God caring for you personally? When, if ever, have you experienced a sense that God does indeed care for you? When does God's care for you seem furthest away?

8. How has your concept of God grown and changed over the course of time? What did you once believe that you no longer believe? What do you now believe that you once didn't believe concerning God? In terms of a relationship with God, what have you lost

and what have you gained?

9. Is speaking with God a part of your life? If so, what are those conversations like? How do you feel as a result of having them? If speaking with God feels foreign to you, what thoughts or ideas make it seem so?

Regardless of your past habits of talking or not talking to God, make a commitment over the next few days to "speak oft with thy Lord as ye would speak to thy brother." You might take a few minutes before or after your meditation or use the time when you first wake up or just before you fall asleep at night. You might pause periodically throughout the day to do this. But whenever you do it, hold in mind a caring, mindful Presence as the One you are addressing. Let your heart dictate the content. It may revolve around some of the questions above or it may concern things going on in your life right now. Just notice what it's like to regularly open in this way to a personal God.

Perhaps the most extraordinary thing about the call to a co-creative relationship with God is the way it makes each and every one of us a potential agent of transformation. For when we are called into partnership with God, we align ourselves with the very forces that brought worlds into existence. Sounds magnificent, doesn't it? Yet how do we begin to exercise some formative influence on a process that seems to have a life of its own and a momentum that is moving at a velocity unknown to previous generations? How do we guard against grandiosity and inflation and choose humbly to undertake the enormous work before us? In the final two chapters of this book, we will explore these questions.

Chapter 17:
Living in Times of Uncertainty

Then, the Destiny of the Soul—as of all creation—is to be one with Him; continually growing, growing, for that association. What seeth man in nature? What seeth man in those influences that he becomes aware of? Change, ever; change, ever. Man hath termed this evolution, growth, life itself . . .   262-88

A great wind is blowing, and that gives you either imagination or a headache.   Catherine the Great*

*I*n 1933, during the depths of the Great Depression, Edgar Cayce was asked whether the world had entered the "great tribulation" prophesied in the biblical book of Revelation. Deflecting his questioner away from thoughts of historical apocalypse, Cayce responded that the great tribulation as well as lesser periods of tribulation are part of the experience of every soul and that they are the natural consequences of the influences we ourselves create in our world. Casting tribulations as times when both the "sphere" we live in and its microcosm—the individual soul—"readjust," the reading points us beyond perceived limitations in times of challenge by saying, " . . . Man may become, with the people of the universe, ruler of any of the various spheres through which the soul passes in its experiences . . . "[265] Unfortunately, there is no expansion on this fascinating allusion to "people of the universe," but we can at least infer from this statement that humanity is not the sole example of personhood in an evolving universe of many spheres. We are clearly part of something much bigger than our earthbound view would suggest. Continuing to point the questioner toward the best personal response to tribulations, the reading concluded that such are times to remember that we are corpuscles in the body of God and to be a "helpmeet" with God in bringing all into oneness. The advice is

---

*Retrieved from searchquotes.com.
[265]281-16

as timely today as it was then. It is a call to be agents of transformation rather than victims of challenging times.

Overwhelmed as we may feel at times when faced with the combined ecological, economic, political, sociological, and spiritual puzzles of our day, the very chaos we experience is a sure sign that an emergent possibility exists—that is, the potential exists for a whole new way of dealing with the human condition and something that we never could have expected can arise to address our problems. As we have already seen, it is the pattern of evolution for things to build to a point where the old system just cannot support any more incremental change and then either leap to a new level entirely or collapse to an earlier stage. The chaos that precedes creative emergence is understandably frightening because we can't predict just how things will play out. If we could, it would not be creative emergence. This means that there is no guarantee that we will make the leap to a new level; collapse to an earlier stage is also possible. We are, after all, free-willed beings and we are told in the readings that even God does not know what we will do with our opportunities.[266] Precisely because of this free will and the uncertainty it entails, the stakes are high. In the words of Teilhard de Chardin:

> Like sons who have grown up, like workers who have become "conscious," we are discovering that something is developing in the world by means of us, perhaps at our expense. And what is more serious still is that we have become aware that, in the great game that is being played, we are the players as well as being the cards and stakes. Nothing can go on if we leave the table. Neither can any power force us to remain.[267]

In this, our penultimate chapter, I bring these things out not to stir up fear, but to drive home just how needed *you* are. You—the one reading this right now—have a crucial role to play in our collective destiny. And despite the human tendency to try to retool old solutions for today's challenges—and the predictable despair when they no

---

[266]1402-2 and 257-113, for example

[267]Teilhard de Chardin, *The Phenomenon of Man*, 229.

longer work—the Cayce readings are clear that there is far more for us to embrace than there is to fear. Nowhere do we find Cayce suggesting that we are anywhere near the end of human beings' time on earth. Reminding us that the evolution which prepared conditions on this earth for the developmental needs of the human species took " . . . many thousands and millions of years . . . ," he predicts that such evolution will continue for " . . . hundreds and thousands of years to come . . . "[268] Whether the shift in language that counts past years in terms of millions and thousands but future years in terms of thousands and hundreds is deliberate and significant, I am not prepared to venture a guess. It is enough for now to think that we have many thousands of years to go, at the very least, before we see the end of this planetary age. The more important thing that remains to be seen is whether we will add our momentum to the inexorable forward-moving overall trajectory of evolution (thus expediting it) or resist (thus bringing on one of the recursive loops that are also a part of the evolutionary story). When we take this choice to heart, it becomes very clear that *now* is the time for us to answer the evolutionary call. It is a time to stop procrastinating and take responsibility *today* for bringing consciousness into our thoughts, our bodies, the world, and creation at large. It is time for us to embrace the unique opportunities of this incarnation and transcend our personal agendas in service to the whole, for time is speeding on.

Riding the Winds of Accelerating Change

If it seems as if everything is moving faster than it used to, you are not imagining things. Few would argue against the point that we are, indeed, living in times of accelerated change. In fact, it would be fair to say that we live in times of positively mind-blowing change. As we already saw in Chapter 2 when we were considering the longer view of time, the rate of change in human culture, industry, and technology is exponential. No wonder we find ourselves hurling into the future at speeds previously unimaginable.

Nowhere is this more apparent than in technology. I sit here writing

---

[268]3744-5

on a tablet device that weighs less than two pounds and can perform functions that I could never dream of when I wrote my first book—even though at the time I marveled at the wonders *that* computer could perform. To give some perspective on the acceleration that has brought us here, futurist Ray Kurzweil says that in the nineteenth century we saw more technological change than in the *nine centuries* preceding it. Then in the first twenty years of the twentieth century, we saw more advancement than in all of the nineteenth century. He estimates that the technological advance of the twenty-first century will be equivalent to 20,000 years of progress at today's rate of change. Because of this, he says, organizations have to be able to redefine themselves at a faster and faster pace.[269] This speaks volumes concerning the institutions, both public and private, that we form in order to pool our efforts and resources to do good in the world. Only those that are able to change dramatically with the times will remain effective and relevant.

As just one small example of the kind of advancement Kurzweil is talking about, the computer in your cell phone today is a million times cheaper, 1,000 times more powerful, and 100,000 times smaller than the computer at MIT in 1965. And it has more computer power than NASA had in 1969 when it first sent astronauts to the moon. As tempted as I am to list more of the amazing breakthrough developments in contemporary technology and compare them to those of just a few years back, the truth is that these marvels will most likely be outdated and possibly even quaint sounding by the time these words find their way into print and into your hands. (I use the word, *print*, loosely of course. Odds are there will be no ink or paper involved for many who are reading this book.) By the time my parents' generation was reluctantly learning to use email, my son's generation had stopped bothering to even look at it, preferring instead to text message. The currently popular "Did You Know?/Shift Happens" videos that periodically circulate on the Internet continue to need updating year after year as they take us on a dizzying trip through not only technological change, but demographic, educational, and sociological

---

[269]Ray Kuzweil and Christ Meyer, "Understanding the Accelerating Rate of Change," retrieved from Kurzweilai.net.

change as well. There is no point listing the factoids with which they
barrage us concerning social networking sites larger than most countries of the world, educational courses where things a student may
learn as a freshman are obsolete by graduation, and the proliferation
of careers in fields that didn't even exist a short while ago. There is no
point in listing them because, again, the information would be seriously out of date by the time this book sees the light of day. The one
thing not likely to be outdated any time soon is the assertion that a
condition of rapid change permeates our culture, our societal structures, our education, our public policies, our healthcare, and even our
spirituality.

There is little in our world that is immune from the rapid change
that characterizes this particular time in our evolution. In the words of
Clare Graves, upon whose work Spiral Dynamics is based:

> The present moment finds our society attempting to negotiate the
> most difficult, but at the same time the most exciting transition the
> human race has faced to date. It is not merely a transition to a new
> level of existence but the start of a new 'movement' in the symphony
> of human history.[270]

To the extent that we are called to participate in what Graves so
poetically calls the "new movement in the symphony of history," we
must both accept the fact of accelerated change and find ways to guide
its direction, for this is the essence of our evolutionary responsibility.
In this regard, Edgar Cayce was once asked how humankind's scientific advances, medical discoveries, and improving mode of living
prove that we are evolving here on earth as well as possibly on other
planes. The linkage between scientific advancement and humanity's
evolution, the reading explained, arises from the fact that these developments involve a growing understanding of and ability to apply
" . . . the laws of the Universe . . . "[271] Our lack of understanding the
scope of the laws we manipulate in our human inventions has led to

[270]As quoted in "The Never Ending Upward Quest," an interview with Dr. Don Beck
by Jessica Roemischer in the Fall–Winter, 2002 edition of *What is Enlightenment?* Retrieved from enlightennext.org.
[271]900-70

unintended negative consequences in the past, this reading goes on to say, thus emphasizing the need for a widening grasp of laws that apply across the domains of biological, cosmological, and spiritual evolution. This is perhaps the greatest challenge and opportunity of our age, for even as we feel caught in a whirlwind of change all around us, it is common for people to feel that we really aren't making much progress in the improvement of human nature. Is this an accurate assessment of our current state of affairs, or is there reason to believe that things are getting better?

Finding Progress in the Center of the Whirlwind

War, hunger, greed, and violence still characterize the human experience in so much of the world. So slow does our change appear to be when it comes to the things that really matter, it is not uncommon to hear people question whether evolution is really continuing within the human race at all. Such has been the lament for as long people have both grasped the vision of what humanity could be and seen what it is in actuality. I recently found myself chuckling at the following rant over our seeming lack of progress in the classic novel *Tristram Shandy* by Laurence Sterne. Though written two and a half centuries ago, it could well describe how many a despairing pessimist sizes things up in the early twenty-first century:

> Tell me, ye learned, shall we for ever be adding so much to the bulk—so little to the stock? Shall we for ever make new books, as apothecaries make new mixtures, by pouring only out of one vessel into another? Are we for ever to be twisting, and untwisting the same rope? For ever in the same track—for ever at the same pace? Shall we be destined to the days of eternity, on holy-days, as well as working-days, to be shewing the relicks of learning, as monks do the relicks of their saints—without working one—one single miracle with them? Who made Man, with powers which dart him from earth to heaven in a moment—that great, that most excellent, and most noble creature of the world—the miracle of nature, as Zoroaster in his book called him—the Shekinah of the divine presence, as Chrysostom—the image of God, as Moses—the ray of divinity, as

Plato—the marvel of marvels, as Aristotle—to go sneaking on at this pitiful—pimping—pettifogging rate?[272]

The archaic language and spelling may be a bit of a stumbling block to some readers, but that's part of the charm, too. It only drives home how very much things do change even when we think they are standing still. Sterne penned this passage in the mid-1700s, a time when slavery was an accepted norm, a time when children could be executed for stealing, a time when women did not yet have a modicum of say over their own lives, and children were often little more than chattel, a time when it was considered natural to fear or denigrate people whose skin, social class, or culture did not match yours. None of these conditions that were commonplace at the time of Sterne's lament seem to auger well for humanity's progress in fulfilling its glorious potential. Yet, with the benefit of hindsight we can see tremendous forward movement that is seldom apparent while it is happening. Sterne's time was also one of burgeoning rational and scientific inquiry which was already germinating into many desirable things: a potent antidote to the superstition that had fueled the Inquisition and the witch hunts, a spur to new experiments in political freedom, the foundation of medical research, a movement beyond parochial thinking that would in time bring the spiritual wisdom of the east and west together, and, eventually, the catalyst to an age of unprecedented sensitivity to human rights. Nor does the fact that we still have a long way to go in all of these areas negate how far we have come in comparison to conditions three centuries ago.

What unforeseen developments might arise from today's accelerated changes in the way we communicate and the tools we use to do it, from our exploration of the inner world of DNA and the outer world of deep space, and from the sheer genius that emerges when people are able to pool their wisdom in ways of undreamed of before the Internet? Witness the remarkable Foldit game, the brainchild of protein research scientist David Baker of the University of Washington. Baker theorized that the collective wisdom of video gamers tasked

---

[272]Laurence Sterne, (1759-1767, p. 159), *The Life and Opinions of Tristram Shandy, Gentleman*, e-book.

with manipulating models of protein structures (folding it in different ways) would outperform computer output on the same task. He was right. Foldit participants, ordinary people without scientific training, each working the protein puzzles on their own computers using the tools provided as part of an online game, successfully deciphered the structure of the protein in an enzyme in a virus that causes AIDS in monkeys and successfully improved the design of the protein in an enzyme used in synthetic chemistry. Because understanding the structure of a protein is important to understanding how it operates in the biological world, this work has implications for biological, medical, and environmental research. It is also an astounding example of how "crowdsourcing" (think "Ask the Audience" on "Who Wants to Be a Millionaire") can be a largely untapped source of innovation and problem-solving ability across the board.

Steven Johnson makes this same point in his book *Future Perfect: The Case for Progress in a Networked Age.* In it, he emphasizes that it is not the technology itself but the networking that the technology makes possible which will lead us to new ways of addressing the challenges before us. He also makes the point that there are many signs of progress in our world, our well-known problems notwithstanding. For example, in the United States the last two decades have shown dramatic decreases in crime, drunken driving, traffic deaths, teen pregnancies, per capita gasoline consumption, air pollution, and divorce rates as well as increases in life expectancy, wage equality between the sexes, college enrollment, and charitable giving. World poverty, though still a problem, has declined by 50 percent in the last fifty years even as the population doubled. While facing the specter of global warming and figuring out what to do about it, Johnson thinks we should also know that we have made great strides in cleaning up our water and air over the past few decades. The natural and widespread bias toward reporting the dramatic and the tragic skews our view of progress, Johnson maintains, and he points to a future where our connectivity will usher in new models for addressing our societal issues.

The fact that the winds of change are blowing all around us means that we live in times of possibility just as surely as we live in times of peril. Wherever we are running into the turmoil and chaos created by our past limitations and mistakes, that is precisely where we are positioned to make evolutionary strides forward. Think about it: Everything we see around us in the physical world evolved as an adaptation to needs imposed by conditions surrounding it. Wings, lungs, thumbs, and brains have all evolved to meet the challenges of survival. And there is usually a lot of trial and error before the adaptive fit is found. According to American theoretical physicist Sydney Dancoff's "Principle of Maximum Error," optimum development occurs when an organism makes the maximum number of mistakes consistent with survival. In other words, every failure up till now is part of what can make our success possible. Or, as the Cayce readings put it, " . . . You only fail if you quit trying . . . "[273]

So what will we do? What *can* we do? How do we take a theoretical framework like evolutionary spirituality and turn it into actual practices that will help build the forward-moving momentum? The remaining pages will explore some of the dimensions of a committed evolutionary path.

Chapter 18:
Agents of Transformation:
Being the Change You Seek

Thus the innate desire to be associated with those doing big things, things having to do with great movements of one nature or another. But remember, it is the tiniest cog that moves the greater machine, and each corpuscle of the body must be in accord with the divine . . .   3578-1

The richness of the world around us is due, in large part, to the miracle of self-organization. Unfortunately, our minds are bad at grasping these kinds of problems. We're accustomed to thinking in terms of centralized control, clear chains of command, the straightforward logic of cause and effect. But in huge, interconnected systems, where every player ultimately affects every other, our standard ways of thinking fall apart.

Steven H. Strogratz[*]

As we look around ourselves at a world in need, it is easy to feel too small, too insignificant, too flawed, too lacking in connections with those in power to truly make a difference. It is common for us to become paralyzed by our own lack of workable solutions. It is tempting to think that these are simply times of collective tribulation and to wait on the sidelines for the next big development before we take any definitive action. Yet this is precisely what we must not do, for we are part of the equation for what that next big development will be. According to Cayce, we all have " . . . individual force toward the great creation and its individual niche, place or unit to perform . . . "[274]

Notice how participation in the "great creation" is intrinsic to the purpose of each and every one of us. Living that purpose, this reading continues, will lead not only to our own development, but more importantly to the "development of the creation of the world." So it all

[*]Stephen H. Strogatz, (2012, p. 34), *Sync: How Order Emerges From Chaos in the Universe, Nature, and Daily Life*, e-book.
[274]3744-5

begins with each of us finding our place of leverage, discovering for ourselves what Cayce called our "individual niche, place or unit to perform." And although that may seem daunting at first, it is really not so hard to discern as we may imagine.

Recognizing Your Soul Purpose

As a practicing life coach and hypnotherapist (and from personal experience as well, I might add!), I am convinced that not living one's soul purpose is the greatest single cause of all our anxiety, discontent, and depression. I am also convinced that the second greatest cause is not knowing what soul purpose is. Please note that I did not say our trouble comes from not knowing what *our* soul purpose is; it comes from not knowing what soul purpose in general is, and as a result missing the opportunity to live it every day. This is a crucially important distinction for anyone called to the evolutionary path of the co-creator. We can all know our purpose, here, now—despite the fact that, from the number of books and courses that promise to help us find our soul purpose, it would seem to be quite a complex mystery to unravel. I see this all the time when people come to me to do hypnotic work in the expectation that their purpose will be revealed in a past-life regression or some other form of communication with the unconscious mind. People seem to be looking for that "aha!" moment when they can say, "So *that's* what I'm supposed to do!" And until that happens, many well-intentioned people find themselves in "spiritual purpose limbo."

The problem is that many of us, in wanting to discover our soul purpose, make the mistake of leaping to the most grand—and therefore most out-of-reach—possibilities first. Maybe we're to write a great book that awakens spiritual consciousness in thousands of people. Or maybe there is some mission we are called to do, working among those who are sick or in poverty or who lack education—who hasn't read those inspirational stories about the one person whose great idea turned into a thriving charitable organization and felt like a slacker by comparison? Maybe we're supposed to take in foster children or become a skilled counselor who works with the addicted or the abused. Maybe the gift of healing is hidden away inside of us, if only we could figure out how to bring it out. Or maybe we have absolutely no idea what we are called to do, despite being tormented with the idea that we *must* do our soul's mission. If any of these situations reminds you of your own inner dilemma as you to try to imagine what it might mean to fulfill your evolutionary purpose, you may be asking the wrong question.

The confusion comes from the fact that soul purpose has meaning simultaneously on three levels: First, we all share a common cosmological purpose; second, we each have a unique place to fill within that purpose; and third, we have a purpose each day that entails aligning our choices, priorities, and behaviors with the highest evolutionary vision we hold. All too often we zero in on the second aspect of soul purpose, thinking it's all about the specific work we will do. We want to solve the puzzle of where we'll go when we get out of bed in the morning and how we will answer the question, "What do you do?" at a social gathering. We can become locked in on answering that one aspect of soul purpose, essentially paralyzing ourselves when it comes to fruitfully living aspects one and three. This emphasis has it all backward. Unless you're already clearly drawn to a particular life's work, it will usually be fruitless to try to discern your one, true life purpose from a place of standstill in your life. For unless we first cultivate the ability to follow the leading of our inner, deeper Self in small, everyday situations, we have little reason to expect that "the" answer will come as a shining moment of revelation. As one Cayce reading expresses it:

> . . . Not some great deed or act, or speech, but line upon line, precept upon precept, here a little, there a little. Not as sounding of trumpets as to what is being accomplished, but in the quiet of thine own conscience lay the plans for that that may be accomplished and in the acts day by day so build that as conforms to *His* way.[275]

The evolutionary path of the co–creator calls us to do *now* the things we already know to do. Many of these things are familiar themes from

---

[275]257–78

earlier chapters: awakening to the true Self as we come out from under successive layers of false ego-self, fostering deepened consciousness of the "I Am" core within us through meditation, embracing the
world of manifestation as the arena of co-creation, seeing in our own
growing edges the evolutionary needs of humanity and therefore doing the work of self-transcendence, exercising will and expanding in
love. Of course we find these daily, ongoing efforts challenging, because they all require us to buck the tide of what we're used to calling
"human nature." Theosophist C.W. Leadbeater does not mince any
words in describing just how demanding such a path can be:

> He who wishes to reform the world must first of all reform himself.
> He must learn to give up altogether the attitude of insisting upon
> rights, and must devote himself utterly to the most earnest
> performance of his duties. He must learn to regard every connection
> with his fellow-man as an opportunity to help that fellow-man, or in
> some way to do him good.[276]

The biggest pitfall in the quest for life purpose is the inclination to
put off implementing a purposeful life until we have the whole plan
laid out before us. Most of us already know far more than we are
applying in our lives, so there is no use waiting around for more
knowledge before we get started! For example, if you know it's important for you to meditate or volunteer at the hospital or spend thirty
minutes a day journaling and you are not doing it, then *start* doing it.
If you're interested in art or energy healing or physical fitness but you
can't quite see how that could organize itself into a life purpose—or
even whether your life purpose is to be found there—don't wait to
find out before you act on your interest. Start doing something with
that field now. Pick up a book, take a class, play around with it in your
free time, and see what comes next.

Look at time-wasters in your day (you know what these are!) and
fill that time with the things you know to do but have been putting
off. And if ever you are in doubt, get quiet and ask, "What should I do
now?" Let me be clear: this question is not about what you should do

---

[276]C.W. Leadbeater, *A Textbook of Theosophy*, 68.

next week, tomorrow, later on, or even an hour from now. It is the practice of asking, "What should I do in this very moment?" If you listen, the answer to that question will always be there. But then you have to follow it. In so doing, you will be learning to listen to that voice that will always lead you, one step at a time, in the direction of your unfolding purpose.

What small step might you take *right now* that would support the momentum of unfolding evolution in your own life? Your path will be as unique as you are, but there are some common elements arising from the Cayce advice to hundreds of individuals that may be helpful in bringing the evolutionary path down to the level of nuts-and-bolts daily living. These relate to aspect number three of soul purpose: aligning our everyday choices, priorities, and behaviors with the highest evolutionary vision that we hold. The ways to do this are many. What follows is not necessarily an exhaustive list, but it's a pretty good place to start.

Core Practices on the Path of the Co-creator

The following practices represent themes that run throughout the body of Cayce advice given to people from all walks of life and religious persuasions who sought to foster their own spiritual development and facilitate the spiritual awakening of the world. None of these is a onetime effort, but rather a way of life—a perspective through which to live the ins and outs of daily experience. For most of us, some will be more easily implemented than others. For all of us, establishing the ability to live these values with consistency is a lifelong effort. They are presented not as a litmus test of whether someone passes muster as a true evolutionary co-creator, but rather as a set of guidelines for anyone who wishes to live life according to an evolutionary ideal. As Samuel Johnson wrote, "Great works are performed not by strength, but by perseverance."

Selfless Service. One of the great challenges to the Cayce work, as it tried to find its niche in the blossoming New Age movement of the late twentieth century, came from the uncomfortable fact that the readings place great emphasis on selfless service rather than the bells and whistles of altered states of consciousness and paranormal experience:

"That which is so hard to be understood in the minds or the experiences of many is that the activities of a soul are for self-development, yet must be selfless in its activity for it, the soul, to develop.[277] In fact, the readings go so far as to say that unless our motivations are selfless, all of our mental and physical desires and purposes will eventually come to naught.[278] For many in the New Age marketplace, this stolid insistence on selflessness and unblinking scrutiny of one's ideals and purposes just lacks a certain sizzle. Statements such as the following can easily be experienced as downright put-off-ish:

> . . . This, then, is rather as the warning: First, as indicated, *find self.* Find what is self's ideal. And as to how high that ideal is. Does it consist of or pertain to materiality, or spirituality? Does it bespeak of self-development or selfless development for the glory of the ideal? And be sure that the ideal is rather of the spiritual.[279]

This somewhat jaundiced view of what often passes for spiritual development has not always won Cayce points in a New Age movement often criticized for its tendency toward narcissism. The readings' "Search for God" system of spiritual development is relatively long on the drudgery of keeping a tight rein on the impulses, rationalizations, and desires of the ego and short on more scintillating topics like esoteric mysteries. As a result, it has not been uncommon for people to think of this body of material as the ground floor—a kind of kindergarten level of spirituality that one leaves behind in order to pursue "deeper" material. "Others, not self"—a refrain that rings through the readings—is a tough thing to market. Yet nothing could be closer to the heart of the readings' view of spirituality, "For each entity, each soul, IS his brother's keeper!"[280] and "In any field of service where thy hands find work to do, serve . . . "[281]

Even those who received readings for health problems were not

---

[277]275-39

[278]633-5

[279]440-8

[280]189-3

[281]3292-1

exempt from the call to service. For example, in a reading given for a thirty-five-year-old man who had been bedridden with his illness for two years by the time he requested his health reading, the Cayce source outlined a detailed course of action that included massage, physical therapy, hydrotherapy, dietary changes, and vitamins—but not before he had identified attitude as the place where healing had to begin, explaining that " . . . each anatomical structure, each atom, each vibration of each organ, must be able to rebuild itself . . . and that such recuperation involved mind, purpose, and body. . . . Not as boastful, not as egotistical, but that each word, each act, each hope, each element of activity, is to be selfless and unto the glory of Creative Forces, or God."[282] The young man was promised that if he heeded this advice, he could look forward to " . . . many days yet of a useful service . . . " In giving healing advice to a young woman who suffered both physical and emotional ailments, he advised her to observe certain dietary, medicinal, and exercise regimens to restore her health, but then added pointedly that she needed to give more attention to the needs of other people " . . . for, as the body knows, it is not *all* of death to die, neither is it all of life *just* to live! but to be of a service to someone else is the *only* way that life is made to be such as to bring contentment, and to find the joy, the pleasure in living."[283] Possibly the readings' most pithy call for service above all else comes in this question asked of one supplicant: " . . . What need is there for a better body, save to serve thy fellow man the better? . . . "[284]

This is rough, brutal even, some may think. It is a hard-core, uncompromising take on what is asked of us as evolving beings. It is definitely not for the faint of heart or the lukewarm, nor is it the elementary level of the spiritual path. But those who choose to hold themselves to the standard of selfless service are promised great reward as well: " . . . For they that do good unto their neighbor lendeth to the Lord, and *he* will repay in those ways that bring peace, harmony and understanding in thine conscience . . . "[285]

[282]2994-1
[283]911-7
[284]1620-1
[285]262-67

Selfless service begins, of course, with compassion. But it needs action to make it real. The Victorian novelist Wilkie Collins could have been describing our own age when he said,

> In my experience, I have observed that people are oftener quick than not to feel a human compassion for others in distress. Also, that they mostly see plain enough what's hard and cruel and unfair on them in the governing of the country which they help to keep going. But once ask them to get on from sitting down and grumbling about it, to rising up and setting it right, and what do you find them? As helpless as a flock of sheep—that's what you find them.[286]

Yet we need not be helpless sheep. There are many forms that service can take. For some it may lead to a life of activism on behalf of those people or causes that awaken their compassion, bringing resources of time, skill, or money to address the need. "How much suffering there is!" exclaimed one reading. "And how happy those should be that have been called to a purposefulness in relieving suffering physically, and most of all in bringing and in giving hope to those who find life's pathway in the material world beset with shadows and doubts and false hopes."[287] The reading goes on to say that we are getting in the way of our own light when we let "the foibles of material things" interfere with our doing what we know to do.

Care for the environment is another way that we engage constructively in the ongoing creative evolutionary process. We can, of course, serve through financial support or active involvement in conservation groups, but we can also serve by exercising stewardship in our personal habits of consumption and disposal of wastes. One reading, well ahead of its day in environmental conscience, quotes " . . . Be thou fruitful and multiply; subdue the earth . . . " from the Genesis story of creation—and then adds the commentary, " . . . It didn't say abuse the earth or that therein, nor use for thine own aggrandizement; for only that that may be personally used from day to day is necessary . . . "[288]

---

[286]Wilkie Collins, *Man and Wife*, (1870, p. 397), e-book.

[287]254-79

[288]520-2

That principle alone, if applied conscientiously by enough people, could transform the course of human experience on this planet. That makes it deeply evolutionary.

Those closest to us are fitting recipients of our service as well. Many who read this will be fighting a sense of being overwhelmed in their lives just to care for small children, sick friends and neighbors, or aging parents as they hold down jobs and meet the demands of daily living. Those whose plates are already full to overflowing may take heart from the fact that Cayce most often advised people to serve right where they were, insisting that we can manifest the glory of the divine just by serving those we meet in our own little corner of the world.[289] "What service should I render to the world in this incarnation?" one questioner wanted to know. "Keep in that thought, in that purpose, in that way of aiding where and when the opportunity presents itself, by the kindnesses, by the encouraging and, as has ever been the principle, find the good and not the evil in the life of every individual."[290] Again and again we read the same advice. A seventy-two-year-old widow wanted to know how she could know and best fulfill her destiny. She was told to do what she knew to do in her daily contacts with those she met, " . . . just being gentle, just being kind, speaking well to those even though they be harsh in their attitude . . . " Like many of us, she apparently didn't think that was significant enough because she next asked "In what way can I best serve my fellow man?" "As given." was the succinct reply.[291] Attitudes such as kindness, hopefulness, patience, forbearance, and not finding fault with people were among the acts of service recommended in the readings. So were small kindnesses such as a smile or a cheery word, which points out that even little courtesies and favors done for others leave results in the lives of the recipients.[292]

Doing Your Part to Leverage the Collective Consciousness:
There is no reason for anyone—even those without the material means

---

[289]397-1

[290]4065-1

[291]851-2

[292]922-1, 2073-1, 705-1, 257-85

or the ability to be involved in external forms of activism—to feel
disempowered as an agent of transformation. For, as we've already
seen, consciousness itself is the leading edge of evolution, and every
one of us can work faithfully in that domain. No one could miss the
mark while heeding this advice from C.W. Leadbeater:

> Any person who habitually thinks pure, good and strong thoughts is
> utilizing for that purpose the higher part of his mental body—a part
> which is not used at all by the ordinary man, and is entirely
> undeveloped in him. Such an one is therefore a power for good in
> the world, and is being of great use to all those of his neighbours
> who are capable of any sort of response. For the vibration which he
> sends out tends to arouse a new and higher part of their mental
> bodies, and consequently to open before them altogether new
> fields of thought.[293]

In this regard, intercessory prayer is something that any one of us
can do. We sometimes have a tendency to devalue intercessory prayer
as a form of active service, saying things like, "I wish there was something I could do, but all I can do is pray for you" or "I don't have the
means to help with that problem in the world but at least I can pray"—
as if prayer is a poor substitute for really *doing* something. But in the
Cayce work intercessory prayer has always been treated as a major
avenue of service. Such prayer is not so much the petitioning of an
external God on behalf of another as it is the channeling of divine
healing energy to someone in need or some situation that could benefit from an infusion of healing light. As activism on the level of
thought, spirit, and energy, prayer is arguably one of the most important things we can do. From the standpoint of the Cayce readings, this
form of service is so valuable that we are called to "consecrate" ourselves to a dedicated time of prayer on a regular basis.[294]

Prayer, meditation, acts of service large and small—all of these facilitate our collective awakening and move us that much closer to new
ways of dealing with the challenges of our day. But as our thoughts

[293]C.W. Leadbeater, *A Textbook of Theosophy*, 34.
[294]281-20

soar to the grand possibilities of a new evolutionary advance and the opportunity we have to be quickeners of consciousness, it's equally important that we keep our feet on the ground and monitor how well we are living these principles in the nitty-gritty aspects of daily experience. After all, it is usually so much easier to see what needs to be done in the world and in other people's lives than it is in our own. In the following question-and-answer exchange from the readings, we can sense the latent inflation on the part of the questioner and feel an "ouch!" at the response he is given:

> (Q) What direction should I take to best serve humanity in getting rid of problems and healing the people, assisting them to adjust to life and get happiness out of earth life? (I am interested in God working through humanity in the earth-life.)
> (A) First live it thyself and then ye are shown the way. It is not by might or power but day by day living. For as He gave, sufficient unto the day is the evil thereof. Do the first things first. Get *self* right before ye attempt to tell others.[295]

Perhaps the greatest vulnerability of the evolutionary path comes in the all-too-human tendency to fall a bit short on living it ourselves and really getting ourselves right before telling others. As one presuming to write a book on the topic, I know that I have had to repeatedly bring myself up short and remind myself to put first things first. That pesky bit about practical application is what trips us up every time! Fortunately, there are some additional helps to be found among the core practices of the evolutionary path.

Balanced Lifestyle: Edgar Cayce was a great proponent of what he called "balance." Balance between work and play, balance among physical, mental, and spiritual pursuits, and balance between inner life and outer expression were all part of the holistically balanced lifestyle recommended in the readings that Cayce gave for countless people. Today this lifestyle is often called "integral" because it integrates the various departments of life into a coordinated whole. Proponents of modern integral practice tell us that there is a synergy that

---

[295]3308-1

comes from attending to the various dimensions of life such as health, spirituality, and service simultaneously and that this synergy brings enhanced results across the board. In other words, your meditation is helped by your health and fitness efforts and vice versa and both have a synergistic relationship with acts of service or creative breakthrough. For students of the Cayce readings this will not be a novel approach, as the readings' insistence on maintenance of multiple practices across a variety of life categories has long been both an inspiration and a challenge for those wishing to adopt the lifestyle recommended in the readings.

That so-called "balanced lifestyle" can be quite a juggling act. Exercise, good diet, meditation, acts of service, civic responsibility, helpfulness to family and friends—these all go hand in hand if one is serious about following the program for growth outlined in the readings. As we've already seen, it's not enough to meditate your heart out, if you are not applying spiritual law to your daily actions. It's not enough to be a stickler for proper nutrition and exercise and care of the body, if you miss the spiritual components of good health or have no purpose beyond yourself.

The readings have always encouraged integral practice and one of the Cayce work's greatest contributions to integralism may be the ideals chart (see Figure 4), which is an integral practice map par excellence. It applies to disparate life areas; it addresses interior realities such as attitudes and emotions as well as exterior realities such as actions and behaviors; and it involves body, mind, and spirit in an integrated whole.

As Figure 4 illustrates, the spiritual ideal is the central value from which all of our intentions are derived. It is the shaping influence of everything we do. (For a refresher on ideals see Chapter 13) In this example, "Being an agent of transformation" is the spiritual ideal. The next circle outward from the center of the chart represents mental ideals. Entries at this level describe the attitudes and emotions we wish to cultivate, as well as the things we may want to build with the creative power of the mind, as is sometimes done with creative visualization. Mental ideals are set with respect to particular life areas. The life areas in our example include "spiritual development," "service work," "family and friends," "recreation," and "care of body." Notice that

Ideals as an Integral Practice Map

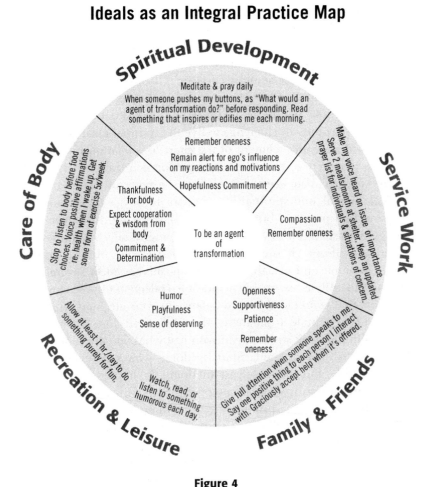

Figure 4

the same mental ideal may be appropriate for more than one life area, such as our example shows with "remember oneness" applying to spiritual development, service work, and personal relationships. The outermost ring represents behaviors and concrete things we will do to manifest the spiritual and mental ideals. These ideals are "physical" because they move our intentions from the internal world of thought and intention to the external world of action. Here again, the same physical ideal (behavior) may apply to more than one life area. In our example, the discipline of prayer shows up as a behavior in both the spiritual development and service work aspects of life.

Do remember that these illustrations are just examples. The specific life areas addressed will be most effective if they are personalized to the user and changed as life priorities change. For example, someone might include "job" as a life area if his or her work situation presented a special opportunity or challenge to live the spiritual ideal. Someone else might devote one segment of the chart to a relationship with a particular person or a condition (either personal or social) that was of current concern. Also, keep in mind that the point of charting one's physical, mental, and spiritual ideals is not to devise an exhaustive self-perfection program, but to strive for balance and to trigger that synergy wherein a few key practices become mutually supportive of one another. If you choose to work with ideals, pick out a few attitudes, emotions, and visualizations that positively affect several life areas and identify a reasonably achievable collection of practices and behaviors that would lead toward balance in your life. Start with just a few and then build from there. This will create forward-moving momentum that may surprise you with just what you are capable of. As St. Francis of Assisi said, "Start by doing what's necessary, then what's possible, and suddenly you are doing the impossible."

Working in Groups. Finally, no description of the core evolutionary practices emphasized by the Cayce readings would be complete without mention of small group work. The validity of Edgar Cayce's emphasis on the small group as a catalyst for spiritual growth is increasingly borne out today, as a growing body of evidence suggests that in certain highly focused group situations we can increase our capacity to tune in to higher states and deeper intelligence.* In short, small group work may well be our most promising avenue to unity consciousness. I speak here not merely of discussion or support groups (as valuable as those groups may be), but rather of a very specific kind of group based on commitment to a common ideal, deep group

---

*For a detailed and fascinating article on this see "Come Together" by Craig Hamilton, which appeared in *What Is Enlightenment? Magazine*, May-June, 2004. The article is readily available online by web search for the title and author.

attunement, and practical application of spiritual law in the members'
lives. Such a group also covenants to leave ego (Cayce would call it
"self") at the door and participate for the sake of the group's common
aim. This is easier said than done, as observation of group dynamics
will readily show how often personal needs for power or healing or
acceptance and validation will drive group members' behavior. On
this point, we may look with new admiration at Cayce's placement of
"Cooperation" at the head of the list of lessons in the "Search for God"
material. Considering that the year was 1931, the story is really quite
amazing.

The first "Search for God" group, a circle of Cayce's friends and associates who had been helped by his readings, came together around
a shared purpose to be channels of light and truth to the world. Turning to the Cayce source for instruction, they sought a series of readings
that could be developed into a guidebook of lessons for the serious
spiritual aspirant. They understood the importance of being of one
mind, too, as evidenced by their opening question: "Outline for us the
steps which we must take that we may become more of one mind, that
we may be of the greatest influence for good." The reading's response
charged them with practicing the first lesson that they would later
present to others: cooperation:

> . . . Let all dwell together in mind as of one purpose, one aim; or,
> *first* learn cooperation! Learn what that means in a *waiting*, in a
> *watchful*, in a world *seeking to* know, *to* see, a sign. There, as has
> been given, will only *be* the sign *given to* those that have drunk of
> the cup that *makes* for cooperation in *every sense* of enlightening
> a seeking desiring world.[296]

The group went on to receive seven more readings on this foundational principle over the next three months before moving on to "Know
Thyself," the next topic in the series of lessons. Along the way, they
plumbed the depths of what it meant to—as their initial reading put
it—"drink the cup that makes for cooperation in every sense." In reading the background reports to these readings as well as the questions

---

[296]262-1

that arose concerning their dreams and visions while working on this material, it is evident that cooperation in action truly did begin to catalyze new ways for deep spiritual wisdom to break through in that small group effort.

The resulting model of small group work that grew from that first experimental Search for God effort was way ahead of its time. It emphasized group meditation and prayer, inclusion of input from members' dreams, commitment to application of the lessons in daily-life experience, and perhaps most important of all, purity of intention; the spiritual ideal was referenced as a continual touchstone. All of this was done in a format that vested all of the group members with leadership responsibility, thus doing away with the teacher-student dichotomy. As one reading said of this endeavor at the time, " . . . The thought or the truths as presented there are *evolutionary* and *revolutionary* in the minds of some, yet are basic truths in the experience of individuals that have lived or experienced or visioned them, and will bear fruit."[297]

More than seventy years later, we see this power of the small group finally coming forth as a recognized carrier of evolutionary consciousness. Speaking of the tremendous power of groups, Dr. Otto Scharmer, Senior Lecturer at MIT and core faculty member of the UN Leaders Program, writes:

> What's new today in the world is that now the first and most accessible gateway into deeper spiritual experience is not individual meditation but group work. What happens is that, in quite a spontaneous way, you tap into this deeper process of awareness and consciousness as a group. And then, once you have done that, you can say, 'Well, I want to sustain this quality in my own life, so therefore I will pick a practice or two to do on a day-to-day level.' I think that for many people today, the collective is the most important teacher on this whole journey, because it allows us to explore a territory that is much less accessible, if at all, for individuals.[298]

---

[297]262-71

[298]As quoted in the article, "Come Together," by Craig Hamilton, *What Is Enlightenment? Magazine* (May–June, 2004), retrieved from enlightennext.org.

From all of this we can see that one of the most exciting possibilities of our time comes from what might happen if small, intentional groups of people committed to the evolutionary path of the co-creator begin to multiply across the planet. And although personal support may not be the primary reason to engage in this kind of group, it is nonetheless a wonderful side benefit. Commitment to a group is a great boost to personal motivation, because we are no longer answerable to only ourselves. When members feel safe with one another and the ego is parked outside, a group can also be a powerful vehicle for the personal work of growing beyond ego's myopia. And certainly anyone who has ever meditated in a group can't help but notice how much more quickly and easily the meditative state is achieved when we are bathed in the group energy field.

Why is it, then, that we so often hold participation in a group as an unfulfilled intention? One difficulty, of course, is that group work, promising though it is, presents a challenge for many people in today's over-scheduled, hectic lifestyle. Another obstacle may come from the fact that sometimes many miles separate us from others who share our ideals. Especially as we move toward a distinctively evolutionary perspective, the pool of like-minded fellow-travelers gets smaller still. For those whose opportunity for face-to-face group work is limited by either schedule or geography, Internet based groups hold fascinating potential. While it remains unclear what the full potential might be for such group cooperation in the world of cyberspace, I have had some profound experiences with Internet-based groups in both the Cayce community and the evolutionary community. In these situations, just as in face-to-face groups, it all comes down to the level of commitment on the part of each participant. When that commitment is there and when group members connect with one another beyond personal needs for affirmation, approval, or other purely personal needs, the collective power transcends the physical boundaries and seems to transmit from heart to heart via keyboards and cyberspace. It's worth giving it a try.

Making a Commitment to Be the Change You Seek

So there we have it. A set of practices for evolutionary advance that entails a committed life of meditation, determination to transcend the small self, care for others, holistic care for ourselves, and coming to-gether in groups that foster unity consciousness. It seems simple, but if Cayce and today's evolutionary thinkers are right, it is really all we need to do. From these efforts, new directions as yet unimagined may develop. "The wise man must remember that while he is a descendant of the past, he is a parent of the future," wrote Herbert Spencer. Cayce takes our formative potentials a step beyond the parenting metaphor when he says, " . . . Know that as thy service is a portion of the Creative Energy or God, as it is exercised it influences the pulse—as it were—of the universe."[299]

Influencing the pulse of the universe. Do we believe it? Are we ready to know that this is just how powerful we are—for the best or the worst? As the Cayce readings remind us, even God does not know what we will do with our power of choice.[300] Will it be evolution or escape? Is it a consciousness set on going back to the beginning or expanding along the currents of an ongoing creation that has been the dynamic pulse of this manifest realm since the Big Bang? We might not know exactly what is to unfold in the years ahead of us, yet the future draws us on. New Thought writer Thomas Troward captures the inner spiritual thrill of this evolutionary call when he says:

> If our speculations lead us to the conclusion that we have reached a point where we are not only able, but also required, by that law of our own being to take a more active part in our own evolution than heretofore, this discovery will afford us a new outlook upon life and widen our horizon with fresh interests and wider hopes.[301]

Can you feel it? We may not know exactly what is on that horizon, for time and human choices have yet to shape what is to come. But as the evolutionary impulse within us warms to full mobilization, the future calls us to new possibilities. The path of the co-creator stretches before us. What will we build as the legacy of the next one hundred

---

[299]1261-1

[300]1402-2, 257-113, for example.

[301]Thomas Troward, (1915), *The Creative Process in the Individual,* e-book.

years? Will this year—whatever year it may be as you are reading this—be the year that you and I do what we know to do more faithfully than ever before? The evolutionary trajectory is truly in our hands. What will we do with it?

Epilogue

So there I was, hanging on to the restraint bar of that elevator car in the Tower of Terror, wondering why I ever chose to get on this ride. As our ascent began, I kept my eyes scrunched closed, telling myself that it would soon be over and I would be back in my real life at home, where everything felt safer. Then, when the car went into its first precipitous drop, all of my fears *really* kicked in. I decided it was just as bad as I'd expected.

But then something interesting occurred. I realized that the fear was simply an interpretation–a choice I was making about how to experience the events at hand. No matter what my fears told me, a deeper part of me knew that nothing could really hurt me on this ride, so I decided to just go with it and see what it would be like to fully engage with the experience, instead of just hunkering down and waiting for it to be over. Once I made that decision, things changed. I began to notice things that I'd missed while I was so busy focusing on waiting for it to be over. To my delight, I noticed that there was a moment, as we dropped, when I was weightless. And there was another thing I began to notice as well. The elevator rises and drops multiple times, and it struck me that with my eyes closed I could not tell whether we were going up or down. The direction was indiscernible. So by the third ascent, I had decided to open my eyes, and I discovered it could be really fun. At the highest point, the doors to the elevator open, affording a panoramic view of the entire park. It was beautiful and even exhilarating. It was like seeing the world from an entirely new, much wider perspective–not the view above it all like you get in an airplane, but not the limited ground view either. I was still in a building with its foundations on the ground, but I could also see way beyond so many of the ground-level obstructions. It was quite awesome. By then I found myself laughing with joy and even looking forward to the next cycle of the ride.

By the time I left the Tower of Terror, I actually felt like a different person than the one who had fearfully gotten in line for the ride. I can't really describe precisely what was different, but I can tell you that it felt like being more alive. I was really glad I had decided to move right through the heart of my fear and take the ride anyway.

About the Author

Lynn Sparrow Christy is a teacher, writer, and hypnotherapist–life coach with more than forty years of experience with both traditional and alternative approaches to spirituality. Her interests in world religions and the pathway of inner awakening led her to the work of the American psychic Edgar Cayce when she was still in her teens. Ongoing engagement with that body of information led to her earlier books *Edgar Cayce and Christian Faith* and *Reincarnation: Claiming Your Past, Creating Your Future*, as well as the home–study courses *Meditation Made Easy* and *How to Discover Your Past Lives*. Over the past several decades, Lynn has conducted numerous seminars in cities throughout North America and several international locations. She is also the developer and online mentor of the Edgar Cayce eGroups *Apprenticed to the Master: Following Jesus in the 3rd Millennium, Life Lessons and Soul Purpose, Transforming Your Karma: Expanding the Influence of Grace in Your Life*, and *The Path of the Co-Creator: Living the Evolutionary Perspective of the Edgar Cayce Readings*. Here in *Beyond Soul Growth: Awakening to the Call of Cosmic Evolution*, she explores the important contribution the Cayce material makes to the burgeoning "evolutionary spirituality" movement.

In addition to her writing and seminar work, Lynn is also a certified Master Hypnotherapist and hypnosis trainer, Neuro–Linguistic Programming (NLP) Practitioner, and life coach. She maintains a private practice in Virginia Beach, where she works with clients on everything from habit change and personal healing to exploration of deep spiritual themes. Maintaining her original ties to the Christian tradition, Lynn has also served as a Licensed Minister with the Christian Church (Disciples of Christ) in Virginia, pastoring two different churches as an interim minister. She lives in Virginia Beach with her husband Larry Christy.

Bibliography
E-Books

Allen, James. (1902). *As a Man Thinketh*. e-book.

Aurobindo, Sri. (1939–40). *The Life Divine*. e-book.

Bailey, Alice. (1922). *The Consciousness of the Atom*. e-book.

Benson, E.F. (Edward Frederic). (1910). *Daisy's Aunt*. e-book.

Bergson, Henri. (1910). *Creative Evolution*. e-book.

Besant, Annie. (1905). *Esoteric Christianity: Or The Lesser Mysteries*. e-book.

____. (1907). *An Introduction to Yoga*. e-book.

Collins, Wilkie. (1870). *Man and Wife*. e-book.

Drummond, Henry. (1883). *Natural Law in the Spiritual World*. e-book.

Leadbeater, C.W. (1912). *A Textbook of Theosophy*. e-book.

Rogers, L.W. (1917). *Elementary Theosophy*. e-book.

Steiner, Rudolf. (2008). *Knowledge of Higher Worlds and Its Attainment*. e-book.

____. (1922). *An Outline of Occult Science*. e-book.

____. (1894). *The Philosophy of Spiritual Activity*. e-book.

Sterne, Lawrence. (1759–1767). *The Life and Opinions of Tristram Shandy, Gentleman*. e-book.

Strogatz, Stephen H. (2012). *Sync: How Order Emerges From Chaos in the Universe, Nature, and Daily Life*. e-book.

Troward, Thomas. (1915). *The Creative Process in the Individual*. e-book.

Woolson, Constance Fenimore. (1880). *Anne*. e-book.

E-Sources

Atkinson, William Walker. (1907). *The Secret of Success*. Retrieved as free PDF from scribd.com.

Atlee, Tom. "Tom Atlee's Take on Conscious Evolution." Retrieved from wikia.com, emphasis original.

Beckett, Samuel. *Proust*. Retrieved from goodreads.com.

Gladson, Jerry A. "Echoes of Millerite Millenarianism among the Founders and Heirs of Brush Run." Retrieved from brushrunchurchbicentenial1811–2011.org.

Hamilton, Craig. "Come Together." *What Is Enlightenment? Magazine* (May–June, 2004). Retrieved from enlightennext.org.

Hubbard, Barbara Marx. "Conscious Evolution Defined." Foundation for Conscious Evolution. Retrieved from barbaramarxhubbard.com.

Kuzweil, Ray and Christ Meyer. "Understanding the Accelerating Rate of Change." Retrieved from Kurzweilai.net.

Nietzsche, Friedrich. Retrieved from brainyquote.com.

Pal Binda, Amrit. "The Importance of Hindu Names." *Hinduism Today* (July, August, September 2005). Retrieved from hinduismtoday.com.

Phipps, Carter. "A Theologian of Renewal." *EnlightenNext Magazine* (December 2009–February 2009). Retrieved from enlightennext.org.

Roemischer, Jessica. "The Never Ending Upward Quest." *What is Enlightenment?* (Fall–Winter, 2002). Retrieved from enlightennext.org.

Sahtouris, Elisabet. "Planetary and Personal Health: Global Health and Agriculture." Retrieved from sahtouris.com.

Schelling, Friedrich. (1809). *Philosophical Inquiries into the Nature of Human Freedom.* Retrieved from en.wikipedia.org.

———. (1800). *System of Transcendental Idealism.* Retrieved from en.wikipedia.org.

Science Mysteries: Pole Shift: "Earth Loses its Balance a Half Billion Years Ago." Retrieved from World-Mysteries.com.

Whitehead, Alfred North. "Religion and Science." *The Atlantic Magazine* (August, 1925). Retrieved from theatlantic.com/magazine.

Print Articles and Journals

Edison, Thomas. *Harper's Magazine* (February, 1890).

Miller, William. *The Christian Messenger* (November, 1844).

Percival, Harold W. "Life." *The Word* (Winter 2001): 5.

Taubman, Howard. "Father of Biophilosophy." *The New York Times* (November 11, 1966).

Print Books

Aurobindo, Sri. *On Yoga II, Tome One.* Pondercherry: Sri Aurobindo Ashram, 1958.

Aurobindo, Sri. *Sri Aurobindo's Major Works, Volume 10: "Essays Divine and Human."* Pondicherry: Sri Aurobindo Ashram, 1993.

Beck, Don Edward and Christopher C. Cowan. *Spiral Dynamics: Mastering Values, Leadership and Change.* Carlton, Victoria 3053, Australia: Blackwell Publishing, 1996, 1999, 2000, 2001, 2002, 2003.

Bell, Rob. *Velvet Elvis: Repainting the Christian Faith.* Grand Rapids: Zondervan, 2005.

Bucke, Richard Maurice. *Cosmic Consciousness.* New York: Penguin Compass, 1991.

Cohen, Andrew. *Evolutionary Enlightenment: A New Path to Spiritual Awakening.* New York: SelectBooks, 2011.

Dowd, Michael. *Thank God for Evolution.* San Francisco/Tulsa: Council Oak Books, 2007.

Forster, E.M. *Howard's End.* New York: Vintage Books, 1954.

Haldane, J.B.S. "Science and Ethics." In *The Inequality of Man*, 113. London: Chatto, 1932.

Hardy, Thomas. *The Dynasts.* London: Macmillan, 1918.

——. *The Life and Work of Thomas Hardy.* Edited by Michael Millgate. Athens: The University of Georgia Press, 1985.

Huxley, Julian. "Evolution and Genetics." In *What Is Science?*, 278. Edited by James R. Newman. New York: Simon and Shuster, 1955.

Johnson, Steven. *Future Perfect: The Case for Progress in a Networked Age.* New York: Riverhead Books, 2012.

Krishna, Gopi. *A Kundalini Catechism.* Darien: The Kundalini Research Foundation, 1995.

Krishna, Gopi. *Kundalini: Empowering Human Evolution.* St. Paul: Paragon House, 1996.

Leadbeater, C.W. *A Textbook of Theosophy.* Chicago: The Theosophical Press, 1925.

Leloup, Jean-Yves. *The Gospel of Mary Magdalene.* Rochester: Inner Traditions, 2002.

Lewis, C.S. *Miracles*. New York: Macmillan, 1947.

——. *Prince Caspian*. New York: HarperCollins, 1951.

Lipton, Bruce. *The Biology of Belief*. Santa Rosa: Mountain of Love/Elite Books, 2005.

Lovejoy, Arthur. *The Great Chain of Being: A Study of the History of an Idea*. Cambridge, MA: Harvard University Press, 1936.

Percival, Harold. *Thinking and Destiny*. Dallas: The Word Foundation, 1987.

Sagan, Carl. *Cosmos*. New York: Random House, 1980.

Teilhard de Chardin, Pierre. *The Phenomenon of Man*. New York: Harper and Row, 1961.

Tyson, Neil deGrasse. *Death by Black Hole: And Other Cosmic Quandaries*. New York: W.W. Norton and Company, 2007.

Wilber, Ken. *The Atman Project: A Transpersonal View of Human Development*. Wheaton, IL: Quest Books, 1996.

——. *A Brief History of Everything*. Boston: Shambhala, 2000.

——. *Eye of Spirit: An Integral Vision for a World Gone Slightly Mad*. Boston: Shambhala, 1997.

——. *Integral Spirituality*. Boston: Shambhala, 2006.

——. *A Theory of Everything*. Boston: Shambhala, 1996, 2000.

——. *Up from Eden: A Transpersonal View of Human Evolution*. Wheaton, Quest Books, 2007.

Williams, Charles. *He Came Down from Heaven and The Forgiveness of Sins*. Berkeley, CA: Apocryphile Press, 2005.

Yogananda, Paramahansa. *The Second Coming of the Christ: The Resurrection of the Christ within You, Vol. 1*. Los Angeles: Self-Realization Fellowship, 2004.

Index

A

Activism, spiritual 234–235, 242–248, 284, 286
Adamic races 44
Allen, James 231
Angel, guardian 109–110
Animal intelligence 25
Anthroposophy 14
Aquarian Age 3, 4
As a Man Thinketh 231
Atkinson, William Walker 219
Atlantis 31, 32, 36, 37, 43
Atlee, Tom 178
Atman Project, The 174
Atonement, the 236
Aurobindo, Sri 14, 19, 24, 34, 38, 143
Awareness
Awareness, of awareness 25, 63–68
Awareness, self-reflective 25–27, 29, 30, 32, 36, 62–63, 65, 96
Axial Age 26, 29, 31

B

Babbage, Charles 160
Bailey, Alice 14, 23, 24, 143, 168, 214, 221
Baker, David 273
Balanced lifestyle 287–290
Beck, Don 174
Beckett, Samuel 1
Becoming xvi, 33, 35, 84, 88, 90–95, 93, 99, 108, 109, 260
Being xiii, xviii, 117, 33, 34, 38, 73, 74, 91, 92–94, 95, 109, 257, 260,
Bell, Rob 249
Benson, E.F. 187
Besant, Annie 95, 110, 153, 222
Big Bang, the 5, 7, 29, 32, 40, 41, 84, 163, 263, 294
Big History Project, the 163
Biology of Belief, The 117, 156
Boehme, Jakob 13, 20
Brief History of Everything, A 174
Bucke, Richard 9, 15, 25–26, 169–170
Buddha 26, 208
Buddha mind 207
Buddhism 82, 102, 246

C

Campbell, Alexander 236n
Catherine the Great 267
Cayce, Edgar
First encounter with ix
Readings of xix, xx, xxi, 3, 15, 16, 17, 18, 19, 21, 22, 23, 24, 27, 31, 32, 33, 36, 37, 39, 40–41, 42, 43, 44–45, 46, 49, 50, 54, 61, 62, 63, 70, 73, 79, 81, 84, 85, 89, 90–91, 92, 93, 96–97, 102, 109, 119, 131, 133, 140, 164, 184, 185, 201, 202, 203, 204, 206, 207–208, 209, 216, 217, 218, 219–220, 221, 222, 229, 231, 234, 235, 238–239, 240–245, 248, 249, 250, 255, 257–260, 261, 262–263, 266, 267, 269, 271, 275, 277, 279, 282, 283, 284, 285, 286, 287, 290, 291, 292, 294
Numerical identification system 3
Cells (biological) 7–8, 23, 28, 116–119, 120, 123–126, 129, 147, 156, 157, 176, 192
Center for Human Emergence–Middle East, The 174
Chakras
As representing themes of human development 132–140, 143, 172–173, 183–185
Opening 140–143
Chambered Nautilus, The 180
Chaos 7, 40, 152, 153, 163, 164, 165, 166, 185, 187, 189–190, 193–197, 199, 201, 202, 204, 215, 222, 244, 268, 274
Chinese medicine 131
Christ Consciousness 137, 145, 208
Christ, Jesus xix, 3, 90, 121, 139, 155, 158, 202, 208, 221, 235, 236, 237, 238, 239, 251, 258
Christian Church (Disciples of Christ), the 236n, 299
Christian, David 163
Christianity 236
Co–creatorship xvii, 4, 16, 17, 18, 21, 46, 49, 56, 84, 91, 94, 99, 164, 248, 249, 261, 279, 281–292
Co–Intelligence Institute, the 178
Cohen, Andrew 190, 254

214, 218, 245, 280, 286, 294
Meditation practices 66-68, 71-74, 122-
127, 140-150
Meridians 131
Miller, William, and the Millerites 236-
237
Moliere 185
Mysticism 137

N

Nadis 131
Names, significance of 89-92
Natural Law in the Spiritual World 13, 22,
81, 155
Neo-Darwinism 220
New Age xiii, xiv, 2, 6, 36, 50, 281, 282
New Biology 220
New Thought 103, 219, 294
Newtonian model 163
Nietzsche, Friedrich 101

O

Omega Point 15, 95
Original sin xiv
Origin of Species, The 12

P

Percival, Harold W. 21, 95
Pheonomenon of Man, The ix, 15
Piscean Age 4
Plato 26, 273
Prayer, general 73-74
Prayer, healing 141, 286
Prigogine, Ilya 194, 200
Principle of Maximum Error 275
Prophecy 141, 235, 237
Prophets, Hebrew 26
Psychic disorders 138
Psychoanalysis 102
Psychosis 134
Psychosomatic disorders 138
Purpose, soul 278-281

R

Reincarnation 81-83, 96
Renaissance, the 2, 3
Revelation, Book of 141, 144, 267
Rogers, L.W. 26, 31, 79, 192

S

Sagan, Carl 20, 21, 25
Sahtouris, Elisabet 193
Salk, Jonas 54
Scharmer, Otto 292
Schelling, Friederich xiii, xviii, 13, 17
Schopenhauer, Arthur 13
Science 3, 6-7, 13, 14, 37, 45, 153, 155-
158, 161, 168, 169, 171, 253
Search for God, A, lessons and study
groups 62, 105, 201, 282, 291-292
Self-organizing systems 194, 200
Service, path of 239, 281-287
Sexuality 172
Social Darwinism 213
Spencer, Herbert 294
*Spiral Dynamics: Mastering Values,
Leadership and Change* 174
Spiral Dynamics 174, 271
St. Francis of Assisi 290
Steiner, Rudolf 14, 50, 221
Sterne, Laurence 272-273
Stone, Barton W. 236
Strogratz, Steven H. 277
Structure of Scientific Revolutions, The 161
Stuck states 165-168, 181-184, 190-191,
199, 200-204
Superego 102

T

Tao Te Ching 34
Technology, advance of 11, 48, 214,
269-270, 274
Teilhard de Chardin, Pierre ix, 15, 18,
19, 20, 28, 30, 45, 47, 54, 62-63, 94,
129-130, 160, 169, 176-177, 196,
221, 222, 246-247, 259-261, 268
Tersteegen, Gerhard 34
Thank God for Evolution 160, 193
Theory of Everything, A 174
Theosophy 31, 38, 79, 103
Thermodynamics, second law of 162
Third eye 137-138, 141, 143
Thomas, Gospel of 202
Thoreau, Henry David 15
Time, cyclic view of 11, 12, 14
Transcendentalism 15
Tristram Shandy 272
Troward, Thomas 294
Tyson, Neil de Grasse 115

A.R.E. PRESS

Edgar Cayce (1877–1945) founded the non-profit Association for Research and Enlightenment (A.R.E.) in 1931, to explore spirituality, holistic health, intuition, dream interpretation, psychic development, reincarnation, and ancient mysteries—all subjects that frequently came up in the more than 14,000 documented psychic readings given by Cayce.

Edgar Cayce's A.R.E. provides individuals from all walks of life and a variety of religious backgrounds with tools for personal transformation and healing at all levels—body, mind, and spirit.

A.R.E. Press has been publishing since 1931 as well, with the mission of furthering the work of A.R.E. by publishing books, DVDs, and CDs to support the organization's goal of helping people to change their lives for the better physically, mentally, and spiritually.

In 2009, A.R.E. Press launched its second imprint, 4th Dimension Press. While A.R.E. Press features topics directly related to the work of Edgar Cayce and often includes excerpts from the Cayce readings, 4th Dimension Press allows us to take our publishing efforts further with like-minded and expansive explorations into the mysteries and spirituality of our existence without direct reference to Cayce specific content.

A.R.E. Press/4th Dimension Press
215 67th Street
Virginia Beach, VA 23451

Learn more at EdgarCayce.org. Visit ARECatalog.com to browse and purchase additional titles.

ARE PRESS.COM

EDGAR CAYCE'S A.R.E.

Who Was Edgar Cayce?
Twentieth Century Psychic and Medical Clairvoyant

Edgar Cayce (pronounced Kay-Cee, 1877-1945) has been called the "sleeping prophet," the "father of holistic medicine," and the most-documented psychic of the 20th century. For more than 40 years of his adult life, Cayce gave psychic "readings" to thousands of seekers while in an unconscious state, diagnosing illnesses and revealing lives lived in the past and prophecies yet to come. But who, exactly, was Edgar Cayce?

Cayce was born on a farm in Hopkinsville, Kentucky, in 1877, and his psychic abilities began to appear as early as his childhood. He was able to see and talk to his late grandfather's spirit, and often played with "imaginary friends" whom he said were spirits on the other side. He also displayed an uncanny ability to memorize the pages of a book simply by sleeping on it. These gifts labeled the young Cayce as strange, but all Cayce really wanted was to help others, especially children.

Later in life, Cayce would find that he had the ability to put himself into a sleep-like state by lying down on a couch, closing his eyes, and folding his hands over his stomach. In this state of relaxation and meditation, he was able to place his mind in contact with all time and space—the universal consciousness, also known as the super-conscious mind. From there, he could respond to questions as broad as, "What are the secrets of the universe?" and "What is my purpose in life?" to as specific as, "What can I do to help my arthritis?" and "How were the pyramids of Egypt built?" His responses to these questions came to be called "readings," and their insights offer practical help and advice to individuals even today.

The majority of Edgar Cayce's readings deal with holistic health and the treatment of illness. Yet, although best known for this material, the sleeping Cayce did not seem to be limited to concerns about the physical body. In fact, in their entirety, the readings discuss an astonishing 10,000 different topics. This vast array of subject matter can be narrowed down into a smaller group of topics that, when compiled together, deal with the following five categories: (1) Health-Related Information; (2) Philosophy and Reincarnation; (3) Dreams and Dream Interpretation; (4) ESP and Psychic Phenomena; and (5) Spiritual Growth, Meditation, and Prayer.

Learn more at EdgarCayce.org.

What Is A.R.E.?

Edgar Cayce founded the non-profit Association for Research and Enlightenment (A.R.E.) in 1931, to explore spirituality, holistic health, intuition, dream interpretation, psychic development, reincarnation, and ancient mysteries—all subjects that frequently came up in the more than 14,000 documented psychic readings given by Cayce.

The Mission of the A.R.E. is to help people transform their lives for the better, through research, education, and application of core concepts found in the Edgar Cayce readings and kindred materials that seek to manifest the love of God and all people and promote the purposefulness of life, the oneness of God, the spiritual nature of humankind, and the connection of body, mind, and spirit.

With an international headquarters in Virginia Beach, Va., a regional headquarters in Houston, regional representatives throughout the U.S., Edgar Cayce Centers in more than thirty countries, and individual members in more than seventy countries, the A.R.E. community is a global network of individuals.

A.R.E. conferences, international tours, camps for children and adults, regional activities, and study groups allow like-minded people to gather for educational and fellowship opportunities worldwide.

A.R.E. offers membership benefits and services that include a quarterly body-mind-spirit member magazine, *Venture Inward*, a member newsletter covering the major topics of the readings, and access to the entire set of readings in an exclusive online database.

Learn more at EdgarCayce.org.

EDGARCAYCE.ORG